occam-2

occam-2
Second edition

John Galletly
University of Buckingham

First published in 1996 by UCL Press.

UCL Press Limited
University College London
Gower Street
London WC1E 6BT

and
1900 Frost Road, Suite 101
Bristol
Pennsylvania 19007–1598

The name of University College London (UCL) is a registered trade mark used by UCL Press with the consent of the owner.

British Library Cataloguing in Publication Data
A catalogue record for this book is available from the British Library.

Library of Congress Cataloging-in-Publication Data

ISBN: 1-85728-362-7 PB

Occam is a Trademark of SGS-THOMSON Microelectronics Ltd.

Typeset in Times New Roman and Courier New.
Printed and bound by
Biddles Ltd, Guildford and King's Lynn, England.

Contents

Contents

Preface

"Entia non sunt multiplicanda praeter necessitatem" – Ockham's Razor

Aims and objectives

This book presents a gentle and structured introduction to *occam* 2, the programming language specifically designed for the *transputer*, a parallel architecture microprocessor developed by INMOS Ltd (now SGS-THOMSON Microelectronics Ltd). The aim of the book is to give a clear and concise description of this novel programming language. The text assumes that the reader has some knowledge of programming. The level is suitable for undergraduate students taking a course in parallel programming, although anyone with a knowledge of programming should be able to follow the text for self-study.

Each language construct is illustrated with an example. The book is organized so that information given in the early chapters is used and reinforced in later chapters.

A formal syntax of occam 2 in terms of BNF has not been included. This may be found in the definitive work by INMOS – *The occam 2 Reference Manual.*

Contents

The contents of this book grew out of an evolving lecture course that I have given to undergraduates at the University of Buckingham since the autumn of 1987. For this second edition, the text has been revised and extended from 11 to 16 chapters, including an expanded chapter on approaches to writing real-world parallel programs in occam. New chapters include material on occam 2.1 extensions, coding hints for performance maximization, and architecture descriptions of the T801 and T9000 transputers.

Chapters 1–9 contain a description of the basics of occam 2. These are introduced in a structured way, so that the reader is gradually led along the learning path. Each of these chapters contains exercises. The reader is encouraged to attempt these so that the instruction contained in the text may be reinforced by practice.

Chapter 10 explains how an occam program, built using the constructs described in the earlier chapters, may be distributed over a network of transputers. Chapter 11 contains a description of occam 2.1 enhancements and Chapter 12 explores approaches by which occam can be used to develop parallel programming solutions to real problems. Algorithmic, geometric and process farming paradigms are illustrated via example programs. Chapter 13 contains hints for achieving better performance with occam programs, and Chapter 14 discusses parallel program design issues such as deadlock, load balancing and routing. Finally Chapters 15 and 16, respectively, describe the hardware architecture and operation of the T805 and T9000 transputers.

John Galletly
University of Buckingham
December, 1995

Acknowledgements

Many colleagues and students have contributed to the development of this book over the years. I wish to thank them all. For this second edition, I would particularly like to thank Alan Pinder of SGS-THOMSON Microelectonics Ltd for his painstaking reading of the draft manuscript and for his constructive criticisms and helpful suggestions. My thanks also go to Jeremy Martin of the University of Oxford for his careful reading of, and enlightened comments, on Chapter 14.

I would like to thank SGS-THOMSON Microelectronics Ltd for their kind permission in allowing the reproduction of their copyright material.

Thanks also to Chris Wadsworth, David Johnston and Brian Henderson of the Rutherford Appleton Laboratory for their kind permission to use their material on the wave equation and ray tracing examples in Chapter 12.

Much of the revision was carried out during two sabbatical terms spent at the Czech Technical University (CVUT), Prague. I would like to thank Professor Vladimir Marik and his colleagues in the AI Group, Department of Control Engineering at CVUT for assistance, use of facilities and a friendly working environment. The second sabbatical was generously supported by the British Council, Prague, whom I also wish to thank.

Thanks are due to the staff at UCL Press for their help and guidance.

Finally, I would like to thank all my friends and family for their continued encouragement and support.

Introduction: the basics

0.1 Occam and the transputer

Conventional programming languages such as Pascal and C operate in a *sequential* fashion – one program statement is executed at a time, the sequential nature being forced by the sequential architecture of conventional computers. This type of architecture was first proposed by von Neumann in 1946, and, by and large, since then the majority of successive generations of widely available computers have kept to the same design – a single processor and memory units linked via a single data bus (Fig. 0.1). Instructions and data are fetched by the processor from memory using the data bus, processed, then any resultant data stored back in memory again using the data bus. This *fetch and store cycle* operates repeatedly to sequence through a program.

However, many real-world problems, such as those involving vision, speech and language processing, simulation and modelling (quantum chromodynamics and fluid-flow analysis, for instance), and digital signal processing, have an inherent parallelism. Solving these problems in a sequential fashion is at best time-consuming and constraining. Such problems would be better solved in a *parallel* fashion i.e. the simultaneous execution of program statements to accommodate

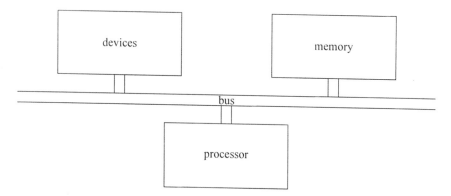

Figure 0.1   Block diagram of conventional sequential computer architecture.

1

their natural parallelism. To achieve this, the algorithms for computing the solutions to these problems would need to be stated in parallel terms. This in turn requires a suitable programming language, having facilities for expressing parallelism, to be available. The parallel computation may then be effected by having a multicomputer system, with each component computer acting on part of the problem, all component computers executing simultaneously. Distributing the processing load over more than one computer, as would be possible with a multicomputer system, should increase the execution performance of the system.

There are several motivations for developing parallel processors. These include:

- performance – obtaining more power as the number of processors in the system is increased;
- time reduction – obtaining results more quickly;
- fault tolerance – providing systems that can still operate, albeit in a degraded fashion, if some processors fail.

Various approaches to the introduction of parallel architectures have been made (Hockney 1988). For example, there has been much research and development in recent years into pipelined vector processors and array processors, together with multiprocessors.

Attempts have been made to extend the simple von Neumann design to multiprocessors for parallel operation, but without much success. It was found that adding more processors to the data bus, after an initial improvement, caused a degradation in the overall performance. This is because of the increased competition for use of the *shared* data bus by each extra processor – a condition known as the *von Neumann bottleneck*. In the von Neumann design only one processor may have access to the bus at any one time. Other processors wanting to use the bus must wait until the bus is free. (This type of architecture is also sometimes referred to as a *shared-memory* system.) The sharing of a single data bus among many processors brings more problems than it solves. The programming languages used for these systems were also, by and large, extensions of existing sequential-mode languages – parallel programming features were added as an afterthought. Conventional programming languages were not initially designed to cope with parallelism.

An interesting and easily understood analogy has been drawn between parallel processing and the construction of a wall by several bricklayers (Fox 1988). This analogy identifies several concepts and problems involved in parallel processing. For example, employing many bricklayers corresponds to using multiprocessors, collaboration between bricklayers corresponds to communication between processors, and so on. This analogy is further explained in Chapter 12.

Much current research is being devoted to the design of new parallel computer architectures and corresponding formalisms for programming languages. Occam (and the transputer) represent one of the success stories.

0.2 A classification of processor architectures

Before introducing occam and the transputer, it will be constructive to set the transputer in context with other parallel processors. There are several different ways that processor architectures may be classified and compared. For example, the classification can depend on the control mechanisms or on the address-space organization. Probably the most common (and simplest) classification of processor architectures is that attributable to Flynn (1972), a classification based on control mechanisms. It classifies processors according to how their instruction stream(s) and data stream(s) – how data is manipulated by the instruction stream(s) – are organized; either singly or multiply. Four classes of architecture result:

- a single instruction stream operating on a single data stream (SISD) – this class describes the traditional, sequential (von Neumann) processor executing a single set of instructions with a single data stream.
- a single instruction stream operating on multiple data streams (SIMD) – several processors execute the same instructions but each operates on different data sets. Parallelism is obtained by performing the same operation simultaneously on many data streams. A *processor array*, such as the Connection Machine CM-200, is an example of a SIMD architecture.
- multiple instruction streams operating on a single data stream (MISD) – an anomaly of the classification scheme, for which no examples seem to exist.
- multiple instruction streams operating on multiple data streams (MIMD) – several processors execute different instruction sets, operating on different data sets. Parallelism is obtained through many processors performing different operations on many data streams. The transputer falls into this class, as do the Sequent Symmetry, the nCUBE 2 and the Connection Machine CM-5.

Flynn's classification has been extended by several authors. For example, Gurd (1988) has refined the taxonomy into subcategories to take account of processors implementing novel models of computation. Thus, Gurd introduces subclasses of SIMD for *vector (pipelined) processors*, and *array (lockstep) processors*, which he further subdivides into global and local memory classes. The MIMD class is, likewise, partitioned into two subclasses: a conventional style (based on multiple communicating processes), which is further split depending on whether memory is global or local, and the unconventional style (not based on the von Neumann model of computation). Examples of this latter style include *dataflow* and *reduction model* processors. Various other authors have put forward other taxonomies for computer architectures. For instance, Kutti (1985) explores the address space or buffer type as a means of classification, whereas Skillicorn (1988) has proposed a scheme that depends on such characteristics as the processor to processor, and processor to memory subsystems.

Several authors have developed theoretical models of parallel computation. For example, Hoare (1985) has developed the *communicating sequential process* model, and Milner has developed the *calculus of communicating systems* (1980). Kumar et al. (Kumar 1994) describe a model of computation based on shared-memory processors known as the *parallel random access machine* (PRAM). Such a model, developed by Valiant (1990), is gaining general favour and credence in the parallel processor research and development community.

0.3 Occam

Occam is a programming language that from the outset was designed to support concurrent applications i.e. those systems whose parts may operate independently and sometimes have a need to interact. The title *occam* is derived from the name of a fourteenth-century Oxford philosopher, William of Ockham (or Occam). He was particularly famous for an adage known as Occam's Razor – "*Entia non sunt multiplicanda praeter necessitatem*". Translated from the Latin, this says "Entities should not be multiplied beyond necessity", or, paraphrasing, "Keep things simple". This encapsulates the whole philosophy of the occam programming language – programming is kept simple. Excess language constructs have not been specified in the occam definition. This simplicity helps understanding and use. As a consequence, occam programs should be more reliable, more efficient and easier to reason about.

Occam is an ideal language for scientific and engineering applications, for industrial process control applications, and for embedded systems, be they for domestic, industrial or military consumption. Its real-time ability, making use of features of the transputer such as the two levels of priority and the two interval timers, endow occam with the facilities necessary for the development of real-time applications.

Various systems for developing and executing occam programs are available. Probably the most common is the TRAM (TRAnsputer Module) concept, introduced by INMOS (now part of the SGS-THOMSON Microelectronics Group) in 1987 (INMOS 1989a). A TRAM is a sub-assembly of one or more transputers and other components, such as memory, on a plug-in card with a simple, standard interface. TRAMs come in several modular physical sizes, and are mounted onto an INMOS motherboard, such as the IMS B008 (which has an interface to an IBM 386 PC or compatible host), and may even be stacked, one on top of another. They are parallel processing building blocks, allowing the design of parallel systems in a modular fashion. Together with the occam toolset software (IMS D7305A), such a system provides an integrated environment for the development and execution of occam programs. The PC host provides keyboard input, display screen output and filestore facilities for the development system, and for occam programs executing on the transputer. Occam programs may be loaded from the PC host via a transputer link, or even may be loaded from ROM. Occam development systems (including transputers) are also available for other computer systems such as VAXes, Suns and Apple Macintoshs, and specialized transputer equipment such as Meiko's Computing Surface. Occam and transputer products are also available from third party developers such as Parsytec and Transtech.

In addition to occam, high-performance compilers for C, FORTRAN, Pascal and Ada programming languages are available for the transputer.

Cross-compilers with run-time systems have also been developed for occam, allowing occam programs to be executed on architectures other than the transputer. Three examples of successful cross-compilers are "occam for the PC" (Poole 1993), SPOC (Debbage et al. 1994) and KROC (Welch & Wood 1996). "Occam for the PC" is a cross-compiler that generates code for IBM 386 PCs or better. SPOC is an occam 2-to-C converter, and produces code that can be fed into a standard C compiler. It has been successfully evaluated on some Unix platforms. KROC is a native-code compiler, currently for Sun Sparc workstations, although releases for other processors are planned. It has other features, such as an interface tool for calling C and assembler libraries. All three cross-compilers include occam 2 language extensions. The code for SPOC and KROC is in the public domain. These and other occam/transputer resources are available from the Internet Parallel Computing Archive (http://www.hensa.ac.uk/parallel/occam and http://www.hensa.ac.uk/parallel/transputer).

0.4 The transputer

Occam was designed specifically for the *transputer*, a parallel architecture microprocessor developed by INMOS. The name transputer is actually a contraction of two words: transistor and computer.

The transputer is a novel VLSI architecture that explicitly supports *concurrency* and *synchronization*. Concurrency of process execution is realized in the transputer by a microcoded process scheduler that time-shares those processes ready for execution. Synchronization is required when different parts of a system, each with different relative times of execution, need to interact or cooperate with each other in some way, for example when passing messages between each other. Each interacting part must be ready and prepared for the interaction to take place. Otherwise, either part may get out of step and the interaction may never take place. The transputer uses a *message-passing* architecture to achieve this synchronization.

The transputer is really a family of related microprocessors each consistent with the basic transputer architecture but with different capabilities and features.

For example,

• IMS T225 – a 16-bit microprocessor.
• IMS T425 – a 32-bit microprocessor.
• IMS T805 – a 32-bit microprocessor plus floating point unit.

Members of this generic architecture have, in general, similar characteristics, but differences do exist.

Although the transputer family contains processors of differing wordlength, the instruction set used by occam has been designed to be independent of the processor's wordlength. However, the difference in wordlength does mean that there are

5

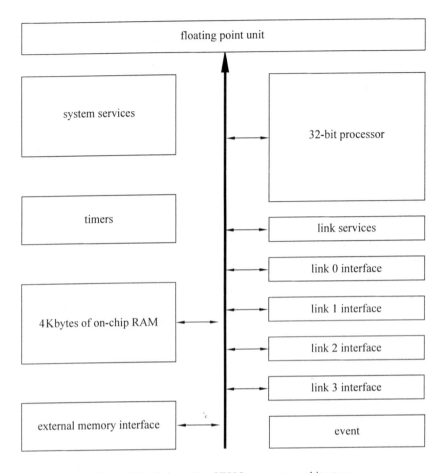

Figure 0.2   Schematic of T805 transputer architecture.

a few variations in behaviour. For example, the default integer size will vary, as will the real-time clock period.

The high performance transputer, the floating-point IMS T805, is an interesting example to study. The T805 comprises a 32-bit microprocessor, a 64-bit floating-point unit, four high-speed serial communications links, 4 Kbytes of on-chip memory and an external memory interface, all on a single chip (Fig. 0.2). Thus, the transputer is really a "microcomputer on a chip".

The T805-30, running at 30 MHz, can deliver 30 Mips, peak performance. (The T805 is available with a choice of clock speed: 20, 25 or 30 MHz.) Its minimal instruction set and its small group of 32-bit registers are designed to maximize execution speed. Importantly, it contains a microcoded priority scheduler that time-shares any number of concurrent processes.[1]

Thus, a single transputer, in addition to executing processes in conventional sequential mode, may execute processes concurrently. Being constructed in hardware, context switching between processes (needed for the concurrent execution of processes on the same processor) is very fast, being of the order of a few microseconds. There is thus a small but finite overhead penalty incurred in the execution of concurrent processes.

Two levels of process priority are supported by the scheduler – priorities 0 and 1, with priority 0 being the higher. At the low priority level, processes are timesliced in execution in round-robin fashion with a timeslice of approximately one to two milliseconds. The high priority level has no timeslicing. Once a high priority process starts execution it runs to completion, unless it requires inter-process communication or a timed delay. High priority processes are executed in preference to low priority processes. A switch from low to high priority occurs in a few microseconds (worst-case interrupt response).

The floating point unit implements the IEEE 754 floating-point arithmetic standard in hardware and provides both single (32-bit) and double (64-bit) length operations. It operates concurrently with the microprocessor and can deliver 4.3 Mflops, peak performance.

Each transputer communication link can transfer data bi-directionally at 2.4 Mbytes per second, with automatic hand-shaking synchronization in each direction, and provides a bi-directional, point-to-point connection between transputers or between transputers and external devices. A single transputer link implements two occam *channels*, one in each direction. Occam uses such channels for inter-process communication. All links operate concurrently with the microprocessor in a DMA, block transfer fashion. Each transputer may thus be linked to up to four other transputers. In this way, networks of transputers of various sizes and topologies may be built up. Each transputer in a network operates as an independent unit communicating as and when necessary with the other transputers to which it is linked. Data is transferred using a simple one byte protocol with acknowledgement, thus ensuring synchronization. Speed options for the communication links are 5, 10 or 20 Mbits per second.

The IMS T805 can directly address a memory address space up to 4 Gbytes. Memory above the on-chip 4 Kbytes is accessed via the external memory interface. The memory interface also supports memory-mapped devices that may use DMA.

In addition, each transputer has two 16- or 32-bit timers (depending on the particular transputer wordlength), one for each of the priority levels. The high priority timer is incremented every microsecond and cycles approximately every 4295 seconds (approximately 71 minutes) on the IMST425 and IMS T805, and approximately every 66 milliseconds on the IMS T225. One second corresponds to 1 000 000 clock ticks. The low priority timer, on the other hand, is incremented every 64 microseconds and cycles approximately every 76 hours on the IMS T425

---

1. In this book, a distinction is drawn between concurrent execution – processes executing in "parallel" on the same processor – and parallel execution – processes executing in parallel on separate processors (Burns 1988). Others authors use these terms interchangeably.

and IMS T805, and approximately every 4 seconds on the IMS T225. One second corresponds to 15 625 clock ticks.

The whole transputer package, comprising a processor (plus a floating-point unit on the T805s), internal memory plus memory interface, and four communications links, is constructed on a chip about $1\,cm^2$ in area.

Apart from the floating-point unit, the T2XX and T4XX series of transputers have the same generic architecture. These transputers rely on software to perform floating-point calculations.

A transputer follows the von Neumann design – the microprocessor, floating point unit, memory and communications links are linked via a 32-bit wide data bus. However, in a multitransputer configuration, a transputer has sole use of its own on-chip and off-chip memory and thus does *not* have to compete with the other transputers for memory accesses for instructions and data on a shared data bus. Consequently, the performance of a network of linked transputers can scale linearly according to the number of transputers in the network – 10 transputers giving ten times the performance, for example. There is no von Neumann bottleneck to degrade performance. Groups of parallel processes comprising an occam program may be distributed over such a network of transputers. Each transputer will execute its own processes – any communication between parallel processes on different transputers being handled by the transputer links – and so the parallel execution of the program will be effected.

However, to gain the expected increase in performance demands some care and attention. An example quoted by Hey (1988a) illustrates this. The timings for the execution of sequential and parallel implementations of the Newton–Raphson method for the evaluation of square roots were measured (using both single- and multitransputer versions). For ten iterations, the results were:

- sequential code on one T414A: 60 μsec
- parallel code on one T414A: 170 μsec
- parallel code on twelve T414As: 30 μsec.

The results may appear strange: a speed-up of only two is achieved with twelve transputers, and the sequential implementation performs better than the parallel one executing on a single transputer! The answer to the puzzle lies in the small but finite overheads associated with setting up parallel processing and performing communication. For a single transputer, in this example, there is far too little computation compared to this overhead. With twelve transputers, this is somewhat alleviated. For any application, the computation and communication loads for each transputer need to be carefully assessed in order to gain maximum performance and efficiency.

Many different network topologies may be created with a system of transputers by connecting up the four transputer links in different ways. These topologies range from pipelines, through rings, to hypercubes. Much of the interest in transputer networks stems from the fact that the networks are readily reconfigurable into different topologies. The different types of transputers can all interwork together, allowing systems to be custom-built and allowing the upgrading of systems as the technology progresses. The construction of networks of transputers is facilitated by the IMS C004 link switch, a 32-link, programmable crossbar switch, which is cascadable, allowing the building of arbitrary networks of transputers. Also available is the IMS C011 link adaptor, which allows parallel-mode external devices to interface to the transputer via the serial communications links.

The normal method of program development using transputers is to design, implement and test the occam program on a single transputer system, and then when satisfied, to distribute the component processes over a transputer network. This necessitates configuring or mapping processes to the transputers in the network – declaring which processes will execute on which transputer. As the inter-process communication protocol does not specify where any two communicating processes reside, this distribution is transparent to the logic of the program.

The architecture of the transputers so closely implements the occam language and occam so completely provides for control of the transputer hardware that, although occam is a high-level language, it may be regarded as the "assembly language" of the transputer. Indeed, this extremely close association between hardware and software is instrumental in producing such a powerful combination as occam and the transputer. (An assembly language for the transputer does exist. Assembly language statements may be inserted into occam code [INMOS: *Transputer instruction set*].)

The transputer is not only useful as a parallel processor *per se*, but is also used as a building block in the development of high-performance, low-cost super parallel computers and in embedded, real-time systems. The three identified industrial application areas for the transputer are imaging, embedded computing and communications.

The internal architecture of the transputer is described in Chapter 15.

0.5 The transputer family history

INMOS announced the first transputer, the T424, in 1984. However, owing to production difficulties, this transputer did not make it to the market place. It was superseded by the introduction of the T414 (in 1985). This transputer was later revised in a 1986 version. The T212 also made an appearance in 1986. The first floating-point version of the transputer, the T800, was launched in 1987. A low cost transputer, the T400, reportedly costing 2 USD per Mip, was introduced in 1989. Since 1985, the transputer family has been gradually extended. A range of 16/32-bit and floating-point products, T2XX, T4XX and T8XX, was developed, including some with military specifications. Some transputers have been designed for specific purposes (for example, the disk processor transputer, M212, and a transputer with just two communication links instead of four, the T400). In 1991, the next generation of transputer was announced, the T9000 series. The T9000 has a vastly improved and extended architecture compared with the first generation. Unfortunately, production difficulties have dogged its commercial introduction, and it was only in

1994 that it was available as a commercial product. A fuller description of the T9000 is given in Chapter 16.

The transputer products currently supported by INMOS are the T225, T400, T425, T450, T805 and T9000, with the T805 being the highest performance member of the first generation. Its performance is however surpassed by the second generation T9000.

0.6 The origins and history of occam

The design of occam was heavily influenced by the work of Hoare (1985) on the theoretical model of communicating sequential processes (CSP), which grew out of a study of process synchronization problems. CSP is a mathematically based notation for specifying the behaviour of concurrent processes. Within the framework of CSP, a program is considered to be a collection of sequential processes, each of which may be executing concurrently with the others. The processes may only interact or *communicate* via inter-process input/output operations – these input/output operations are the only interaction allowed between processes. The communicating processes are fully synchronized, in that when a process reaches an input(output) operation, it waits for the corresponding process to reach the matching output(input) operation. At this point the input/output operation is performed – the processes are in *synchronization* – and then both processes resume their execution at their own speeds. There is no queuing or buffering of messages.

A complex system may be completely (mathematically rigorously) specified in CSP. As indicated above, CSP embodies a notation for expressing the execution and interaction of a system comprising a collection of concurrent processes. The table shown below contains a few examples of statements in CSP notation.

P ; Q – process P is followed sequentially by process Q

P || Q – process P executes concurrently with process Q

P {b} Q – process P is executed if Boolean b is true, else process Q is executed

b * P – process P is executed while Boolean b is true

x := e – expression e is assigned to variable x

c ! e – the value of expression e is output

c ? x – a value is input and assigned to variable x

In a similar fashion, the occam language contains statements that allow the development of serial and/or concurrent processing of programs. An occam program comprises a collection of processes. Any concurrent processes that need to interact are completely synchronized i.e. communicate with each other in the fashion of CSP. An occam program (a collection of processes) may reside on a single transputer or a network of interconnected transputers (Fig. 0.3). In the former case the transputer shares its time between the concurrent processes – a sort of pseudo-parallelism. (Because the necessary process switching to perform concurrent processing is built in hardware on the transputer, it is inherently fast and does provide pseudo-parallelism.) In the latter case the processes are distributed in some way over the network of transputers and each transputer executes the processes allocated to it. This is true parallelism.

Occam is not just a programming language. It has been used in design as a specification language for both software and hardware systems. Indeed, occam was used in the design specification of the T800 and T9000 transputers! Occam's rich formal semantics allow program transformation and proof. Mathematical proof techniques that allow an occam program (or specification) to be verified for correctness have been developed. The algebraic semantics of occam comprise several laws that define the language and allow one occam program to transformed into different, but semantically equivalent, occam program (Roscoe & Hoare 1986).

A very readable description of how to develop a specification of a program in CSP, followed by its implementation in occam 2, is given in the book by Mett et al. (1994).

The first version of the occam language (called proto-occam or occam 1) was introduced in 1982. This was superseded by the next version, occam 2, in 1986. A complete and authoritative definition of the occam 2 syntax has been published by INMOS (1988a).

In parallel with the announcement of the T9000 transputer, in 1991, INMOS published a specification for an extended language, occam 3 (or occam 91, as it was also called). Occam 3, a superset of occam 2, introduces features to facilitate the modularization of large programs, the construction of libraries, data structuring and channel types. A subsequent revision to the occam 3 draft was issued in 1992 (Barrett 1992). The major innovations in occam 3 are the following:

- **RECORD** and **UNION** data structure types, in addition to arrays.
- remote call channels, which allow parameters to be passed from a process to a "remote" procedure (one that is executed by another process), in much the same way as client–server remote procedure calls function in conventional distributed systems. Both processes may be on different transputers.
- shared channels, which support a many-to-one connection between processes (instead of the usual point-to-point connection). The shared channel is claimed exclusively by a process and is automatically relinquished when the claiming process goes out of scope.
- channel records that permit the declaration of bi-directional channels between two communicating processes. The channel record encapsulates the individual uni-directional channels into one structure.
- modules, which provide a mechanism for structuring processes – allowing a set of processes to be declared as a unit to provide information hiding and encapsulation.
- libraries, which provide another mechanism for structuring processes – permitting the implementation of abstract data types and system services, avail-

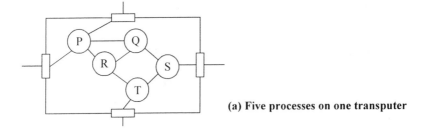

(a) Five processes on one transputer

(b) Five processes on two transputers

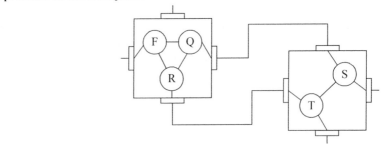

(c) Five processes on five transputers

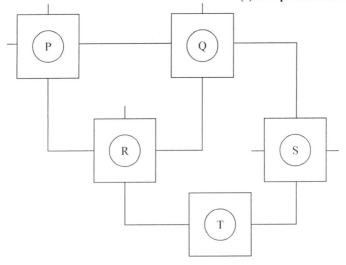

Figure 0.3 Illustration of the distribution of occam processes to a network of computers.

able to any number of concurrent programs. A library is a re-usable unit of program.

At the time of writing, INMOS has no plans to support occam 3. INMOS, however, did announce in 1994 proposed language extensions to occam 2. Extended occam 2 (commonly known as occam 2.1), implements a subset of the occam 3 enhancements plus some other extensions. SGS–THOMSON expects to release these extensions in the IMS DX405 occam toolset, due in 1995/96.

This book is concerned with the description of occam 2. Extended occam is dealt with in Chapter 11.

A very readable account of the role and the future of occam is provided by Welch (1990).

In order to further the dissemination of information about occam and the transputer, some national User Groups have been formed, principally in Europe, North America, Australasia and Japan. These groups have over 5000 members worldwide and include both academic and industrial users. Newsletters and technical papers are published and international conferences are held twice yearly. An international journal, *Transputer Communications*, is devoted to occam and transputer issues. Occam and transputer information and resources are available from the Internet Parallel Computing Archive (http://www.hensa.ac.uk/parallel/occam and http://www.hensa.ac.uk/parallel/transputer).

Chapter 1

Occam basics

1.1 Introduction

As explained earlier, occam is based on the process model of CSP – an occam program comprises a collection of communicating sequential processes; individual processes executing in sequence, groups of which may be executing in parallel. Those processes executing in parallel may communicate with each other only via synchronized input/output operations.

Following the CSP model, the three most common basic, or *primitive*, processes in occam are defined to be

- the assignment process – assign a value to a variable,
- the input process – input a value into a variable, and
- the output process – output a value from a variable

The remaining primitive processes are **SKIP** and **STOP**; the former being a process that terminates immediately, the latter being a process that never terminates. These seemingly harmless processes play important roles in an occam program. Their functions will be described in more detail shortly.

More higher-level processes may be built from these "building blocks" using occam *constructions*. A construction encompasses a collection of component processes, the whole being yet another occam process. Thus, a process in occam may be as simple as a single statement (one of the primitive processes) or more "complex" (a collection of processes built from primitive processes using constructions). The process formed by a construction may itself be used as the component of another construction. So a hierarchical or nested structure of occam processes may be formed. Constructions are introduced by occam reserved words. The most important and interesting of these are **SEQ**, the sequential construction, **PAR**, the parallel construction, and **ALT**, the alternation construction. Others will be described in Chapter 5.

Occam is a *typed* language (see Ch. 2). The name and type of program objects such as constants and variables must be declared before use. Data declaration statements are prefixed to the processes concerned. Scoping rules apply so that data is local to the process following the declaration. Processes nested within other processes may access this data; these nested processes are within the *scope* of the enclosing process. However, processes within a parallel construction may only communicate data via an occam *channel* – a shared, common variable may *not* be used to communicate values between parallel processes. The channel is used for communication between parallel processes. The need for this constraint will be explained shortly. Another way of saying this is that occam uses the *message-passing* paradigm for sharing data.

The syntax of occam is reasonably straightforward. Each occam language statement (a primitive process, a construction reserved word, etc.) occupies a line by itself. Importantly, *the components of a higher-level process are indented by two spaces with respect to the construction reserved word*. This indention reflects the block structure of the occam program and replaces the BEGIN and END statements of conventional block-structured languages such as Pascal. Processes at the same level will have the same indention. The end of any level of indention marks the end of the process. The level of indention of a process marks the region of its validity. The process is defined only within the range of its indention, as is the scope of its local variables.

A long occam statement may be continued over more than one line, provided that the statement is broken immediately after an operator (see Ch. 3), a comma, a semi-colon, an assignment operator (: =) or one of the occam reserved words **IS**, **FROM** or **FOR**. The continuation lines must be indented at least as far as the initial line of the occam statement.

1.2 Primitive processes

The primitive processes – assignment, input and output – are described in this section. The variables used in the examples are assumed to have been declared previously. How this is done in practice is left until Chapter 2.

1.2.1 Assignment
The assignment process assigns a value to a named occam program variable. It has the form

```
variable := expression
```

where
- `variable` is an occam program variable identifier, and
- `expression` is an occam expression. The value of the expression is assigned to the variable.

In occam an expression may take many forms. For the moment consider an expression to be a constant, a variable or some simple arithmetic combination of these. Expressions will receive further coverage in Chapter 3.

The data type of the expression must be the same as the data type of the variable to which the value of the expression is being assigned (see Ch. 2). For example,

```
Index := 0
```

is an assignment process that assigns a value of zero to the integer variable `Index` (see Ch. 2 for a definition of occam types), and

```
Left := Limit - Index
```

is an assignment process that assigns the value resulting from the evaluation of the arithmetic expression, `Limit - Index`, to the variable `Left`.

Multiple assignments may be made within one statement if required. For example,

```
Total, Index := 0, Index + 1
```

is similar to the two separate assignments

```
Total := 0
```

and

```
Index := Index + 1
```

Multiple assignments may be used in occam to interchange the values of variables. For example,

```
Item1, Item2 := Item2, Item1
```

successfully swaps the values of variables *Item1* and *Item2*, and has a similar effect to the statements executed in sequence

```
Temp  := Item1
Item1 := Item2
Item2 := Temp
```

where *Temp* is a temporary variable.

Note that, in a multiple assignment, the components of the right-hand side of the assignment statement are evaluated in parallel, that is, simultaneously, and then are assigned to the left-hand side components in parallel. This means that the statement

```
Total, Index := 0, Index + 1
```

16

is equivalent to

```
SEQ
  PAR
    Temp1  :=  0
    Temp2  :=  Index + 1
  PAR
    Total  :=  Temp1
    Index  :=  Temp2
```

and is not quite the same as either the sequential assignment (see §1.3)

```
SEQ
  Total  :=  0
  Index  :=  Index + 1
```

or the parallel assignment (see §1.4)

```
PAR
  Total  :=  0
  Index  :=  Index + 1
```

This could lead to problems for the unwary.

1.2.2 Input and output

The input and output processes operate via channels and provide inter-process communication between concurrent processes. A channel is a *one-way* communications link between *two* concurrent processes. The channel is used to pass data from one concurrent process to another. A channel is shared between only two communicating processes – one process may output on the channel, the other may input. No more than *one* process may use the channel for either input or output. Data that has been assigned or input by a process within a parallel construction may only be shared with another process in the construction via an occam channel. Both the input and output processes must be ready before the data transfer can take place; that is, there is complete synchronization of channel communications. This synchronization is automatically provided by occam.

The channel is realized in practice by using memory locations, if the communicating processes are resident on the same transputer, or by the transputer's communications links, if the communicating processes are on different transputers. The channel is a feature of the occam language and is implemented transparently by the occam environment. The actual implementation of channels is described in Chapter 15.

1.2.2.1 Input   The input process allows a value to be input from an occam channel and that value to be assigned to a named variable (Fig. 1.1). The input process has the form

```
channel ? variable
```

where
- `channel` is an occam channel identifier,
- `variable` is an occam variable that receives the value input along the channel, and
- `?` is the occam operator for channel input.

Figure 1.1   The input process.

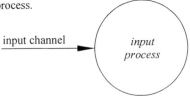

The input value must be of the same data type as the named variable (see Ch. 2). For example,

```
InChan ? Data
```

inputs a value via the channel `InChan` and assigns that value to the variable `Data`.

1.2.2.2 Output   The output process outputs the value of an expression along a named channel (Fig. 1.2). It has the form

```
channel ! expression
```

where
- `channel` is an occam channel identifier,
- `expression` is an occam expression (see Ch. 3 for more details)
- `!` is the occam operator for channel output.

Figure 1.2   The output process.

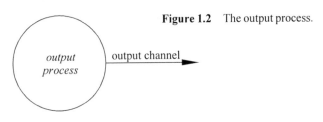

For example,

```
OutChan ! Data
```

outputs the value of the variable Data to the channel OutChan, and

```
OutChan ! 2 * Data
```

outputs twice the value of the variable Data.

1.3 The SEQ construction

The sequential construction causes component processes to be executed one after the other. This is just the normal mode of execution of conventional computers. However, because with occam the programmer has the option of executing processes in sequence or in parallel, sequential execution *must* be explicitly specified. Sequential execution is not a default in occam as it is in conventional programming languages.

Each sequential construction is introduced by the reserved word **SEQ**, and this is followed by a list of processes to be executed in sequence.

The sequential construction has the format

```
SEQ
  process 1
  .
  .
  .
  process n
```

where process 1 . . . process n represents a collection of processes to be executed in sequence and each one must be indented by two spaces from the **SEQ** reserved word. These processes are the components of the **SEQ** construction and each may be one of the primitive processes or a more "complex" process. The component processes are executed in the sequential order specified.

The **SEQ** construction terminates when the last of the component processes terminates. (In occam, a process, be it primitive or complex, is said to *terminate* if it successfully finishes execution – see §1.9 of this chapter.) An **SEQ** construction without any component processes behaves as a **SKIP** process.

Example 1.1

```
SEQ
  Index := 0
```

```
Limit  := 100
Left  := Limit - Index
```

is a sequential process that assigns a value of 0 to the variable `Index`, a value of 100 to the variable `Limit` and the arithmetic difference of `Limit` and `Index` to `Left`. (As commented on earlier, these variables must have been previously declared.) The assignments are executed one after the other, that is, in sequence. The **SEQ** construction ends when the last of its component processes terminates – in this case the assignment to `Left`.

Example 1.2

```
SEQ
   A  := 6
   B  := A + 2
   C  := A * B
   D  := 4
   D  := 2 * D
```

is a sequential process containing a mixture of simple and arithmetic expression assignments.

Example 1.3

```
SEQ
   Chan ? Data
   Data := Data + 1
```

is a sequence of statements comprising an input, via channel `Chan`, and an assignment.

Example 1.4

```
SEQ
   In ? Num
   Out ! Num
```

shows a process that inputs a value from the channel `In` and outputs that value on the channel `Out`. The **SEQ** construction in this example behaves as a simple buffer (Fig. 1.3). This illustrates occam's usefulness in the fabrication of "building block" processes.

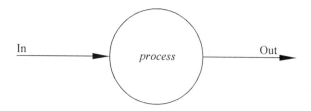

Figure 1.3   A simple buffer process.

Example 1.5

```
SEQ
    InChan ? Num
    OutChan ! Num * Num
```

is a process that inputs a value from the channel InChan and outputs the square of that value on the channel OutChan.

Note that in these examples the cooperating processes in the communication have been left unspecified. Proper communication between processes will be discussed shortly.

1.4 The PAR construction

The parallel construction causes component processes to be executed concurrently, each at its own rate. Each process within a parallel construction starts execution at the same time as all the other processes within the same parallel construction. (Note: If the component processes reside on a single transputer, then the processes will be executed concurrently or in pseudo-parallel. If the component processes are placed on separate transputers – such as a network of transputers – then the processes will be executed in true parallel.)

A parallel construction comprises the occam reserved word **PAR**, followed by a list of processes to be executed in parallel.

The parallel construction has the format

```
PAR
    process 1
    .
    .
    .
    process n
```

where process 1 . . . process n represent a collection of processes to be executed in parallel, and each one may be one of the primitive processes or a

21

more "complex" process. These processes are the components of the **PAR** construction. Each of the component processes must be indented by two spaces from the **PAR** reserved word.

The **PAR** construction terminates only after all of the component processes have terminated. The component processes do not necessarily terminate together, since they are quite likely to be different processes. A **PAR** construction without any component processes behaves as a **SKIP** process.

Example 1.6

```
PAR
  Comm1 ? Item1
  Comm2 ? Item2
```

represents two inputs executing concurrently, a value being input into variable `Item1` via channel `Comm1` and another value being input into variable `Item2` via channel `Comm2` (Fig. 1.4).

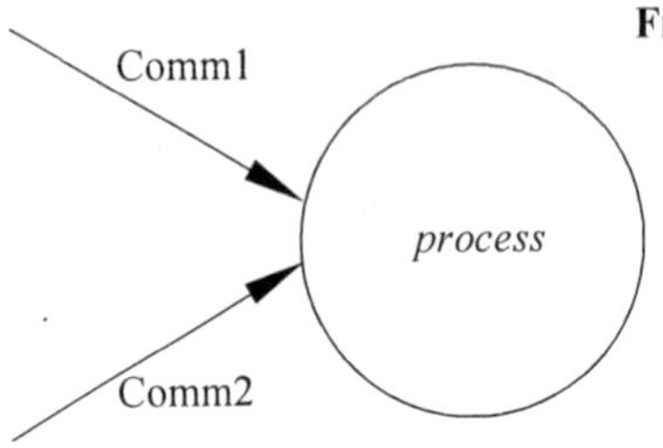

Figure 1.4   A two-channel **PAR** process

The fact that each process within a **PAR** construction starts execution at the same time as all the other processes within the construction means that the named order of processes within a parallel construction is immaterial. (The same is *not* true for the **SEQ** construction since, as its component processes are executed in sequence, the named ordering is essential.) For example,

```
PAR
  Comm1 ? Item1
  Comm2 ? Item2
  Comm3 ? Item3
```

is equivalent to

```
PAR
  Comm3 ? Item3
  Comm2 ? Item2
  Comm1 ? Item1
```

or any other permutation of component process order.

22

1.5 The **ALT** construction

The alternation construction allows a particular process from a list of component processes, or *alternatives*, to be selected for execution. In the simplest case, *each* component process is prefaced or *guarded* by an input process, which is known as an *input guard*. Which alternative is selected for execution depends on which input guard has input available first. The process associated with the first input guard to be ready is the one chosen for execution. Thus, essentially the **ALT** construction selects an available input from several input channels (Fig. 1.5). For a discussion of what happens if two or more input guards are ready at the same time, see Chapter 5.

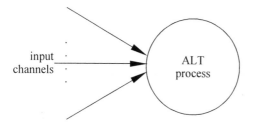

Figure 1.5 The **ALT** process.

input channels · · · → ALT process

An alternation construction is introduced by the occam reserved word **ALT** and this is followed by a list of processes guarded by inputs. The alternation construction has the format

```
ALT
  input_guard 1
    process 1
  .
  .
  .
  input_guard n
    process n
```

where input_guard 1 . . . input_guard n are the input guards and process 1 . . . process n represent the associated processes, each one of which may be one of the primitive processes or a more "complex" process. Each input guard must be indented by two spaces from the **ALT** reserved word and each associated process indented a further two spaces.

After the execution of the selected process, the **ALT** construction terminates.

Example 1.7

```
ALT
  InChan1 ? Data1
    OutChan ! Data1
```

```
InChan2 ? Data2
   OutChan ! Data2
InChan3 ? Data3
   OutChan ! Data3
```

is an alternation construction that has three alternatives, each guarded by an input process. If the input on channel `InChan1` becomes ready first, then its associated process (`OutChan ! Data1`) is the one that is executed, and similarly for the other two input guards. If placed in a loop, this **ALT** process behaves as a multiplexor, accepting data from several input channels and feeding that data down a single output channel (Fig 1.6).

ALT enables the creation of event-driven software, a particular event being associated with a particular input channel. The **ALT** construction is treated more thoroughly in Chapter 5.

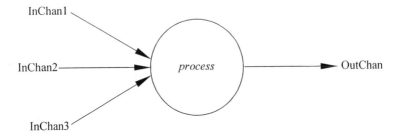

Figure 1.6 A three-channel **ALT** process.

1.6 Nested constructions

As discussed earlier, constructions may be nested within other constructions. In this way it is possible to build "complex" occam processes from simpler ones.

Example 1.8

```
PAR
  SEQ
    Index := 0
    Chan1 ! Index
  SEQ
    Limit := 100
    Chan2 ! Limit
```

represents a parallel process with two component sequential processes. These sequential processes, being the components of a **PAR** construction, execute concurrently.

Example 1.9

```
PAR
  SEQ
    Result := 42
    Comm ! Result
  SEQ
    Comm ? Answer
```

is a parallel process with two sequential components, one containing an output process, the other containing an input process. Note that both the input and output processes are using the same channel – the sequential processes executing concurrently have the ability to communicate via this channel (Fig. 1.7). The components of a parallel process may only communicate via the same named channel and this channel may only link *two* processes. Note also that the communication is strictly one-way – in this case output from the first sequential process, input into the second sequential process.

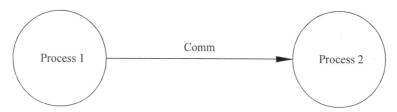

Figure 1.7 Two processes communicating via a channel.

In general, with two communicating processes, at some point one process will wish to output to the other process. This output will not continue until the execution of the second process reaches the appropriate input. Correspondingly, the second process may reach the input before the first process is ready to output. In this case the input is suspended until the first process wishes to communicate. The communication is fully synchronized for occam by the transputer microcode.

1.7 Two-way channel communication

It should be reiterated that the same channel may not be used for both input and output within the same process. Two-way communication between processes requires *two separate* channels.

Example 1.10

```
PAR
  SEQ
    Value := 21
    Comm1 ! Value
    Comm2 ? Answer
  SEQ
    Comm1 ? Data
    Comm2 ! 2 * Data
```

is a parallel process with two sequential components. Each sequential component has two distinct channels, Comm1 and Comm2 (Fig. 1.8). These channels allow two-way communication between the components of the **PAR** construction. The first component outputs via channel Comm1 and inputs via channel Comm2, and the second component inputs via channel Comm1 and outputs via channel Comm2.

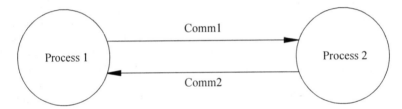

Figure 1.8   Two-way communication between processes.

1.8 Deadlock

When processes are participating in two-way communication, it is important to order the respective input and output processes in such a way so as to avoid *deadlock*. Deadlock is a situation that arises when one or more processes for some reason cannot proceed. They are held up waiting for an "event" that will never happen. Special care is needed to ensure that communicating processes are not held up waiting for an input or output that cannot proceed.

Example 1.11

```
PAR
  SEQ
    Chan1 ! Data1
    Chan2 ? Data2
  SEQ
    Chan2 ! Item2
    Chan1 ? Item1
```

The first sequential process tries to output on Chan1 but is held up until the corresponding input is ready in the second sequential process. (The input on Chan2 by the first sequential process cannot be executed until the output on Chan1 has succeeded.) However, the second sequential process can never reach this input because it will be held up as it tries to output on Chan2. There is deadlock: neither process can proceed (Fig. 1.9).

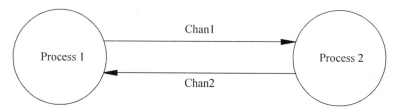

Figure 1.9   Possibility of deadlock between processes.

   As demonstrated above, deadlock can be a real problem when processes participate in two-way communication. The problem in this case usually arises from the sequential ordering of the communicating processes. Deadlock may be avoided by carefully ordering the sequence of inputs and outputs. Other possibilities of avoiding deadlock are the use of a **PAR** construction instead of a **SEQ** for the inputs and outputs – if the sequences of inputs and outputs are independent – or the use of an **ALT** construction to avoid sequencing the inputs. However, each case needs be carefully considered for the best solution and a cavalier approach to the problem must be avoided at all costs.

Example 1.12

```
PAR
  SEQ
    Chan1 ! Data1
    Chan2 ? Data2
  SEQ
    Chan1 ? Item1
    Chan2 ! Item2
```

where the sequence of input and output in the second sequential process has been reordered to remove the deadlock.

Example 1.13

```
PAR
  SEQ
    Chan1 ! Data1
```

```
    Chan2 ? Data2
PAR
    Chan2 ! Item2
    Chan1 ? Item1
```

where the **SEQ** construction of the second sequential process has been replaced by a **PAR** construction to remove the deadlock. Since the input and output in this new parallel process now execute concurrently and not in sequence, they will not be held up by their ordering. The same effect may have been gained by replacing the first **SEQ** construction by a **PAR**, or replacing both **SEQ** constructions by **PAR**s, provided the logic of the program allows these inputs and outputs to be independent.

It must be stressed that these are artificial examples used to illustrate a point. What is possible in practice depends on the logic of the program. A more thorough discussion of deadlock in occam programs appears in Chapter 14.

1.9 SKIP and STOP

SKIP and **STOP** are the two remaining occam primitive processes.

SKIP starts, does nothing and then terminates immediately. It behaves like a null process; program execution continues afterwards with any subsequent process. A seemingly innocuous statement, it has many uses (see Ch. 5, for example).

STOP starts, does nothing but never terminates. Program execution is held up at a **STOP**, as it never terminates. It behaves like a process in a tight loop, which loops for ever. As such, it is to be used with caution; usually it will be used in circumstances that are illegal in the logic of the program. A run-time error usually causes a rogue process to behave as a **STOP** process.

1.10 Termination of occam programs

In occam, a clear distinction is made between the notions of *terminated* and *stopped* when applied to processes. When a process finishes execution cleanly, it is said to have *terminated*. A process that has *stopped*, however, is in an error condition. A process may stop as a consequence of executing a **STOP** process or after incurring a run-time error.

The organization required to terminate a program comprising a collection of parallel processes needs special care, and the onus for doing this falls on the programmer. Parallel processes need to be terminated in an orderly fashion. A parallel process must *not* be terminated before any processes communicating with it have been informed, as these processes will be deadlocked if they are dependent on some communication from the terminated process: they will wait forever for input or output from the terminated process. Pountain & May (1987) have proposed some simple guiding principles for correctly terminating occam processes:

- processes must be informed via a channel communication when to terminate. For example, by receiving a Boolean flag or a special integer value as a termination notice.
- a process must pass on any termination notice to other communicating processes before terminating itself. Not all processes may be informed at once. It takes time for this termination notice to spread around the system.
- channels, and *not* shared variables, must be used for delivering the termination notice.

A full, worked example of termination handling appears in Chapter 12 – the example dealing with the computation of the Mandlebrot set.

Welch (1989) describes several pitfalls – common but erroneous approaches to implementing termination – that await the unwary occam programmer. He then offers a simple but elegant solution for securely and efficiently spreading a "poison" to all processes of a system via existing channels. The method also solves a much more important problem: how to perform a general (or partial) reset of a collection of parallel processes.

Welch's method relies on the distribution of a termination notice (or poison) to all processes, and is a generalization of the method outlined above. The poison, which is spread via existing process channels, is represented by a special data value or a tagged protocol (see Ch. 8). The procedure is as follows:

- a process exits its main processing cycle if it inputs poison on any channel
- the process remembers on which input channel(s) the poison arrived
- the process feeds poison down all of its output channels (No more output is then sent out down these channels.)
- the process throws away any input received on any channel until poison arrives down that channel. (Thereafter, no more input will be received down that channel.)
- the process terminates when it has received poison from all its input channels.

For the termination problem, Welch actually questions the need to terminate parallel processes and suggests that a more practical solution is to allow the processes to run forever by embedding each one in a non-terminating (**WHILE TRUE**) loop. Such an approach clearly obviates the need for clean termination conditions, and also means a reduced overhead in code.

The same method may be applied, quite securely, to resetting a (sub)network of processes to a known state, with the "reset" signal replacing the poison. During the reset period, there may be some data loss.

1.11 Comments in occam programs

A comment in an occam program is introduced by the double dash (- -), and is terminated by the end of the line on which it appears. Comments must be indented at least as far as the statement on the preceding line. A comment may be added on the same line as a process.

Example 1.14

```
SEQ
-- A comment here
      -- or here is legal
   .

   .

   .

      SEQ
-- BUT not here!
```

Example 1.15

```
SEQ
   Index := 0            -- initialize Index,
   Limit := 100          -- Limit
   Left := Limit - Index  -- and Left
```

1.12 Debugging occam programs

In general, it is fair to say that debugging a parallel program can be more difficult than debugging a sequential one; the nature of parallelism can open a new dimension of errors. One of the most common errors in an occam program is deadlock, a condition described in §1.8. A multitransputer program is correspondingly more difficult to debug than its single-transputer counterpart. Because of its problematic nature, tools have been developed to aid the programmer in the debugging task.

For instance, the INMOS occam 2 toolset includes a network debugger, containing such facilities as direct memory display, instruction disassembly, processor data display, and breakpointing. It can be used in interactive or post-mortem mode. The former allows the breakpoint debugging of executing programs, whereas the latter permits stopped programs to be debugged using the contents of memory. The program may be analyzed in terms of its source code.

Yet a further debugging tool is the INMOS product, INQUEST, available for PC and Sun hosts. This provides a windows-based interactive debugging environment, plus performance analysis facilities. INQUEST is currently available with the T9000, but will be provided in all future toolsets.

1.13 I/O with external devices

The occam language definition does *not* contain a specification of I/O procedures for allowing communication by occam programs with external devices, such as the keyboard, display screen or filestore of the host computer. Instead, these procedures are supplied in software libraries. Thus, for instance, the INMOS occam 2 toolset contains several such libraries containing procedures and functions for reading numbers and characters from the keyboard, writing to the screen, and creating and accessing files. Also included are libraries containing numerical conversions such as logarithmic and trigonometric functions. This book does not contain any further description of these libraries. To allow an occam program to input data from and output results to external devices, the appropriate library documentation should be consulted.

1.14 Exercises

1. An assignment, such as `Left := Limit - Index`, may be written as a **PAR** construction comprising two parallel processes (with `Left` in one parallel process and `Limit` and `Index` in the other). Write down a suitable **PAR** construction to do this.

2. Comment on the validity of the following occam code fragments.

   (a)

   ```
   PAR
     SEQ
       Item := 0
     SEQ
       Item := Item + 1
   ```

   where the variable `Item` has been declared *outside* the **PAR** construction.

   (b)

   ```
   SEQ
     Chan ? Item
     Chan ! Data
   ```

   (c)

   ```
   PAR
     SEQ
       Chan1 ! A
       Chan2 ? B
     SEQ
       Chan2 ! C
       Chan1 ? D
   ```

   (d)

   ```
   PAR
     PAR
   ```

31

```
        Chan1 ! A
        Chan2 ! B
     PAR
        Chan2 ? C
        Chan1 ? D
```

(e)

```
   PAR
      SEQ
         Chan1 ? A
         Chan2 ? B
      SEQ
         Chan2 ! C
         Chan1 ! D
```

3. Rewrite the following occam program fragment to remove the deadlock
   (a) by reordering the sequence of inputs and outputs, and
   (b) by using a **PAR** construction as described in the text (assuming the sequence
       of inputs and outputs is independent).

```
   PAR
      SEQ
         Chan1 ? A
         Chan2 ? B
      SEQ
         Chan2 ! C
         Chan1 ! D
```

Chapter 2

Data basics

2.1 Introduction

In occam, program objects such as constants and variables must be declared before use; the name or *identifier* of the program object and its type must be specified. There are several typed objects used in occam
  • data types: the familiar integer, floating-point, etc. types,
  • channels: inter-process communication links that allow values to be communicated between concurrent processes
  • timers: special input-only channels that provide access to the transputer's real-time clock facility.
Channels and timers will be dealt with in Chapters 8 and 9 respectively. Data types (and simple channels) will be discussed in this chapter.

2.2 Identifiers

Occam is a strongly typed, hierarchical block-structured language. That is to say, program objects such as constants and variables, together with their data type, must be declared before they are used. Moreover, operations defined for a particular data type, for example addition or comparison, may be performed only with constants and variables of that data type. Program objects may be declared throughout the program at the head of a suitably indented process, making the objects local to that process.

The identifier of a constant or variable in an occam program:
  • may be of any length
  • must start with a letter, but may include digits and full-stops
  • is case-sensitive.
Occam has several reserved words which must always be written in capital letters. Within this book, reserved words will appear in **boldface** type. A constant or variable identifier must not clash with a reserved word. As occam is case-sensitive, the identifiers *count* and *COUNT*, for example, represent different objects.

There are two common conventions in use for writing an identifier in an occam program:

33

• the identifier is written in lower-case letters, but with an initial capital letter. For example,

```
Count
Temperature
Average
```

If the identifier comprises more than one word, the initial letter of each word will a capital. For example,

```
SensorReading
CharacterCount
EndOfFile
```

• the identifier is written in lower-case letters. For example,

```
count
temperature
average
```

If the identifier comprises more than one word, each word is separated by a full stop. For example,

```
sensor.reading
character.count
end.of.file
```

This book adopts the former convention.

The following are *invalid* occam identifiers

```
1Data       – starts with a digit
count$      – includes a $ character
Time_Out    – includes an underscore character
TIMER       – clashes with an occam reserved word
```

2.3 Data types

The basic or *primitive* data types available for constants and variables in occam 2 are given by the following reserved words:

```
BYTE        – a small integer (0 to 255) or a character
INT16       – a signed integer occupying 16-bits
INT32       – a signed integer occupying 32-bits
INT64       – a signed integer occupying 64-bits
```

REAL32   – a signed real occupying 32-bits
REAL64   – a signed real occupying 64-bits
BOOL   – a truth value.

A further data type, **INT**, is also defined. This type represents a signed integer, occupying an implementation-defined number of bits. For a T2XX transputer (16-bit wordlength), **INT** values lie in the range –32768 to 32767, whereas for a T4XX and a T8XX transputer (32-bit wordlength), **INT** values lie in the range – 2147483648 to 2147483647. Integers (**INT**, **INT32** and **INT64**) are represented internally in twos complement form.

The real types, **REAL32** and **REAL64**, internally use the ANSI/IEEE floating point standard representation, with 1 sign bit, 8 or 11 exponent bits, and 23 or 52 fraction bits respectively. The range for **REAL32** values is –3.40282348 E38 to 3.40282347 E38, and the range for **REAL64** values is –1.7976931348623158 E308 to 1.7976931348623157 E308.

The **BYTE** type, representing an unsigned integer in the range 0 to 255 or a character, is stored in 8-bits. The **BOOL** type is also stored in 8-bits, – **TRUE** having the numeric value 1, **FALSE** having the numeric value 0 – although this is not part of the occam language definition.

2.4 Literals

A *literal* is the textual representation of a known value, and may be used, for example, to assign a constant value to a variable or define a constant within an occam process. The format of the literal will depend on the data type required. Importantly, for literals of type **BYTE**, **INT16**, **INT32**, **INT64**, **REAL32** or **REAL64**, the data type *must* be explicitly specified within brackets immediately following the literal value, wherever the literal is used in any occam statement. The exceptions to this rule are:

• integer literals of type **INT**
• single character and character string literals
• Boolean literals.

No explicit typing is required for these literals.

2.4.1 Integer literals

Integer literals are signed, decimal or hexadecimal (whole) numbers. Valid data types for integer literals are **INT**, **INT16**, **INT32** and **INT64**. Additionally, the **BYTE** data type may be used for an integer literal *if* the literal numeric value lies in the range 0 to 255 (*but* their use in expressions is restricted to comparisons; see Ch. 3). Examples of *valid* integer forms are:

–273
32767
–90

(The unary minus is an arithmetic operator, and has well defined usage rules; see Ch. 3. Thus, strictly speaking, the above negative forms are expressions, not literals.)

Examples of *invalid* integer forms are:

6,536 – comma not allowed
13.0 – decimal point not allowed for an integer.

Example 2.1

```
AbsoluteZero := -273
```

assigns the integer value –273 to the **INT** variable AbsoluteZero. (No explicit typing is required for **INT** literals. If no data type is specified for an integer literal, then by default type **INT** is assumed.)

```
Count := Count + 1
```

adds the integer value 1 to the **INT** variable Count and then assigns the result to Count.

```
Maximum := 32767(INT16)
```

assigns the integer value 32767 to the **INT16** variable Maximum.

```
SmallNumber := 32(BYTE)
```

assigns the byte value 32 to the **BYTE** variable SmallNumber.

An integer literal may also be expressed as a *hexadecimal* (base 16) number. Such a number must be preceded by a hash (#). Examples of hexadecimal integers are:

```
#FC
#1FFF
```

Example 2.2

```
BitMask := #1F
```

assigns the integer value #1F to the **INT** variable BitMask.

2.4.2 Real literals
A real literal is a signed decimal number (with the decimal point and fractional part), optionally followed by an exponent value. Allowable data types for real lit-

erals are **REAL32** and **REAL64**. Examples of *valid* real forms are:

```
2.0
-0.00005
1.0E-6
-1.3E+3
```

Examples of *invalid* real forms are

```
235          - no decimal point
-5,000.0     - comma not allowed
2.           - no fractional part
```

Example 2.3

```
Epsilon := 1.0E-6(REAL64)
```

assigns the real value 1.0E-6 to the **REAL64** variable Epsilon.

```
Double := 2.0(REAL32) * Single
```

multiplies the **REAL32** variable Single by the real value 2.0 and then assigns the result to the **REAL32** variable Double.

2.4.3 Character literals
A character literal is a single character enclosed by single quotes (' '). Single characters are represented internally by their numeric ASCII code values as a single byte. Examples of character literals are:

```
'J'
'E'
'G'
```

Example 2.4

```
Char := 'M'
```

assigns the single character 'M' to the **BYTE** variable Char. (No explicit typing is required for a character literal.)

```
A, E, I, O, U := 'a', 'e', 'i', 'o', 'u'
```

assigns the characters 'a', 'e', 'i', 'o', 'u' to the **BYTE** variables A, E, I, O, U respectively.

It is possible to specify that a character be of type **INT** instead of the default

BYTE type. To do this, the **INT** type must be specified in brackets after the character. For example,

```
Return := '*c'(INT)
```

specifies that the character `'*c'` (carriage return) is to be of non-default type and assigns the character to the **INT** variable `Return`.

Certain characters, for example single and double quote marks, and non-printable control characters, for example carriage return and tab, are specified with a different format as follows

```
*code
```

where `code` is a specific letter for each character. The following table lists those characters that must be specified with this format.

```
*c   – carriage return
*n   – line feed
*t   – tab
*s   – space
*'   – single quote
*"   – double quote
**   – asterisk
```

Alternative denotations for `*c`, `*n`, `*t` and `*s` are `*C`, `*N`, `*T` and `*S` respectively.

Example 2.5

```
Asterisk := '**'
```

assigns the character `'**'` (asterisk) to the **BYTE** variable `Asterisk`.

```
Space := '*s'
```

assigns the character `'*s'` (space) to the **BYTE** variable `Space`. Note that the space character may be represented as

```
Space := '*s'
```

or

```
Space := ' '
```

Any character may also be written in the form

```
*hex_code
```

where `hex_code` is the ASCII value (expressed in hexadecimal) of the character.

Example 2.6

```
Bell := '*#07'
```

assigns the character constant having value #07 (control G) to the **BYTE** variable `Bell`.

2.4.4 String literals

A string literal is a character string enclosed by double quotes ("). Strings are represented internally as an array of bytes of the corresponding ASCII code values (see Ch. 4.5). Examples of character strings are

```
"Greetings!"

"Time flies"
```

Example 2.7

```
Message := "Hello"
```

assigns the character string `"Hello"` to the variable `Message`. Since a string is treated as a byte array, `Message` would be declared as a **BYTE** array variable of size 5.

```
Greetings := "Have a nice day*c*n"
```

assigns the character string "Have a nice day" plus the carriage return and line feed characters to the **BYTE** array variable `Greetings`.

```
Prompt := "***>"
```

assigns the character string comprising two asterisks and angle bracket to the **BYTE** array variable `Prompt`.

2.4.5 Boolean literals

A Boolean literal is a truth value, denoted by the occam reserved words **TRUE** and **FALSE**. Booleans are represented in occam as a single byte.

Example 2.8

```
EndOfFile := FALSE
```

assigns the Boolean value **FALSE** to the **BOOL** variable EndOfFile.

2.5 Declarations

The identifiers and types of all constants and variables in an occam program must be declared before use, each declaration statement being terminated by a colon (:). The colon "fixes" or binds the declaration to the process that immediately follows it. The declarations are *local* to that following process and any component processes (see §2.7). Any declaration statement must be indented by the same amount as the process to which it belongs.

Occam does not force a particular ordering on any declarations. A common ordering within an occam process is as follows (Pountain & May 1987):
• channels
• timers
• abbreviations (constants)
• variables.
Channels must be declared before the **PAR** in which they are used.

This chapter introduces simple (i.e. scalar) constants and variables. Later chapters (4 and 7) show how structured constants and variables may be declared using arrays.

2.5.1 Simple constants
A simple constant is an example of an occam *abbreviation*. Abbreviations are an important feature of occam and will be described fully in Chapter 7. A constant declaration specifies the data type of the constant and assigns that constant a value. It has the format

```
VAL type constant IS constant_expression :
```

where:
• type is the data type of the constant. The inclusion of type is optional and may be omitted, since the type of the constant may be determined from the type of constant_expression
• constant is the occam identifier of the constant
• constant_expression is the value assigned to the constant, and may be a literal or an expression (see Ch. 3) that evaluates to a constant value. The data type of constant_expression must be the same as type, if type is specified.

Example 2.9

```
VAL BYTE Limit IS 255(BYTE) :
VAL INT Emergency IS 999 :
VAL INT OneThousand IS Emergency + 1 :
VAL INT16 Maximum IS 32767(INT16) :
VAL REAL32 Pi IS 3.14159(REAL32) :
VAL REAL32 TwoPi IS 2.0(REAL32) * Pi :
VAL REAL64 Epsilon IS 1.0E-6(REAL64) :
```

are simple constant declarations that use the long-hand form of specification. For example, Limit is specified to be of type **BYTE** and have a byte value of 255, Emergency is specified to be of type **INT** and have an integer value of 999, and Pi is specified to be of type **REAL32** and have a real value of 3.14159. The declarations for OneThousand and TwoPi are examples of expressions that evaluate to constants.

As noted above, type may be omitted if the type of the constant may be determined from the data type of constant_expression. Thus, the above constant declarations may be written less tediously as shown below, but without the additional compiler check.

Example 2.10

```
VAL Limit IS 255(BYTE) :
VAL Emergency IS 999 :
VAL OneThousand IS Emergency + 1 :
VAL Maximum IS 32767(INT16) :
VAL Pi IS 3.14159(REAL32) :
VAL TwoPi IS 2.0(REAL32) * Pi :
VAL Epsilon IS 1.0E-6(REAL64) :
```

In accordance with the previously stated rule, explicit typing of **INT**, single character, character string and Boolean literals may be omitted. This is illustrated in the following example.

Example 2.11

```
VAL Space IS ' ' :
VAL Bell IS '*#07' :
VAL Initial IS 'J' :
VAL Asterisk IS '**' :
VAL Message IS "Hello" :
VAL Prompt IS "*c*n>" :
VAL Updating IS TRUE :
```

41

In the above, the character string constants, `Message` and `Prompt`, are effectively byte arrays of size five and three respectively (see Ch. 4).

Example 2.12

```
VAL Pi IS 3.14159(REAL32) :
VAL TwoPi IS 2.0(REAL32) * Pi :
SEQ
  Radius := 12.0(REAL32)
  Circumference := TwoPi * Radius
  RadiusSquared := Radius * Radius
  Area := Pi * RadiusSquared
```

shows the use of constant declarations in an occam fragment. (The occam variables, `Radius`, `Circumference`, `RadiusSquared` and `Area`, must also be declared; how this is done will be explained in the next section.)

2.5.2 Variables

A variable declaration specifies the data type of a variable. It has the format

```
type variable :
```

where
  • `type` specifies the data type of the variable
  • `variable` is the occam identifier of the variable.

Example 2.13

```
BYTE Char :
INT Index :
REAL32 Average :
BOOL EndOfFile :
```

declare variables `Char` of type **BYTE**, `Index` of type **INT**, `Average` of type **REAL32**, and `EndOfFile` of type **BOOL**.

More than one variable of the same type may be declared within the same specification, the identifiers being separated by commas. For example,

```
INT Count, Sum :
REAL32 Average, Total, Error :
BOOL EndOfLine, EndOfFile :
```

Example 2.14

```
VAL Pi IS 3.14159(REAL32) :
VAL TwoPi IS 2.0(REAL32) * Pi :
REAL32 Radius, RadiusSquared, Circumference, Area :
SEQ
   Radius := 12.0(REAL32)
   Circumference := TwoPi * Radius
   RadiusSquared := Radius * Radius
   Area := Pi * RadiusSquared
```

shows a previous example, but this time with the variables declared.

2.6 Simple channels

The channels used by a process must be declared in the same way as the constants and variables used by the process must be declared. As noted in Chapter 1, two processes wishing to communicate must each use the *same* channel. One process will be the output process, the other will be the input process.

A channel has an associated *protocol*. The protocol defines the type of data (i.e. the data type and format of the variables) to be transferred along the channel in any communication; the associated protocol effectively types the channel. The channel syntax allows for this protocol to be explicitly specified. Thus, it must be declared whether the channel will support the transfer of three integer values, an integer followed by two real values, or whatever. Protocols will be described fully later on in this book (Ch. 8). For now, only *simple* protocol channels – channels that allow the communication of a single value of a single data type at a time – will be considered. Channels may be used over and over again for the communication of data as specified by the protocol, that is, they support bursts of communication. This communication is achieved using the *input* and *output* primitives described in Chapter 1. A channel specification has the format

```
CHAN OF type channel :
```

where
   • type is the data type supported by the channel
   • channel is the occam identifier of the channel.

Example 2.15

```
CHAN OF BYTE Input :
```

declares a channel named Input, which will support the successive transfer of

43

single bytes.

Example 2.16

```
CHAN OF INT Error :
```

declares a channel named `Error` capable of communicating single integers.

More than one channel of the same type may be specified within the same declaration, the individual identifiers being separated by commas. For example,

```
CHAN OF BOOL Flag, Semaphore :
```

declares two channels, `Flag` and `Semaphore`, of type **BOOL**.

Example 2.17

```
CHAN OF BYTE Chan :
PAR
  BYTE Data :
  SEQ
    Data := 100(BYTE)
    Chan ! Data
  BYTE Value :
  SEQ
    Chan ? Value
```

depicts two sequential processes executing concurrently, but communicating with each other via the named channel Chan (Fig. 2.1). Note that the channel declaration is placed before the **PAR** construction. This is necessary because the communicating processes within the **PAR** must both have access to the channel specified in the declaration. This is all tied up with the concept of scope, which will be discussed in the next section. Note also how the variables for the input and output processes – Value for the input process, Data for the output process – have been declared. These variables are *local* to their respective processes (see next section for a full explanation).

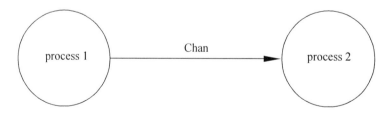

Figure 2.1   Two communicating **SEQ** processes.

Example 2.18

```
CHAN OF REAL32 Chan1, Chan2 :
PAR
  REAL32 Item, Result :
  SEQ
    Chan1 ! Item
    Chan2 ? Result
  REAL32 Data, Value :
  SEQ
    Chan1 ? Data
    Chan2 ! Value
```

depicts two sequential processes executing concurrently. Two-way communication between the two processes is achieved by specifying two channels. Local variables have again been specified for the communicating processes. Note the ordering of the input and output processes in both components of the **PAR** construction. This ordering avoids deadlock, as discussed in Chapter 1.

2.7 Scope

As discussed above, the named objects of an occam process, such as constants, variables and channels, must be declared in advance of any process in which they are used. The *scope* or range of definition of a named object is the range of definition of the process that immediately follows its declaration. (Scope also includes any declarations that are between the declaration of the named object and the following process.) The range of definition of a process is determined by its indention, and so the scope of named objects is defined by the indention of the following process. The named objects are said to be *local* to that process and any component processes.

Example 2.19

```
INT Item :          -- declaration of Item
INT Data :          -- scope of Item
SEQ                 --
  Item := 1024      --
    .               --
    .               --
    .               --
  SEQ               --
    Data := Item + 1024  --
```

45

In this example, the variable Item is available to the inner **SEQ** construction since this variable is still in scope. (The same comment applies to the variable Data.)

Example 2.20

```
CHAN OF INT Comm :      -- declaration of Comm
PAR                     -- scope of Comm
   INT Value :          --
   SEQ                  --
      Value := 512      --
      Comm ! Value      --
   INT Result :         --
   SEQ                  --
      Comm ? Result     --
```

shows how the channel Comm, being declared at the outermost level, has a scope that covers the whole program fragment. Thus, the channel is common to *both* component sequential processes – as it *must* be for inter-process communication.

Example 2.21

```
CHAN OF INT Comm :
PAR
   INT Value :          -- declaration of Value
   SEQ                  -- scope of Value
      Value := 512      --
      Comm ! Value      --
   INT Result :         -- declaration of Result
   SEQ                  -- scope of Result
      Comm ? Result     --
```

illustrates the scope of the variables in the inner processes of the previous example.

A consequence of scoping is that the value of a variable is undefined outside the scope of the declaration. This means that program objects with different scopes may have the same name but lead independent existences, that is, they are totally separate objects, and may even have different types.

Example 2.22

```
CHAN OF BYTE Chan :
PAR
   BYTE Char :          -- first declaration of Char
   SEQ                  -- scope
      Char := 'J'       --
```

46

```
Chan ! Char        --
BYTE Char :        -- second declaration of Char
SEQ                -- scope
   Chan ? Char     --
```

A variable named Char is declared for both sequential processes. However, these variables are quite separate, each being local to its own sequential process. Channel Chan is declared outside the **PAR** construction and so the channel is common to both component processes.

If an object is declared within the scope of an existing object with the *same* name, then all references to that name refer to the more recent declaration, that is, the more recent declaration takes precedence in a clash of scope. The older declaration is suspended for the duration of the scope of the more recent declaration, but resumes its role afterwards.

Example 2.23

```
BYTE Item :        -- declaration as BYTE
SEQ                -- scope as BYTE
   Item := 50 (BYTE)
   INT Item :      -- declaration as INT
   SEQ             -- scope as INT (BYTE
                   -- declaration
                   -- masked)
      Item := 500  --
      Chan2 ! Item -- gives 500
   Chan1 ! Item    -- gives 50 (BYTE declaration
                   -- restored)
```

where Chan1 is specified as type **BYTE**, and Chan2 is specified as type **INT**. In this example, the second declaration of variable Item masks the first declaration for the duration of the second's scope. Any reference to Item during this period will refer to the second declaration. Thus, the output via channel Chan2 produces the value 500 as the second declaration is in force here. However, the output via channel Chan1 produces the value 50, since the first declaration is back in force; the second one is no longer in scope.

Any variable should be assigned a value – either by direct assignment or input – before being used. Occam does not itself initialize any variable before use. Chapter 7 explains how an occam procedure may be executed many times. It is important to realize that occam does not guarantee that the value of a local variable be kept from one execution of a procedure to the next. If a value of a variable needs to be retained between executions, then the variable must be declared in a higher-level process. Such a variable is called a *free* variable.

A free variable is available to **PAR** component processes so long as that variable

47

is not assigned to or input by the component processes.

2.8 Exercises

1. Which of the following are valid occam identifiers?
(a)   `chan`
(b)   `CHAN`
(c)   `Raw.Data`
(d)   `Raw Data`
(e)   `Raw_Data`

2. In terms of scope, comment on the validity of the following occam code fragments.
(a)

```
INT Count, Limit :
REAL32 Factor :
BYTE Limit :
```

(b)

```
BYTE Small :
SEQ
  Small := 55
```

(c)

```
BYTE Small :
SEQ
  Small := -1(BYTE)
```

(d)

```
REAL32 Real :
SEQ
  Real := 3.0(REAL32)
```

(e)

```
INT INDEX
SEQ
  Index := 0
```

(f)

```
CHAN OF BYTE Chan :
PAR
  BYTE Char :
  SEQ
    Char := 'J'
    Chan ! Char
  SEQ
    Chan ? Char
```

(g)

```
CHAN OF BYTE Chan :
PAR
  BYTE Char :
  SEQ
    Char := 'G'
    Chan ! Char
  INT Char :
  SEQ
  Chan ? Char
```

(h)

```
CHAN OF INT Chan1 :
CHAN OF BYTE Chan2 :
PAR
  INT Item :
  SEQ
    Chan1 ? Item
  BYTE Item :
  SEQ
    Item := 250(BYTE)
    Chan2 ! Item
```

(i)

```
CHAN OF INT Chan1 :
CHAN OF BYTE Chan2 :
INT Item :
PAR
  SEQ
    Chan1 ? Item
```

```
BYTE Item :
SEQ
  Chan2 ? Item
```

(j)

```
INT Count, Index :
SEQ
  Index := Count
```

(k)

```
INT Count :
SEQ
  Count := 0
  INT Index :
  SEQ
    Index := Count
```

(l)

```
INT Index :
SEQ
  .
  .
  .
  INT Count :
  SEQ
    .
    .
    .
    Index := Count
```

Chapter 3

Operators

3.1 Introduction

Constants and variables may be used in occam as operands that may be combined with operators to form simple expressions. The expressions so formed may be combined again with further constants, variables or expressions to form more complex expressions. There is a range of operators available in occam to allow the formation, for example, of arithmetic and Boolean expressions. Most operators are *dyadic*, requiring two operands, but some are *monadic*, requiring one operand. Other objects, such as array elements and tables (Ch. 4), are also classed as operands and these may also participate in the formation of expressions.

Expressions may be assigned to a variable, output to a channel or take part in a condition evaluation.

Occam enforces strong typing:
- operands of any operator must be of the same data type
- the type of any variable being assigned to in an assignment statement must be the same as the type of the expression being assigned.

The repertoire of operators available covers:
- arithmetic
- relational
- Boolean
- bitwise
- shift operations.

3.2 Arithmetic operators

Constants, variables and literals of *integer* or *real* data types may be combined with arithmetic operators to form arithmetic expressions, with the proviso that the operands must be of the *same* data type, either explicitly or via type conversion. (Type conversion is discussed later in this chapter.) The type of the resultant expression is the same as that of its operands.

The basic arithmetic operators are:

51

```
+    - addition
-    - subtraction
*    - multiplication
/    - division
REM - remainder (from division)
```

The subtraction operator may be used as both a monadic and a dyadic operator. For example,

```
MinInt  := -32768                            -- monadic
RoomLeft := BufferSize - NumberInBuffer  -- dyadic
```

The resultant value from an integer division is truncated, that is, rounded towards zero. For example,

```
11 / 6     - result is 1
(-11) / 6 - result is -1
```

This example introduces the concept of *precedence brackets*; the order of evaluation of operators in an occam expression must be specified with precedence brackets. Operator precedence is an important feature of occam and is described shortly.

An alternative denotation of **REM** is \. Both denotations may be used interchangeably. For example,

```
11 REM 6  - result is 5
(-11) \ 6 - result is -5
```

Note that the result of a real arithmetic expression is rounded to the closest value that can be represented by the real type (see §3.1.4 of this chapter for a discussion of rounding).

Example 3.1

```
INT Index, Seconds, Minutes:
REAL32 Average, Sum, Count, Double, Value:
SEQ
  . . .
  Index := Index + 1
  Seconds := 60 * Minutes
  Count := Count + 1.0(REAL32)
  Average := Sum / Count
  Double := 2.0(REAL32) * Value
```

is an occam fragment containing examples of arithmetic operations, where values

52

for the variables Index, Minutes, Count, Sum and Value are assumed to have been already assigned. Note the use of typed literals in the expressions. As explained in Chapter 2, except for type **INT** integer, single character, character string and Boolean literals, the type of any literal must be explicitly specified within brackets immediately following the literal value.

Example 3.2

```
REAL32 Data :
SEQ
  InChan ? Data
  OutChan ! Data / 2.0(REAL32)
```

is an example of an arithmetic expression being used in an output process, where the protocol of the channels, InChan and OutChan, is specified to have type **REAL32**.

An arithmetic operation is considered to be invalid if the result produced is out of range of the given type; for example, arithmetic overflow or underflow, and division by zero.

A few specialized arithmetic operators are available.

3.2.1 Modulo arithmetic operators

Modulo arithmetic produces values that neither overflow nor underflow. Instead, values wrap around cyclically, either from the most positive value to the most negative or from the most negative value to the most positive, depending on the particular values of the operands and operator. For example, modulo arithmetic values, using **INT16** types, cycle round as follows:

```
. . . -1, 0, 1, . . . 32766, 32767, -32768, -32767,
. . . -1, 0, 1, . . .
```

There are three modulo arithmetic operators available. These are

```
PLUS  - modulo addition
MINUS - modulo subtraction
TIMES - modulo multiplication
```

The respective operands must be of the *same integer* type.

Example 3.3

```
VAL INT16 MaxInt IS 32767(INT16) :
INT16 Result :
SEQ
```

```
Result := MaxInt PLUS 1(INT16)-- value is -32768
Result := MaxInt PLUS 2(INT16)-- value is -32767
```

Example 3.4

```
VAL INT16 MinInt IS INT16(-32768) :
INT16 Result :
SEQ
  Result := MinInt MINUS 1(INT16)-- value is 32767
  Result := MinInt MINUS 2(INT16)-- value is 32766
```

Such arithmetic is most useful in connection with timers (Ch. 9).

3.2.2 *MOSTPOS and MOSTNEG*

The operators **MOSTPOS** and **MOSTNEG**, when applied to an *integer* type, produce the most positive and the most negative values respectively of that type.

```
MOSTPOS type
MOSTNEG type
```

For example,

```
MOSTPOS INT32
```

produces a value of 2147483647.

3.2.3 *Operator precedence*

In contrast with other languages, occam does *not* have a hierarchy of operator precedence. In Pascal, for example, the arithmetic expression 2 + 3 * 4 unambiguously produces the value 14 and not the value 20 since, in Pascal, the * operator takes precedence over (is evaluated before) the + operator. Such an expression is *illegal* in occam.

The reason for this is that operators in occam have equal precedence: there is no preferred order for evaluating terms containing operators. The required order of evaluation of multi-operator expressions must be explicitly specified with the use of brackets. For example,

```
(A + B) + C is legal
A + (B + C) is legal
but A + B + C is illegal
```

and

```
(3 * 2) + 6 is legal, result = 12
```

```
3 * (2 + 6) is legal, result = 24
but 3 * 2 + 6 is illegal
```

Complex expressions may contain nested bracketed terms to indicate the order of evaluation.

Example 3.5

```
Expression := ((R + S) / 2) + T
Discriminant := (B * B) - (4.0(REAL32) * (A * C))
DifferenceOfSquares := (X * X) - (Y * Y)
```

shows the use of precedence brackets in valid assignment statements.

These remarks concerning operator precedence also apply to the other operators, and not just the arithmetic operators.

3.2.4 Data conversion

Occam allows an operand declared as one primitive type to be expressed as certain other primitive types; for example, a real type to be expressed as an integer and vice versa, an integer type to be expressed as a byte and vice versa. This mechanism is known as *data conversion*. Data conversion allows, for example, the writing of a mixed data type expression, that is, an expression with operands of different *declared* types. Any data conversion must be specified explicitly by writing the target type ahead of the operand due to be converted:

```
type operand
```

where `type` is the target type and is one of the primitive data types. Data conversion is classed as an operation. Consequently, any conversion appearing in an expression must be enclosed within precedence brackets.

Example 3.6

```
INT Number :
SEQ
  InChan ? Number
  OutChan ! BYTE (Number + (INT '0'))
```

where the channels, InChan and OutChan, are specified as type **INT** and **BYTE**, respectively. This occam fragment shows an integer number (assumed to lie in the range 0–9) being converted to the corresponding ASCII character for output. The conversion proceeds by adding the integer value of character ' 0 ' (the base value) to the number. (In the ASCII representation of characters, the character ' 0 ' has a numeric value of 48, ' 1 ' has a value of 49, . . . and ' 9 ' has a value of 57.) This produces the corresponding ASCII value of the number. Note the use of the type conversions. The integer value of character `'0'` is obtained by the **INT** conversion, and the final value converted to type **BYTE**.

Conversion between the real types is allowed (*but* see the discussion on **ROUND** and **TRUNC** in this section), as is the conversion between the integer types, with the proviso that any conversion is valid only if the result is in the range of values supported by the target type. For example, an **INT32** variable with a value 32 768 cannot be converted to type **INT16**, as the value is too large to be represented in **INT16**.

Example 3.7

```
REAL64 Double1, Double2 :
REAL32 Single :
SEQ
   Single := 3.144 (REAL32)
   Double1 := 6.6666666 (REAL64)
   Double2 := (REAL64 Single) * Double1
```

shows the conversion of a **REAL32** variable to **REAL64**.

Data conversion between integer (or byte) and Boolean types is possible as long as the conversion is in range. (Boolean values are represented in occam by the byte values 0 and 1.) For example,

```
BOOL 1 converts to TRUE.
INT FALSE converts to 0.
BOOL 2 is, however, invalid.
```

The conversion between real and byte types, and real and Boolean types, is not specifically allowed, but may be staged via an integer conversion. For example,

```
Real := REAL32 ROUND (INT Byte)
```

demonstrates the two-stage process of converting a byte type to a real.

Data conversion between integer and real types causes complications because of the difference in internal representation of these two types. (Integer types are represented in twos complement form – a single sign bit plus 15, 31, or 63 bits for the integer value – and real types are represented by the ANSI/IEEE floating point standard; see Ch. 2.) It is necessary to state in these cases whether the conversion is to incorporate a rounding or truncation of the result. This is achieved by inserting the occam reserved word **ROUND** or **TRUNC** between the target type and operand.

```
type ROUND operand
type TRUNC operand
```

The effect of **ROUND** is to round the operand value to the nearest number. When the operand value is equidistant from the two nearest numbers, rounding is to the nearest even number. The effect of **TRUNC** is to round the operand value towards zero. For example, the effect of **ROUND** is shown by

```
INT ROUND  3.4 (REAL32)    -- result is  3
INT ROUND -3.4 (REAL32)    -- result is -3
INT ROUND  3.8 (REAL32)    -- result is  4
INT ROUND -3.8 (REAL32)    -- result is -4
INT ROUND  3.5 (REAL32)    -- result is  4
INT ROUND -3.5 (REAL32)    -- result is -4
INT ROUND  2.5 (REAL32)    -- result is  2
```

and the effect of **TRUNC** is shown by

```
INT TRUNC  3.4 (REAL32)    -- result is  3
INT TRUNC -3.4 (REAL32)    -- result is -3
INT TRUNC  3.8 (REAL32)    -- result is  3
INT TRUNC -3.8 (REAL32)    -- result is -3
INT TRUNC  3.5 (REAL32)    -- result is  3
INT TRUNC -3.5 (REAL32)    -- result is -3
```

The same observations apply to the conversion of integers to reals. For example,

```
REAL32 TRUNC 4         -- result is 4.0
REAL32 ROUND 4         -- result is 4.0
```

The effect of **ROUND** and **TRUNC** on the same integer does not necessarily produce the same real value if the integer value cannot be exactly represented in the real representation.

The conversion of a value of type **REAL64** to type **REAL32** is allowed, provided that the value is in the range of the **REAL32** type. Moreover, the conversion must specify a truncation or rounding. For example,

```
SmallReal := REAL32 ROUND BigReal
```

shows such a conversion.

3.3 Relational operators

Relational operators allow operands to be compared; for example, to test whether an operand is less than or equal to another operand. The result of the comparison is a Boolean value, that is, **TRUE** or **FALSE**. The expression formed by a relational operator and its operands is a Boolean expression.

```
=    - equal
<>   - not equal
<    - less than
>    - greater than
<=   - less than or equal to
>=   - greater than or equal to
```

Operands, which may be constants, variables or expressions, used with the equality (=) and inequality (<>) operators may be of *any* primitive data type, but the operands used with the remaining relational operators *must* be of *byte*, *integer* or *real* types only. Both operands must be the *same* data type.

Characters and strings may be compared with relational operators, according to their ASCII ordering. For example, if Comp is declared to be of type **BOOL**, then

```
Comp := (7 = 14) evaluates to FALSE
Comp := (7 < 9) evaluates to TRUE
Comp := (6.9(REAL32) >= 1.3(REAL32)) evaluates to
        TRUE
Comp := ('Z' > 'A') evaluates to TRUE
Comp := ("Hello" > "Greetings") is invalid because
        arrays cannot be compared
```

(Note that the parentheses around each of the Boolean expressions in the above examples are not really required but their inclusion perhaps aids readability.)

Example 3.8

```
Count = Limit
```

is a Boolean expression that evaluates to the value **TRUE**, if the value of Count is equal to the value of Limit, and to **FALSE** otherwise, and

```
Error <= Epsilon
```

evaluates to **TRUE** if the value of Error is less than or equal to the value of Epsilon, and to **FALSE** otherwise.

Example 3.9

```
BOOL Flag :
BYTE Char :
SEQ
```

```
InChan ? Char
Flag := (Char > 'A')
```

where the protocol of the channel InChan is declared to be of type **BYTE**. In this occam fragment, Flag is assigned the value **TRUE** if Char has a value greater than the ASCII value of **'A'**.

3.4 Boolean operators

Boolean operators comprise the usual logical connectives, **AND**, **OR** and **NOT**. They allow the logical combination of Boolean operands, either simple Boolean variables or Boolean expressions. The result is a Boolean value, **TRUE** or **FALSE**.

```
AND - Boolean and
OR  - Boolean or
NOT - Boolean not
```

For example,

```
(Count < Limit) OR (Error > Epsilon)
```

is the logical or combination of the Boolean expressions, Count < Limit and Error > Epsilon. The value of the resultant expression depends on the current value of the numeric variables being compared.

Example 3.10

```
(Value >= Minimum) AND (Value <= Maximum)
```

is a combination of Boolean expressions representing a test that evaluates to the value **TRUE** if a value falls within the range defined by Minimum and Maximum.

Boolean expressions are typically used in control expressions (see Ch. 5), examples of which are

```
WHILE Active
```

where Active is a Boolean variable, and

```
WHILE NOT (Running OR Waiting)
```

where Running and Waiting are Boolean variables.

Example 3.11

```
BOOL Flag :
BYTE Char :
SEQ
  InChan ? Char
  Flag := (Char >= '0') AND (Char <= '9')
```

sets the value of Flag to **TRUE** if Char is an ASCII digit.

Example 3.12

```
BOOL Level1, Level2:
SEQ
  PAR
    InPin1 ? Level1
    InPin2 ? Level2
  OutPin ! NOT (Level1 AND Level2)
```

represents a simplistic software simulation of a NAND logic gate, the inputs proceeding in parallel, followed by the production of the output. (A NAND operation is defined as being the negation of an AND operation.) It is assumed that the channels, InPin1, InPin2, and OutPin, have been specified as **CHAN OF BOOL**.

The requirement of precedence brackets is relaxed for Boolean operators: brackets may be omitted between expressions containing multiple Boolean operators. For example,

```
Bool1 OR Bool2 OR Bool3
```

is a valid combination of Boolean operands.

3.5 Bitwise operators

These dyadic operators allow various operations, for example, setting and masking, to be performed on the individual bits or pattern of bits comprising the value of a constant, variable or expression of *integer* type. One operand represents the value being operated on; the other represents the bit pattern that operates on this value, and itself may be a constant, variable or expression of *integer* type.

```
BITAND  - bitwise and
BITOR   - bitwise or
><      - bitwise exclusive or
BITNOT  - bitwise not
```

The operands must be of the *same integer* type.

Alternative denotations for bitwise and, or and not are /\, \/, and ~ respectively.

Example 3.13

```
Int /\ #7F
```

shows the bitwise "anding" of a variable `Int` with the constant #7F. The bit pattern of #7F is 0111 1111, and so this operation will set to zero all but the 7 low-order bits of `Int`. This expression may be written equivalently as

```
#7F /\ Int
```

Example 3.14

```
Int \/ #1F
```

shows the bitwise "oring" of a variable *Int* with the constant #1F. The bit pattern of #1F is 0001 1111, and so this operation will set to one the 5 low-order bits of `Int`.

Example 3.15

```
UpperCaseChar := LowerCaseChar /\ #DF
```

converts a lower-case ASCII character to its upper-case equivalent (both assumed to be represented by *integer* variables) by anding with the bit pattern 1101 1111 (#DF). (Lower- and upper-case ASCII characters differ by the setting of the fifth bit.)

Example 3.16

```
BITNOT (Int1 BITOR Int2)
```

computes the NOR value for variables `Int1` and `Int2`, NOR being defined as the negation of the OR operation.

Example 3.17

```
StatusRegister := StatusRegister >< #4000
```

uses a mask of #4000 to invert the fourteenth bit of `StatusRegister`.

Example 3.18

```
INT Pulse1, Pulse2:
SEQ
  PAR
    InPin1 ? Pulse1
    InPin2 ? Pulse2
  OutPin ! BITNOT (Pulse1 BITAND Pulse2)
```

represents a variation on the simulation of a logic gate, this time using integer types, and channels specified as **CHAN OF INT**, together with bitwise operators. Other, more complex, digital circuits may be simulated quite easily in occam using the simple logic gates as building blocks. However, deadlock problems can easily arise in such circuits. One solution is to introduce a propagation delay into the gate model (Welch 1987).

3.6 Shift operators

The bits comprising the value of an *integer* constant, variable or expression may be shifted left or right a specified number of bit positions (Fig. 3.1).

```
<<  - shift left
>>  - shift right
```

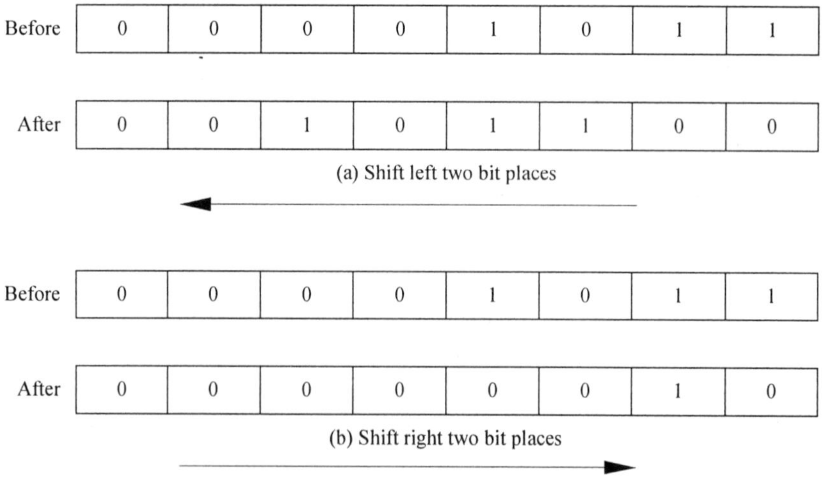

Before	0	0	0	0	1	0	1	1

After	0	0	1	0	1	1	0	0

(a) Shift left two bit places

Before	0	0	0	0	1	0	1	1

After	0	0	0	0	0	0	1	0

(b) Shift right two bit places

Figure 3.1   Example of shifting.

The number of bit positions to be shifted is given by the second operand. This operand, which itself may be a constant, variable or an expression, must be of type **INT**. The number of bits to be shifted must not be greater than the number allowed for the integer type of the first operand. The bit positions of the first operand, vacated by the shift operation, are filled with 0 bits. Note that the sign bit of the first operand is shifted, and there is no check for overflow.

For example,

```
Int << 2
```

shifts the value of the variable `Int` left by two bit positions, and

```
Int >> 8
```

shifts the value of `Int` right by eight bit positions.

Such shifting is similar to multiplying or dividing by powers of two if the shifted value is treated as unsigned. For example,

```
7 << 30
```

evaluates to (-2^{30}).

Example 3.19

```
If Int = 7 * 2²⁸ then
```

```
Int << 2
```

becomes (-2^{30}).

Example 3.20

```
INT16 Packet, TerminalNumber :
BYTE Char :
SEQ
  InChar ? Char
  InInt16 ? TerminalNumber
  Packet := (TerminalNumber << 8) \/ (INT16 Char)
```

forms a composite `Packet`, comprising `TerminalNumber` in the top 8 bits, and `Char` in the bottom 8 bits.

63

3.7 Exercises

1. Comment on the validity of the following occam expressions and fragment:

    (a) `100 - 5 * 5`
    (b) `(100 - (5 * 5) + 20)`
    (c) `100 - (5 * 5) > Limit`
    (d) `100 - (Count > Limit)`
    (e)
    ```
    INT16 Result:
    SEQ
      Result := 32767(INT16) + 1(INT16)
      Result := 33(INT16) * 10
      Result := 330(INT16) * 100(INT16)
    ```

2. Write down the resultant value for the following occam expressions:

    (a)   **NOT TRUE**
    (b)   **TRUE OR** BooleanValue
    (c)   **TRUE AND** BooleanValue

    where BooleanValue has a value **TRUE** or **FALSE**.
    What happens if **TRUE** is replaced by **FALSE** in the above expressions?

3. Write down the resultant values for the following data conversions:

    (a)   **BYTE TRUE**
    (b)   **BYTE FALSE**
    (c)   **BOOL** 0
    (d)   **INT ROUND** 3.142(**REAL32**)
    (e)   **INT TRUNC** 3.142(**REAL32**)
    (f)   **REAL32 TRUNC** 3
    (g)   **REAL32 ROUND** 3

4. Write an occam program that will set bit 4 of an integer variable.

5. Write a set of occam programs that will simulate various logic gates, for example, AND, OR and NOR.

6. Write an occam program that will give the number of hundreds, tens and units in the three-digit integer, 123.

7. Write an occam program that will simulate an XOR gate, composed of AND and OR logic gates. (Hint: A XOR B = ((NOT A) AND B) OR (A AND (NOT B)))

Chapter 4

Arrays

4.1 Introduction

Occam 2 has only one *structured* type defined – this is the multidimensional array. Arrays provide the ability to address an ordered sequence of objects of the same type via a common name. These objects comprise the *components* of the array. Arrays may be formed from any of the primitive data types, or the channel or timer types (channel and timer types are described in Chs 8 and 9 respectively). They must be named in a declaration statement before use; they are bound by the usual scoping rules to the process immediately following their specification.

4.2 One-dimensional arrays

The format of a one-dimensional array declaration is

```
[size]type array :
```

where
  • `size` is the number of components in the array
  • `type` is the type of the array components
  • `array` is the array identifier.
The *size* must be a positive non-zero value of type **INT**, enclosed within square brackets. It may be represented by a literal, a previously declared constant or an expression that evaluates to a constant (but *not* by a variable). The type may be one of the primitive data types, or the channel or timer types. If the type is one of the primitive data types, then operations may be performed on single components, sections of the array or on the whole array itself. Only single components of channel or timer arrays may be referenced. The mechanism for accessing the various parts of an array – single components, sections or the whole array – will be described in this chapter.

65

Example 4.1

```
[50]REAL32 Readings :
```

declares an array Readings having 50 components, each component being of
type **REAL32**.

In the example above, Readings is regarded as an array of type [50]**REAL32**.
This is quite general in occam; the array type is determined by *both* its size and
the type of its components. For occam arrays to have the same type, they must have
the same size and components of the same type.

Example 4.2

```
[10]BOOL Flags :
```

is the declaration for an array Flags of type [10]**BOOL**.

Example 4.3

```
VAL Panel IS 25:
[Panel]CHAN OF BYTE Switches:
```

declares an array of 25 channels named Switches, each channel being capable
of communicating single byte values. Such a channel specification is just the array
extension of a simple channel protocol.

Example 4.4

```
[26]BYTE Alphabet :
[5]BYTE Vowels :
```

declares two arrays, Alphabet and Vowels, of type [26]**BYTE** and [5]**BYTE**
respectively.

Arrays of the same type may be specified in the same statement. For example,

```
[16]BYTE WhitePieces, BlackPieces :
```

declares two arrays, each of type [16]**BYTE**.

Example 4.5

```
VAL Size IS 16 :
[Size]TIMER Clock, Watch :
```

66

specifies two timer arrays, `Clock` and `Watch`, each with 16 components. (Timers are special channels connected to the transputer internal clock – see Ch. 9.)

A whole array may be input, output or assigned to. In such operations, the whole array is accessed by referencing the array identifier. In any assignment or input, the array type must be strictly observed.

The following example illustrates how an array may be transferred from one parallel process to another. The example also shows how a simple channel protocol may be extended to cope with the transfer of arrays of values (more of this in Ch. 8).

Example 4.6

```
CHAN OF [10]INT Chan : -- extension of simple
                        -- channel for the
                        -- transmission of an array
PAR
  [10]INT Array1 :
  SEQ
    .
    .                   -- assign values to Array1
    .

    Chan ! Array1
  [10]INT Array2 :
  SEQ
    Chan ? Array2
```

Note the specification of the arrays and the channel. Both array variables, `Array1` and `Array2`, and the channel, `Chan`, must be of type `[10]INT`, that is, the array type is strictly observed. An alternative to extending the simple channel protocol is the transfer of single array components within a loop. The loop is executed the required number of times in order to transfer the whole array. This approach is further explored in Chapter 6.

Note the difference between

```
[10]CHAN OF INT Chan :
```

and

```
CHAN OF [10]INT Chan :
```

The former is an *array of ten channels*, each capable of transmitting a *single* integer; the latter is a *single channel* capable of transmitting an *array of ten integers* (Fig. 4.1).

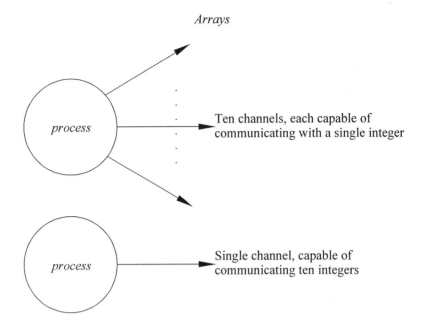

Figure 4.1   An array of channels and a channel for an array.

4.3 Multidimensional arrays

Multidimensional arrays are specified in an analogous manner, the size of each dimension being enclosed within square brackets. For example, a two-dimensional array is specified as

```
[size_1][size_2]type array :
```

where `size_1` and `size_2` are the number of components in each dimension.
    For example,

```
[17][15]REAL32 Grid :
```

represents a two-dimensional array `Grid` with 17 components, each of which is a 15-element one-dimensional array.
    The array `Grid` may be regarded as an array of an array of type `[15]REAL32`. In general, multidimensional arrays may be considered as arrays of array types.
    The format for the declaration of a general multidimensional array is

```
[size_1][size_2] . . . [size_n]type array :
```

where, again, size_1, size_2, . . . size_n are the number of components in each dimension.

Example 4.7

```
[20][1980]BYTE DisplayScreen :
[8][8][8]REAL32 Cube :
[5][4]REAL64 Matrix :
```

are examples of multidimensional array declarations.

Similar to one-dimensional arrays, whole multidimensional arrays may be
input, output or assigned to. Again, in any assignment or input, the array type must
be strictly observed. For example,

```
CHAN OF [5][4]REAL64 Comm :
PAR
  [5][4]REAL64 AMatrix :
  SEQ
     .
     . -- assign values to AMatrix
     .
     Comm ! AMatrix
  [5][4]REAL64 BMatrix :
  SEQ
     Comm ? BMatrix
```

shows the transfer of a two-dimensional array between two parallel processes.

4.4 Array subscripts

The position of an object within an array (i.e. a component of an array) is given
by the array index or *subscript*. The subscript may be a constant (literal or occam
constant) or an expression involving constants and/or variables, but *must* always
be of data type **INT**. The initial subscript of an array is 0. A component of an array
is referenced via

```
array[subscript]
```

The *subscript* must always lie within the bounds of the array (i.e. equal to or greater
than 0 and less than size).

For example, the declaration

```
[50]REAL32 Readings :
```

69

would have 50 components as follows

```
Readings[0]
Readings[1]
Readings[2]
     .
     .
     .
Readings[49]
```

The individual components of an array may be used in exactly the same way as an unstructured occam variable – for example, array components may be used in assignment, input and output statements, and may be used as operands in expressions.

Example 4.8

```
Readings[3]  := Readings[2] + 3.0(REAL32)
Readings[I]  := 12.0(REAL32)
Sum := Readings[0] + Readings[1]
Readings[I + J] := Value
Total := Total + Readings[I + J]
Display ! Readings[15]
```

where the subscripts I and J are of type **INT**. These are all legal examples involving the use of array components (provided the expressions involving I and J evaluate to valid subscripts for the array Readings).

Example 4.9

```
[3]REAL32 X, Y, Z :
SEQ
  Z[1]  := (X[2] * Y[3]) - (X[3] * Y[2])
  Z[2]  := (X[3] * Y[1]) - (X[1] * Y[3])
  Z[3]  := (X[1] * Y[2]) - (X[2] * Y[1])
```

is an occam program fragment that computes the vector cross-product of arrays X and Y.

Components of channel and timer arrays may only be used in the same way as their unstructured equivalents, as part of an input or output process. Only single components of these types of arrays may be referenced. References to sections of an array or to the whole array are invalid for channel and timer arrays.

70

Example 4.10

```
[10]CHAN OF INT Sensors :
INT Voltage, Temperature :
PAR
   Sensor[0] ? Voltage
   Sensor[1] ? Temperature
   .
   .
   .
```

shows an occam fragment that has declared an array of ten channels, Sensor. These channels may only be accessed individually, as shown.

Components of multidimensional arrays are accessed in an analogous manner to their one-dimensional counterparts. In occam, multidimensional arrays are stored in *row-major* order. This means that, for example, with a two-dimensional array, the second subscript will vary more rapidly than the first, and so on, for each extra dimension.

For example, the components of an array declared as

```
[18][16]REAL32 Grid :
```

are stored in memory in the following order

```
Grid[0][0]
Grid[0][1]
Grid[0][2]
   .
   .
   .
Grid[0][14]
Grid[0][15]
Grid[1][0]
Grid[1][1]
Grid[1][2]
   .
   .
   .
Grid[17][14]
Grid[17][15]
```

Example 4.11

```
Grid[7][7] := 0.0(REAL32)
```

71

```
Grid[I] [J]   := REAL32 ROUND (I + J)
Grid[I + J] [I + J]  := 0.0(REAL32)
```

where the subscripts I and J are of type **INT**. These are all legal examples involving the use of array components (provided the expressions involving I and J evaluate to valid subscripts for the array Grid).

Care must be taken with the use of arrays in **PAR** constructions. The rules for their use say that an array may be used in more than one component process, provided that the values of the array subscripts are constants and provided that the parts of the array accessed in each component process do not overlap.

When arrays are referenced within a loop, the accesses may be made more efficient with the use of segments and abbreviations (Ch. 7).

4.5 Segments

Consecutive components of an array comprising a *segment* or a slice of the array may be referenced as a single unit. The format for an array segment is

```
[array FROM first FOR count]
```

where
   • array is the array name
   • first is the subscript of the first component of the segment
   • count is the number of components.
Both first and count must be of data type **INT**. The value of count must be non-negative and must be so constrained that the components referenced lie within the bounds of the array. A segment is just another array comprising the referenced components of the original array. For example,

```
[Readings FROM 10 FOR 5]
```

picks out the eleventh, twelfth, . . . and fifteenth components of the array Readings, that is,

```
Readings[10], Readings[11], . . . Readings[14].
```

Segments may take part in input, output and assignment processes. In an assignment, the array type of the segment must be observed: the data type and number of components of the left- and right-hand sides of the assignment must be the same. Like any other array, a segment may be subscripted. For example,

```
[Readings FROM 10 FOR 5] [1]
```

corresponds to Readings [11].

Example 4.12

```
[100]INT Array1, Array2 :
SEQ
  .
  . -- assign values to the first 50 components
  . -- of Array1
  .
  [Array2 FROM 0 FOR 50] := [Array1 FROM 0 FOR 50]
```

copies the first 50 components of Array1 to Array2.

Example 4.13

```
[2]CHAN OF [50]REAL32 Sensor :
[100]REAL32 SensorReadings :
SEQ
  PAR
    Sensor[0] ? [SensorReadings FROM 0 FOR 50]
    Sensor[1] ? [SensorReadings FROM 50 FOR 50]
  .
  . -- process sensor readings
  .
```

inputs the two halves of the array SensorReadings as separate inputs.

Example 4.14

```
[30]INT WholeRange :
[10]INT MiddleRange :
SEQ
  MiddleRange := [WholeRange FROM 10 FOR 10]
  .
  . -- modify contents of MiddleRange
  .
  [WholeRange FROM 10 FOR 10] := MiddleRange
```

copies part of the array WholeRange into the array MiddleRange and back again after some processing.

Example 4.15

```
CHAN OF [1000]REAL32 Chan1 :
CHAN OF [1000]REAL32 Chan2 :
```

73

```
[2000]REAL32 Digitizings  :
SEQ
  .
  . -- assign values to Digitizings
  .
  PAR
    Chan1 ! [Digitizings FROM 0 FOR 1000]
    Chan2 ! [Digitizings FROM 1000 FOR 1000]
```

outputs the two halves of the array `Digitizings` on two separate channels.

4.6 Strings

In occam, a string of characters is an array of bytes, each byte being the ASCII representation of a character of the string. As such, string constants and variables may be manipulated in the fashion of arrays. For example,

```
[10]BYTE Message  :
SEQ
   Message := "Greetings!"
```

Here

```
Message[0] equals 'G'
Message[1] equals 'r'
   .
   .
   .
Message[9] equals '!'
```

(Note that the number of characters in the string must match the declared size of the array.)

Example 4.16

```
VAL Message IS "Hello"  :
```

is equivalent to

```
VAL [5]BYTE Message IS "Hello"  :
```

and may be accessed as such. This point will be covered in more detail in Chapter 7 on abbreviations.

4.7 Size of arrays

The number of components of an array may be determined at run time with the **SIZE** operator. This is particularly useful with procedures (Ch. 7) for writing general-purpose array handling code; the size of the actual array is not a constraining factor, it can be determined at run-time with the **SIZE** operator. The format is

```
SIZE array
```

where `array` is an array identifier. The result is a value of type **INT**, which is the number of components of the array.

Example 4.17
The statement

```
NoOfComponents := SIZE Signal
```

would assign a value of 32 to `NoOfComponents`, if `Signal` is an array that has been specified as having 32 components. `NoOfComponents` must be specified as being of type **INT**.

The **SIZE** operator may also be used with multidimensional arrays.

Example 4.18

```
INT Num1, Num2 :
[5][4] REAL64 Matrix :
SEQ
  Num1 := SIZE Matrix[0]
  Num2 := SIZE Matrix
```

assigns a value of 4 to `Num1` and a value of 5 to `Num2`. The same result for `Num1` would be realized with statements of the form

```
Num1 := SIZE Matrix[1]
```

or

```
Num1 := SIZE Matrix[2]
```

and so on, up to

```
Num1 := SIZE Matrix[4]
```

4.8 Tables

A table allows an array to be generated from would-be components. It provides a convenient notation for defining arrays of constants or initializing arrays of variables. The individual components, each of which may comprise any occam expression, must all be of the same data type. Within a table statement, the components are separated by commas and enclosed with square brackets.

```
[component_1, . . . component_n]
```

where component_1, . . . component_n are the individual components of the table. For example,

```
VAL [10] INT Primes IS [2, 3, 5, 7, 11, 13, 17, 19, 23, 29] :
```

shows the use of a table in an abbreviation to define an integer array constant, Primes.

Initialization of an array of variables may be performed by assignment as follows

```
[10] INT TenPrimes :
SEQ
   TenPrimes := [2, 3, 5, 7, 11, 13, 17, 19, 23, 29]
```

Other data types besides integers may be used in a table. For example,

```
VAL [10] BYTE Digits IS ['0', '1', '2', '3', '4', '5', '6',
                         '7', '8', '9'] :
```

depicts the definition of a byte array constant, CharDigits, with the ten ASCII digits.

Example 4.19

```
[50] INT Array :
SEQ
   [Array FROM 0 FOR 10] := [0, 0, 0, 0, 0, 0, 0, 0, 0, 0]
```

initializes the first ten components of the array of variables, Array.

Multidimensional tables are allowed. The number of subcomponents in each component of the table must be the same.

Example 4.20

```
[5] [2] BYTE Vowels :
SEQ
   Vowels := [ ['a', 'A'], ['e', 'E'], ['i', 'I'], ['o',
              'O'], ['u', 'U'] ]
```

It has been observed that multidimensional arrays may be considered as arrays of array types. For example, the array in the example above may be treated as a one-dimensional array of type [2] **BYTE** or a two-dimensional array of type **BYTE**. In the same way, the components of multidimensional arrays may be accessed as arrays of array types. For example, consider again the array, Vowels, in the example above. This array is stored in the order

```
Vowels[0][0] -- value 'a'
Vowels[0][1] -- value 'A'
Vowels[1][0] -- value 'e'
Vowels[1][1] -- value 'E'
Vowels[2][0] -- value 'i'
Vowels[2][1] -- value 'I'
Vowels[3][0] -- value 'o'
Vowels[3][1] -- value 'O'
Vowels[4][0] -- value 'u'
Vowels[4][1] -- value 'U'
```

Components may be referenced treating the array as one-dimensional of type [2] **BYTE** – for example, Vowels[1] would reference ['e', 'E'] – or treating the array as two-dimensional of type **BYTE** – for example, Vowels[3,1] would reference 'O'. Thus, Vowels[1] picks out all those components with an initial index of 1.

4.9 Exercises

1. Devise suitable array specifications for:
   (a) the colours of traffic lights (the initial letter of each colour)
   (b) a chessboard (8 rows by 8 columns), with each square capable of holding an integer
   (c) the print positions of printer paper (66 rows by 132 columns), with each position capable of holding a character
   (d) a Scrabble board (15 rows by 15 columns), with each square capable of holding a character
   (e) the names of the months (the first three characters of each name)

2. Distinguish between:

   ```
   [8]CHAN OF REAL64 Chan :
   ```

   and

   ```
   CHAN OF [8]REAL64 Chan :
   ```

3. Write an occam fragment for transferring a [25] **REAL32** array between two component processes of a **PAR** process.

4.
    (a) Write down the component of the middle square of a Scrabble board (15 rows by 15 columns).
    (b) The first word placed on a Scrabble board must lie horizontally across the middle square. If the first word is "ACE", what are the components of the Scrabble board that will hold this word?

5. Consider the following occam fragment:

```
INT Num1, Num2, Num3 :
[15][10][5]INT64 ThreeD :
SEQ
  Num1 := SIZE ThreeD[0][0]
  Num2 := SIZE ThreeD[0]
  Num3 := SIZE ThreeD
```

What are the values assigned to Num1, Num2 and Num3?

6. Comment on the validity of the following tables:
    (a)

    ```
    [256(INT16), 300]
    ```

    (b)

    ```
    ['a', ['b', 'c']]
    ```

    (c)

    ```
    ["Hello", "Greetings"]
    ```

Chapter 5

Constructions

5.1 Introduction

Higher-level processes in occam are built from other (simpler) processes using *constructions*. A hierarchy of nested processes, each built with a construction, may be formed. Earlier the **SEQ**, **PAR** and **ALT** constructions were introduced. Apart from **SEQ**, **PAR** and **ALT**, the other occam constructions provide for:
- condition
- selection
- repetition.

This chapter deals with the **ALT** construction in more detail, and also describes the constructions for dealing with condition, selection and repetition.

5.2 The alternation construction

The alternation (**ALT**) construction selects a process for execution from several *alternatives*. In the simplest case, each alternative process is *guarded* by an input process (which may be a timer input). This is called an *input guard*. The selection of which alternative process to execute is made according to which of the inputs is ready first. The alternation construction terminates successfully after execution of the selected process. Other guards comprise the combination of a Boolean expression with an input process, and the combination of a Boolean expression with a **SKIP** process. These other guards will be dealt with shortly.

The operation of the **ALT** construction, *in principle*, is non-deterministic – that is, if more than one input is available at the *same* time, an arbitrary one is chosen and its associated process executed. However, the occam definition does not actually specify which input will be chosen in such circumstances and so the *actual* input chosen may well vary from implementation to implementation. In particular, the INMOS implementation of the occam compiler is such that the *indefinite postponement* of alternative processes is possible if one input is effectively always available. The same alternative process may be repeatedly chosen as *the one* for execution, thus starving the other alternatives of execution. This problem is revisited and addressed in Chapter 9.

79

The format of the basic **ALT** construction is:

```
ALT
  input_guard_1
    process_1
    .
    .
    .
  input_guard_n
    process_n
```

Each input guard must be indented two spaces from the **ALT** reserved word. Each associated process is further indented two spaces.

The implementation of the **ALT** construction executes very slowly on the transputer (see Ch. 15). This is especially true for **ALT**s with many alternatives; the execution time has a linear dependence on the number of channels.

Example 5.1

```
ALT
  Input1 ? Data
    Output ! Data
  Input2 ? Data
    Output ! Data
  Input3 ? Data
    Output ! Data
  Input4 ? Data
    Output ! Data
```

represents an occam simulation of one iteration of a 4-to-1 multiplexor: data is accepted from any one of four input channels, whichever is available, and output on a single channel (Fig. 5.1). (This fragment needs to be embedded in a loop to simulate a free-running multiplexor.)

Example 5.2

```
VAL Terminator IS '?' :
BYTE Char, Any :
ALT
  InChan ? Char
    OutChan ! Char
  Stop ? Any
    OutChan ! Terminator
```

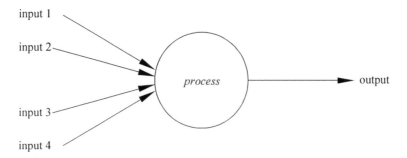

Figure 5.1   A simple multiplexor process.

represents one iteration of a simple buffer, which is stopped by a signal (Any) on the Stop channel (Fig. 5.2). On receipt of a stop signal, the process outputs a terminator character. In the event of inputs being simultaneously available on the InChan and Stop channels, which of the alternatives that is chosen is undefined. (But see the comment concerning the Inmos occam compiler implementation above.) A solution to this difficulty is to be found with the priority **ALT** (Ch. 9).

5.2.1 Boolean guards
An extension of the simple input guard is the combination of a Boolean expression with the input. In this case a process is selected for execution if the Boolean expression is true *and* the input is ready. The format of this type of guard is

```
Boolean_expression & input process
```

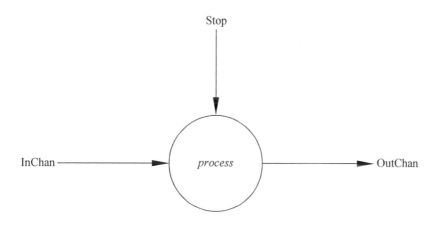

Figure 5.2   A simple buffer process with a stop channel.

81

Example 5.3

```
ALT
  (State = Receiving) & Chan1 ? Signal
    .
    . -- perform processing in receiving state
    .
  (State = Transmitting) & Chan2 ? Signal
    .
    . -- perform processing in transmitting state
    .
  (State = Idle) & Chan3 ? Signal
    .
    . -- perform processing in idle state
    .
```

depicts an occam fragment of an **ALT** construction with Boolean guards. Which alternative is chosen depends now not only on the availability of an input, but also on the truth value of the associated Boolean expression. In the example above, input may be available on one of the channels Chan1, Chan2, or Chan3, but which alternate is chosen will now also be governed by the value of the variable State.

5.2.2 SKIP *guards*

This variation of guard comprises a combination of Boolean expression with the **SKIP** process. The format is

```
Boolean_expression & SKIP
```

This type of guard may be considered as a *catch-all* for the input part of a Boolean guard. If the Boolean expression is true, the **SKIP** acts as a ready input. For example,

```
ALT
  Flag & Chan1 ? Message
    .
    .     -- perform processing
    .
  Flag & Chan2 ? Message
    .
    .     -- perform processing
    .
  (NOT Flag) & SKIP
    .
```

82

```
  .     -- perform processing

  .
```

shows an occam fragment of an **ALT** construction with a **SKIP** guard. If Flag is
FALSE, the **SKIP** guard alternative is chosen. If Flag is **TRUE**, which alternative
is chosen depends on the availability of inputs on the channels, Chan1 and
Chan2.

Caution is needed in the use of the **SKIP** guard. It is always busy while the
Boolean expression is true, so it may always be taken, in preference to the other
guards. It is recommended always to use the priority **ALT** construction (Ch. 9) with
the **SKIP** guard. This allows the **SKIP** guard to be given the lowest priority of the
guards in the given construction, and thus permits one of these other guards to be
taken instead.

A further extension of this is a catch-all for both the Boolean and input parts of
the guard. This is the **TRUE** & **SKIP** combination. Such a guard, since it is always
ready, is really only useful when used with the priority **ALT** construction (Ch. 9).
This construction allows alternates to be placed in a priority order and the ready
guard may be used in some circumstances as the lowest-priority alternate guard.
Note that the different types of guard may be used in the same **ALT** construction.
The example above contains both Boolean guards and a **SKIP** guard.

5.2.3 Output guards
The occam definition only admits input guards. Output guards are *not* supported.
Thus, although

```
ALT
    Chan1 ? Data1
        Process1
    Chan2 ? Data2
        Process2
```

is legal, the following code, with the input guards replaced by "output guards", is
most certainly illegal.

```
ALT
    Chan1 ! Data1
        Process1
    Chan2 ! Data2
        Process2
```

Output guards were omitted from the occam definition, as their inclusion would
have greatly complicated the communications protocol. In some circumstances, it
might require knowledge of the state of the entire network to resolve, instead of
just the local state. This is not really possible to implement sensibly, especially on

multiprocessor systems. However, sometimes it would be convenient to be able to use such guards in an occam program (Jones 1987). It is possible to simulate the *observable* effect of an output guard with an input guard. One solution requires two distinct channels. Instead of writing

```
ALT
    OutChan ! Message
        .
        .  -- perform any other actions
        .
```

the **ALT** has to be rewritten as

```
ALT
    ServiceChan ? Prompt
      SEQ
        OutChan ! Message
        .
        . -- perform any other actions
        .
    -- communicating process
    SEQ
      ServiceChan ! Prompt
      OutChan ? Message
```

In the **ALT**, the output guard is replaced by a valid input guard for a service channel, ServiceChan. This channel is used to trigger the action of an output guard – a message is output on the channel OutChan in the subsequent **SEQ** process. The communicating process sends a prompt along the service channel whenever it is ready to receive a message.

5.3 The conditional construction

The conditional construction allows a process to be executed, provided an associated condition is satisfied, that is, found to be true. The construction consists of the reserved word **IF** followed by a list of choices. A choice comprises a Boolean expression: a condition, plus an associated process. The Boolean expression is known as a *guard*.

The format of the conditional construction is:

```
IF
    Boolean_expression_1
      process_1
```

.

.

.

```
Boolean_expression_n
  process_n
```

Each Boolean expression is indented by two spaces from the **IF** keyword, and each associated process is indented by a further two spaces from its Boolean expression. Note that each Boolean expression is evaluated in the sequence stated in the construction. The associated process of the *first* Boolean expression found to be true is executed, and then the conditional construction terminates successfully.

Note that **IF** guards comprise purely static Boolean tests, whereas **ALT** guards comprise dynamic inputs, the choice in the latter case being made from those channels ready to provide an input.

Example 5.4

```
IF
  Data > 0
    Output ! "Positive"
  Data = 0
    Output ! "Zero"
  Data < 0
    Output ! "Negative"
```

If the value of Data is greater than zero, the message "Positive" is output; if the value of Data is equal to zero, the message "Zero" is output; and if the value of Data is less than zero, the message "Negative" is output.

If none of the Boolean expressions within the **IF** construction is found to be true, the construction behaves as a **STOP** process, that is, it never terminates. It is therefore important that all possible conditions in any **IF** construction are specified. In the example above, it is possible for the variable, Data, to have a positive, zero or negative value. Hence, three conditions are specified within the **IF** construction to test for these values.

The Boolean literal **TRUE** may be used as a guard in conjunction with a process to provide a catch-all and eliminate the **STOP** behaviour. Such a combination must be placed at the *end* of the conditional. **TRUE** always evaluates to true, so, if none of the preceding guards is true, the **TRUE** guard will be taken and its associated process will be executed. For example,

```
IF
  Data > 0
    Output ! "Positive"
  Data = 0
```

```
     Output ! "Zero"
  TRUE
     Output ! "Negative"
```

where the Boolean expression testing for a negative value has been replaced by
the **TRUE** process.

Yet a further possibility is to make the associated process the **SKIP** process.
This produces a catch-all, which does no processing at all. For example,

```
  IF
     Data > 0
        Output ! "Positive"
     TRUE
        SKIP
```

where a message is now output when the data has positive values. Zero and negative values are catered for by the catch-all.

Example 5.5

```
  IF
     (Char >= 'a'(INT)) AND (Char <= 'z'(INT))
        Char := Char BITAND #DF
     TRUE
        SKIP
```

is an occam fragment that converts lower-case alphabetic characters to upper-case
ones. (The variable Char is assumed to have been declared as type **INT**.) Characters that are not lower-case alphabetic are caught by the **TRUE** guard and no conversion processing is performed on these characters.

Example 5.6

```
  IF
     Signal <= Maximum
        SKIP
     TRUE
        STOP
```

shows the use of **STOP** to halt a process if something untoward happens.

5.3.1 Nested conditional
As well as being followed by a choice, a conditional construction may alternatively
be followed by another conditional, producing a hierarchy of nested conditionals.

So constructs such as the following are possible:

```
IF
   Boolean_expression
      IF
         Boolean_expression
            process
```

and even

```
IF
   IF
      Boolean_expression
         process
```

– the latter construct being most useful with replication (see Ch. 6). For example,

```
IF
   Colour = Red
      IF
         Suit = Hearts
            Rank := 3
         Suit = Diamonds
            Rank := 2
   Colour = Black
      IF
         Suit = Spades
            Rank := 4
         Suit = Clubs
            Rank := 1
```

shows a nested **IF** construction. An outer **IF** comprising two choices testing the value of the variable Colour; and, within each of these choices, inner **IF**s testing the value of the variable Suit.

Example 5.7

```
IF
   Num1 > Num2
      IF
         Num1 > Num3
            Max := Num1
         TRUE
```

```
        Max  :=  Num3
   Num2  >  Num3
     Max  :=  Num2
   TRUE
     Max  :=  Num3
```

is an occam fragment for comparing the values of three numbers, and assigning
the largest value to the variable Max.

5.4 The selection construction

The selection construction allows a process to be selected from a list of processes
according to the value of an expression. Processes are guarded by *case* expressions,
the combination of process and case expression being known as an *option*. Each
case expression must evaluate to a different *constant* value. The value of a variable
expression, called a *selector*, is matched against the value of each of the case
expressions in turn. If a match is found – the selector has the value of a case expression – the associated process of the option is executed and then the selection terminates successfully. If no match is found, the construction behaves as a **STOP**
process. The selection construction comprises the **CASE** reserved word and selector, followed by zero or more options. There must be at least one case expression
in any option. Both the selector and case expressions must be of the same type,
either integer or byte.

```
CASE selector
  case_expression_1
    process_1
    .
    .
    .
  case_expression_n
    process_n
```

Each case expression must be indented by two spaces with respect to the **CASE**
reserved word; each associated process is indented by a further two spaces from
its respective case expression.

Example 5.8

```
VAL North IS 0 :
VAL South IS 1 :
VAL East IS 2 :
VAL West IS 3 :
```

```
INT Direction, XCoord, YCoord :
SEQ
  XCoord := 0
  YCoord := 0
  InChan ? Direction
  CASE Direction
    North
      YCoord := YCoord + 1
    South
      YCoord := YCoord - 1
    East
      XCoord := XCoord + 1
    West
      XCoord := XCoord - 1
```

The value of the selector, Direction is compared with each case expression, North, South, East and West, *in turn*. If Direction has one of these values, the associated process is executed, *otherwise* the selection behaves as a **STOP** process.

A limb of the selection may be guarded by more than one case expression, if required. Multiple case expressions must be separated by commas. For example,

```
CASE Suit
  Heart, Diamond
    Colour := Red
  Club, Spade
    Colour := Black
```

If the selector, Suit, has a value equal to Heart or Diamond, then the variable Colour is assigned the value Red. If Suit has a value equal to Club or Spade, then Colour is assigned the value Black.

Example 5.9

```
CASE Month
  February
    Days := 28
  April, June, September, November
    Days := 30
  January, March, May, July, August, October, December
    Days := 31
```

sets the variable Days to the appropriate value for non-leap-year months.

Example 5.10

```
CASE Operator
  '+'
    Result := Operand1 + Operand2
  '-'
    Result := Operand1 - Operand2
  '*'
    Result := Operand1 * Operand2
  '/'
    Result := Operand1 / Operand2
```

shows the use of characters as selectors and constant expressions in a **CASE** construction.

5.4.1 The **ELSE** case expression

This case expression behaves as a catch-all for the **CASE** construction. If none of the case expressions matches the selector, the **ELSE** case expression is taken and the component process executed. The **ELSE** case expression may be conveniently placed at the end of the **CASE** construction.

```
ELSE
  process
```

Example 5.11

```
CASE Day
  Saturday, Sunday
    State := WeekEnd
  ELSE
    State := WorkDay
```

If the selector, Day, is Saturday or Sunday, then the value WeekEnd is assigned to the variable State; otherwise the value WorkDay is assigned to State.

Example 5.12

```
CASE Month
  February
    Days:= 28
  April, June, September, November
    Days:= 30
  ELSE
```

```
Days := 31
```

If selector Month has the value February, then the variable Days is assigned the value 28; otherwise, if Month has the value April, June, September or November, then Days is assigned the value 30, else Days is assigned the value 31.

5.5 The repetition construction

A loop may be created within an occam program with a **WHILE** construction. It has the format

```
WHILE Boolean_expression
  process
```

The component process must be indented by two spaces with respect to the **WHILE** keyword.

If the Boolean expression evaluates to the value **TRUE**, the component process is executed. On termination of the component process, the procedure is repeated. The loop is repeated an indefinite number of times and only terminates when the Boolean expression becomes false. Some action that alters the value of the Boolean expression must take place within the loop to enable loop termination.

Example 5.13

```
VAL Eof IS '.' :
BYTE Char :
SEQ
  Char := ' '
  WHILE Char <> Eof
    SEQ
      InChan ? Char
      OutChan ! Char
```

depicts a **WHILE** loop that repeatedly inputs and outputs a character until a '.' character is input. This character acts as a terminator for the **WHILE** loop.

Example 5.14

```
VAL Eof IS '.' :
VAL Space IS ' ' :
BYTE Char :
INT CountOfSpaces :
```

```
SEQ
  CountOfSpaces := 0
  Char := ' '
  WHILE Char <> Eof
    SEQ
      InChan ? Char
      IF
        Char = Space
          CountOfSpaces := CountOfSpaces + 1
        TRUE
          SKIP
```

is an occam fragment that counts the number of spaces in a piece of text; a character repeatedly being input until a ' . ' character is found.

A non-terminating loop (one that repeats for ever) may be effected with the Boolean expression set to **TRUE**. For example,

```
WHILE TRUE
  BYTE Char :
  SEQ
    InChan ? Char
    OutChan ! Char
```

represents a simple buffer process: it repeatedly accepts a character then outputs it (Fig. 5.3).

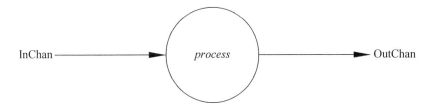

Figure 5.3   A simple buffer process.

Example 5.15

```
BYTE Char :
INT Number :
SEQ
  Number := 0
  InChan ? Char
  WHILE (Char >= '0') AND (Char <= '9')
```

```
SEQ
  Number := (Number * 10) + ((INT Char) - (INT '0'))
  InChan ? Char
```

shows an occam program fragment that forms an integer from ASCII digits (i.e. characters). The integer is formed by subtracting the numeric value of the character '0' from the ASCII digit. As more digits are input, the previous number is scaled up by a factor of ten.

Example 5.16

```
VAL Eof IS '?' :
BOOL Going :
SEQ
  Going := TRUE
  WHILE Going
    SEQ
      InChan ? Char
      OutChan ! Char
      IF
        Char= Eof
          Going := FALSE
        TRUE
          SKIP
```

represents a **WHILE** loop, which repeatedly inputs and outputs a character, governed by a Boolean variable, Going. The loop repeats until a '?' is input, which has the effect of setting Going to **FALSE** and terminating the **WHILE** loop.

Example 5.17

```
INT Number, Maximum, Minimum :
SEQ
  Minimum := MOSTPOS INT
  Maximum := MOSTNEG INT
  Input ? Number
  WHILE Number <> 0
    SEQ
      IF
        Number < Minimum
          Minimum := Number
        Number > Maximum
          Maximum := Number
        TRUE
```

93

```
        SKIP
   Input ? Number
```

depicts an occam fragment that sets the variables Maximum and Minimum to the largest and smallest numbers read, respectively.

5.6 Exercises

1. Devise alternative occam code that will replace the **TRUE** guard in the following occam program fragment, but still keep the sense of the program.

```
IF
   Data < 0
     .
     . - some process
     .
   Data = 0
     .
     . - some process
     .
   TRUE
     SKIP
```

2. Devise alternative occam code that will replace the **TRUE** guard in the following occam program fragment, but still keep the sense of the program.

```
BOOL Running :
SEQ
   .
   . -- some process
   .
   IF
      Running
        .
        . -- some process
        .
      TRUE
        SKIP
```

3. Write an occam fragment that will determine the larger of two integers, and will assign the larger to the variable Max and the smaller to the variable Min. Extend this to determine the largest of three integers.

4. Write a **WHILE** loop to convert a positive integer number to ASCII digits for output as characters. (Your program fragment should cater for the output of leading spaces. Assume a maximum of ten digits.) Extend the fragment to cope with negative and positive integers.

5. A double buffer is a process in which one buffer is used to input while another buffer is used to output the previous input. Two simple ways of implementing such a buffer in occam are essentially via:
   • a **PAR** construction comprising two **SEQ**s
   • a **SEQ** construction comprising two **PAR**s.
   Write occam programs that will implement a double buffer following these two schemes.

6. Extend the *days in the month* example given in the text to cater for leap years.

7. Write an occam program fragment that will output a text message for each different vowel input.

8. Write an occam fragment to implement a *round robin* **ALT** with two alternatives, i.e. an **ALT** in which each input is guaranteed to be eventually serviced. This may be done, for example, by using a Boolean flag that selectively enables successive alternatives of the **ALT**.

Chapter 6

Replicators

6.1 Introduction

Many programming languages possess a feature to enable the formation of loops
that are repeated a definite, specified number of times; for example, a **FOR** loop in
Pascal. Occam, too, has an analogous, but much more powerful and interesting,
feature applying specifically to processes. It is known as *replication*: a process may
be replicated a stated number of times. Replication not only applies to the **SEQ** construct but also to the **PAR**, **IF** and **ALT** constructs. Any of these constructs may be
appended with a *replicator*, which specifies a replication count. A following process is then replicated the stated number of times. The format of the replicator is

```
index = start FOR count
```

where
- index is the occam identifier of the replicator index. Within the replication
  loop, the index behaves as an ordinary occam variable, assuming values
  between start and (start + count) −1. The value of the index must not
  be changed by the replicated process, but may be used to reference the replicated process within the loop. The replicator statement also serves to declare
  the index identifier (as data type **int**)– the index should not be re-specified
  elsewhere.
- start is an expression, the value of which is the initial value of index.
- count is an expression, the value of which is the number of times the process
  is replicated. A count value of zero causes the construct to behave like the
  SKIP process for a replicated **SEQ** or PAR, and to behave like a **STOP** process
  for a replicated **IF** or **ALT**.

The replicator index is incremented in steps of one from the value *start* for *count*
values. The data type of start and count must be **INT**.

6.2 Replicated SEQ

A replicated **SEQ** executes the replicated processes in sequence. The format is

96

```
SEQ index = start FOR count
  process
```

where `process` is the process to be replicated, and which must be indented by two spaces from the preceding **SEQ**. The replicated **SEQ** is analogous to a **FOR** loop in conventional programming languages, since each execution of the replicated process is performed in sequence.

Example 6.1

```
[1024]INT Buffer :
SEQ Index = 0 FOR 1024
  Buffer[Index] := 0
```

initializes the contents of a 1024 component buffer, `Index`, taking values 0 to 1023. A "flattened out" version of this replication would behave as if it had been defined as

```
[1024]INT Buffer :
SEQ
  Buffer[0] := 0
  Buffer[1] := 0
  Buffer[2] := 0

  .

  .

  .

  Buffer[1023] := 0
```

Example 6.2

```
VAL INT NumberOfRows IS 50 :
VAL INT NumberOfColumns IS 100 :
[NumberOfRows][NumberOfColumns]REAL32 Matrix :
SEQ

  .
  . -- initialize matrix

  .

  SEQ Row = 0 FOR NumberOfRows
    SEQ Column = 0 FOR NumberOfColumns
      OutChan ! Matrix[Row][Column]
```

shows an occam fragment that outputs the contents of a two-dimensional matrix. It is assumed that the channel, `OutChan`, has been specified as type **REAL32**. (This example is very inefficient – it is used only as an illustration. It is much better to output the matrix as `OutChan ! Matrix`.)

Example 6.3

```
SEQ Index = 0 FOR SIZE String
  OutChan ! String[Index]
```

depicts an occam fragment to output an array of bytes (representing a character string), a character at a time.

Example 6.4

```
VAL Count IS 3 :
[Count]REAL64 Vector1, Vector2 :
SEQ
  DotProduct := 0.0(REAL64)
  SEQ Index = 0 FOR Count
    DotProduct := DotProduct + (Vector1[Index] *
      Vector2[Index])
```

depicts an occam fragment for calculating the dot product (Vector1[1] * Vector2[1] + Vector1[2] * Vector2[2] + Vector1[3] * Vector2[3]) of two vectors.

6.3 Replicated PAR

A replicated **PAR** executes the replicated processes in parallel. It has the format

```
PAR index = start FOR count
  process
```

where process, the replicated process, is indented by two spaces with respect to the **PAR**. For the replicated **PAR** only, both start and count must be constants, not variables, as parallel processes cannot be created dynamically.

The replicated **PAR** is a vital feature of the occam language. It allows the construction of various structures of concurrent processes. A common use of the replicated **PAR** is the generation of a *pipeline*: a set of communicating processes executing in parallel. Each process in the pipeline inputs data from the preceding process, and outputs data to the succeeding process, performing some processing of the data (Fig. 6.1). The pipeline thus produces an overlapped operation – each component process of the replicated **PAR** executing concurrently with every other component process, input and output being automatically synchronized between processes.

Figure 6.1   Pipeline of processes, with data passed along the pipeline.

Example 6.5

```
[1025]CHAN OF INT Buffer :
PAR Index = 0 FOR 1024
  INT Item :
  SEQ
    Buffer[Index] ? Item
    Buffer[Index + 1] ! Item
```

represents the heart of a 1024-item FIFO buffer process – comprising a concatenation of 1024 simple buffer processes. This concatenation is constructed by the parallel replication of a simple buffer process. In this example, an item is input by the first simple buffer process via the channel Buffer[0], then passed on to the next simple buffer process via the channel Buffer[1], and so on down the line. If the above replicated **PAR** process was "flattened out", it would look like:

```
[1025]CHAN OF INT Buffer :
PAR
  INT Item :
  SEQ
    Buffer[0] ? Item
    Buffer[1] ! Item
  INT Item :
  SEQ
    Buffer[1] ? Item
    Buffer[2] ! Item
       .
       .
       .
  INT Item :
  SEQ
    Buffer[1023] ? Item
    Buffer[1024] ! Item
```

This process requires "topping and tailing" – processes need to be provided to cater for the initialization and termination phases of the pipeline. These processes, typ-

ically, would be provided as procedures (Ch. 7). The body of such processes for
the initialization and termination phases would look like

```
-- initialization
INT Data :
SEQ
   .
   . -- input or produce an item of data
   .
   -- inject the data into the buffer
   Buffer[0] ! Data
```

and

```
-- termination
INT Data :
SEQ
   -- extract the data from the buffer
   Buffer[1024] ? Data
   .
   . -- consume or output an item of data
   .
```

The initialization and termination processes provide interfaces between the pipeline buffer and the outside world.

The full pipeline program will be an amalgam of these three processes: *initialization*, *pipeline* and *termination*. Each process may execute concurrently with the
other two. This can be arranged in occam by allowing each process to be the component of an outer **PAR** process. The synchronization of the communication
between each component process will be automatically guaranteed by occam. As
a final step, each of the three processes must be enclosed within a loop to ensure
a stream of data passes along the pipeline. In this fashion, the composite process
is capable of buffering up to 1024 items. For example:

```
PAR
   initialization process
   pipe process
   termination process
```

or, written out in full,

```
CHAN OF INT InChan, OutChan :
[1025]CHAN OF INT Buffer :
PAR
```

```
-- initialization
WHILE TRUE-- loop to produce stream of
          -- data
  INT Data :
  SEQ
    .
    .         -- input or produce an item of data
    .
    Buffer[0] ! Data
-- pipeline
PAR Index = 0 FOR 1024
  WHILE TRUE
    INT Item :
    SEQ
      Buffer[Index] ? Item
      Buffer[Index + 1] ! Item
-- termination
WHILE TRUE-- loop to consume stream of
          -- data
  INT Data :
  SEQ
    Buffer[1024] ? Data
    .
    .          -- consume or output an item of data
    .
```

The program as written above is rather idealized, in that it runs for ever (via the **WHILE TRUE** statements). In order to introduce some reality into it, termination must be considered. Chapter 2 discussed how a system of parallel processes may terminate, for example, by setting a Boolean flag as a termination notice, and by allowing each process to receive, to act on and to pass on this termination notice. In terms of the pipeline, each process must receive the termination notice from the preceding process and pass on the termination to the succeeding process. This may be accomplished by a small modification to each of the above processes; the **WHILE** is now terminated on some Boolean condition, and the body of the process now contains a test for the termination condition. For example,

```
-- initialization
BOOL Terminate :
SEQ
  Terminate := FALSE
  WHILE NOT Terminate
    INT Data :
    SEQ
```

101

```
InChan ? Data
IF
  Data = Eof
    SEQ
      Terminate := TRUE
      Buffer[0] ! Data
  TRUE
    Buffer[0] ! Data
```

This example assumes that the value used as the terminator is not present as ordinary buffer data; for example, the terminator may be a negative value if the buffer data comprised only non-negative values.

The pipeline and termination processes may be similarly extended.

The pipeline is a very potent concept in occam. This type of structure may be very usefully employed to inject concurrency into an algorithm (Ch. 12) and so produce more efficient processing. For example, the technique may be used for writing parallel sorters (Pountain & May 1987) and parallel prime number generators (Burns 1988). In order to do this, the conditions need to be arranged so that each pipeline process can, in fact, execute concurrently with each other pipeline process, that is, there is overlapped execution. In the case of the FIFO buffer, this means that there must be a stream of data continually entering and leaving the buffer, so that it is kept at maximum capacity. A pipeline in which each process executes one after the other produces no benefit.

6.4 Replicated ALT

In common with the other constructs, an **ALT** may be replicated. The format is

```
ALT index = start FOR count
  input_guard
    process
```

where input_guard and process are replicated. The input guard must be indented by two spaces from the **ALT**, and the process indented a further two spaces.

The other types of alternative guard, Boolean and **SKIP**, may be used instead of an input guard.

The replicated **ALT** is useful for building a *multiplexor* – a process that accepts inputs from a set of channels and sends the outputs to a single channel.

Example 6.7

```
INT Value :
ALT Index = 0 FOR 10
```

```
InChan[Index] ? Value
  OutChan ! Value
```

where the channels have been declared as

```
[10] CHAN OF INT InChan :
CHAN OF INT OutChan :
```

This occam fragment produces ten **ALT**s, each inputting from a different channel
(InChan[0] . . . InChan[9]), but outputting to the same channel,
OutChan (Fig. 6.2). A "flattened out" version of this alternation would look like

```
INT Value :
ALT
  InChan[0] ? Value
    OutChan ! Value
  InChan[1] ? Value
    OutChan ! Value
  .
  .
  .
  InChan[9] ? Value
    OutChan ! Value
```

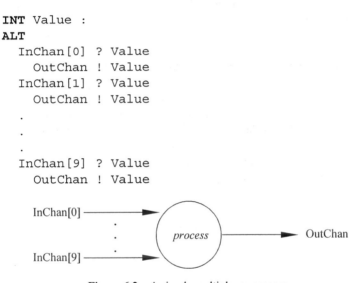

Figure 6.2   A simple multiplexor process.

Example 6.8

```
BOOL Going :
SEQ
  Going := TRUE
  WHILE Going
    BYTE Char :
    INT Any :
    ALT
      ALT Index = 0 FOR 10
        InChan[Index] ? Char
          OutChan ! Char
      Stop ? Any
```

```
Going := FALSE
```

is a variation of the multiplexor theme: the replicated alternatives perform the multiplexor process, and a further channel, Stop, provides a means of interrupting the multiplexor (Fig. 6.3). Note the interesting use of nested alternations. A replicated **ALT** cannot have a "catch-all", so it must be nested within an outer **ALT** to accommodate a catch-all in the outer **ALT**. In this example the catch-all is the code

```
Stop ? Any
   Going := FALSE
```

This allows the multiplexor to be stopped by the sending of a signal down the channel Stop.

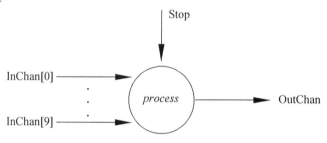

Figure 6.3   A multiplexor process with a stop channel.

The semantic difficulty of the **ALT** construct carries over to its replicated version; which of the alternatives is chosen when more than one input is ready at the same time? This is only resolved with the priority **ALT** (Ch. 9).

6.5 Replicated IF

Several similar choices may be generated with a replicated **IF** statement. This has the format

```
IF index = start FOR count
   Boolean_expression
      process
```

where Boolean_expression and process are replicated. The guard must be indented by two spaces with respect to the **IF** keyword, and the process indented a further two spaces.

A common use of a replicated **IF** is in performing a sequential search; for example, searching for a particular number in a list or a particular character in a string.

104

Example 6.6

```
IF
   IF Index = 0 FOR SIZE List
      List[Index] = RequiredNumber
         SEQ
            Found := TRUE
            Position := Index
   TRUE
      SEQ
         Found := FALSE
         Position := -1
```

shows a replicated **IF** construct being used to search for a particular number in a list. The position of the *first* occurrence of the number is recorded. Note the use of nested conditionals. This device serves the same purpose as nested alternations: to allow a catch-all for the replicated construct. In this way, if the list does not contain the required number, the process does not behave as a **STOP** process.

6.6 Processes as data structures

An occam process need not only represent the conventional active processing element of a program. The exciting, innovative nature of occam allows the novel construction of data structures from processes, using replication to generate the required structure. A data structure node is defined as a collection of operations within a process, and the process is replicated to form the structure. Thus, a binary tree, for example, may consist of several processes (representing the nodes of the tree) linked via channels (representing the branches of the tree) (Burns 1988).

Consider the representation of a binary tree. Apart from the leaf nodes, the root and intermediate nodes can each be represented as a process with six channels: one input and one output channel to the parent node, and one input and one output channel to each of the left and right child nodes (Fig. 6.4). (It is assumed that the parent of the root node is a user interface process.) Each leaf node can be represented by a process with two channels – one input and one output channel to the parent node.

For simplicity, consider a balanced binary tree of height three (Fig. 6.5). The node processes (root, intermediate and leaf) may be most succinctly generated by specifying these processes to be occam procedures (see Ch. 7). These procedures are then replicated the required number of times to form the tree. The root and intermediate nodes may be represented by a procedure with six channel parameters (assumed to be of type **INT** for this example), and the leaf nodes may be represented by a procedure with two channel parameters.

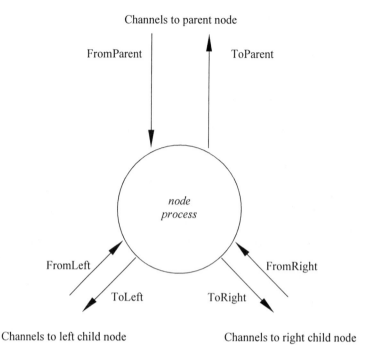

Figure 6.4   Process and channels for a binary tree node.

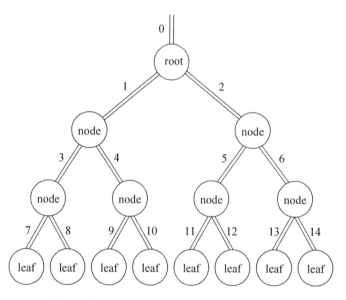

Figure 6.5   Binary tree showing channel numbers.

Thus, the procedure (see Ch. 7) heading for the Node process is

```
PROC Node(CHAN OF INT FromParent, ToLeft, ToRight,
                      ToParent, FromLeft, FromRight)
```

and the procedure heading for the Leaf process is

```
PROC Leaf(CHAN OF INT FromParent, ToParent)
```

(The variables within the brackets are the formal, that is, dummy, parameters of the procedures.) The operations of each node will be performed by processes defined within the procedure. An array of channels is used to provide specific channels, that is, actual parameters of each node generated by the replication. The data structure may now be generated with two replicated **PAR** constructs, one for the root and intermediate nodes, and one for the leaf nodes. By inspection, the tree can be seen to have seven intermediate nodes and eight leaf nodes. If the channels are numbered as shown in Figure 6.5, then for a node with a parent channel numbered N, the left and right child channels will be numbered $2*N + 1$ and $2*N + 2$, respectively. Thus, the data structure may be generated as

```
[15]CHAN OF INT Down, Up :
PAR
  User(Down[0], Up[0])
  PAR Index = 0 FOR 7
    -- generate root and intermediate nodes
    VAL Parent IS Index:
    VAL Left IS (2 * Index) + 1 :
    VAL Right IS (2 * Index) + 2 :
    Node(Down[Parent], Down[Left], Down[Right],
         Up[Parent], Up[Left], Up[Right])
  PAR Index = 7 FOR 8
    -- generate leaf nodes
    Leaf(Down[Index], Up[Index])
```

The index values of each replicated **PAR** construct are chosen to match the channel numbers (Fig. 6.5).

6.7 Exercises

1. Write an occam fragment to display 20 asterisks on the screen.

2. Write a fragment using a replicated **SEQ** to display the alphabet on the screen.

3. Using replication, write an occam program fragment to search for a particular character in a string.

4. Write a program fragment to perform the matrix multiplication of two two-dimensional square matrices.

5. Modify the pipe and terminate processes given in the text so that they cope with the termination notice.

6. Write a pipeline process to raise each number in a list to the nth power.

7. Write an occam fragment that will act as a multiplexor for a series of inputs. As well as performing the multiplexing function, the multiplexor should output the number of the relevant input port, preceding the data.

8. Write an occam fragment to implement a circular buffer as an array, using the **ALT** construct to discriminate between the enqueue and dequeue operations.

Chapter 7

Abbreviations, procedures and functions

7.1 Abbreviations

An *abbreviation* is an occam language feature for producing a succinct alias, or new name, for an occam expression or element. Within an occam process the abbreviation is then used instead of the original expression or element. This feature allows simplification of complicated occam statements. Essentially, the abbreviation behaves as a macro for the expression or element. In execution the effect of an abbreviation is equivalent to the substitution of the abbreviation name by the original expression or element. The usual scoping rules apply to an abbreviation. When a new name is in force because of an abbreviation, the old name of the expression or element may not be used within the scope of the abbreviation. As remarked in Chapter 2, the constant declaration is a simple form of abbreviation. Abbreviations are categorized as being either *expression* abbreviations or *element* abbreviations.

7.1.1 Expression abbreviations
Expression abbreviations are used to abbreviate the *values* of expressions. The value of an abbreviated expression must remain *constant* while the abbreviation is in scope. The simplest format is

```
VAL type name IS expression :
```

where
  • `type`, the type of the abbreviation, is one of the occam data types (either scalar or array). The inclusion of `type` is optional and may be omitted, since it may be determined from the data type of the `expression`.
  • `name` is the occam identifier of the abbreviation.
  • `expression` is a valid occam expression, such as a constant, a variable, an array component or some combination of these. The type of the expression must be the same as `type` if `type` is specified. Any variables used in `expression` must not be changed by assignment or input within the scope

of the abbreviation. Any array component used in the expression must have a valid subscript.

The use of the reserved word **VAL** underlines the constant value of this type of abbreviation.

Example 7.1

```
VAL Return IS '*c' :
VAL AbsoluteZero IS -273 :
VAL TwoPi IS 2.0(REAL32) * 3.14159(REAL32) :
VAL BufferFull IS Count > Limit :
VAL INT16 Maximum IS 32767(INT16) :
VAL REAL32 Volume IS (Length * Breadth) * Height :
VAL REAL64 Error IS Theory - Experiment :
```

So, for example, TwoPi may be used to represent the value of the expression 2.0(**REAL32**) * 3.14159(**REAL32**), and Volume may be used to represent the value of the expression (Length * Breadth) * Height, calculated with the current values of the variables Length, Breadth and Height at the time Volume is referenced. Hence, the assignments

```
Circumference := (2.0(REAL32) * 3.14159(REAL32)) * Radius
ThisVolume := (Length * Breadth) * Height
```

may be written more succinctly with the use of abbreviations as

```
Circumference := TwoPi * Radius
ThisVolume := Volume
```

where TwoPi and Volume are declared as above.

As noted above, because of the restriction to constant values, it is important that the value of any *variable* used in the expression is not changed by either assignment or input within the scope of the abbreviation, that is, while the abbreviation is active. So, for example, Length, Breadth and Height must remain constant within the scope of Volume.

Example 7.2

```
VAL TerminalMask IS #FF << 8 :
```

or

```
VAL Shift IS 8 :
VAL Mask IS #FF :
VAL TerminalMask IS Mask << Shift :
```

shows the use of abbreviations to define a further abbreviation.

Other versions of the expression abbreviation allow for an abbreviation of a table of expressions or an array of values. Such a mechanism is convenient for data initialization. The format is

```
VAL [size]type name IS expression :
```

or

```
VAL []type name IS expression :
```

where the second alternative demonstrates that the actual specification of the array size is optional. Again the specification of type may be omitted as it may be determined from the data type of the expression.

Example 7.3

```
VAL [10]INT Primes IS [2, 3, 5, 7, 11, 13, 17, 19, 23, 29] :
SEQ Index = 0 FOR 10
  Chan ! Primes[Index]
```

depicts the use of a table to initialize an array. The type may be omitted as it may be determined from the table components, so the above abbreviation may be written as

```
VAL Primes IS [2, 3, 5, 7, 11, 13, 17, 19, 23, 29] :
```

The first version is useful when it is required to emphasize the size of the array.

Example 7.4

```
VAL [5][2]BYTE Vowels IS [['a','A'], ['e','E'], ['i','I'],
                         ['o','O'], ['u','U']] :
```

and

```
VAL Vowels IS [['a','A'], ['e','E'], ['i','I'],
              ['o','O'], ['u','U']] :
```

are equivalent initializations of the two-dimensional array, Vowels.

Example 7.5

```
VAL WhiteQueen IS ChessBoard[3][0] :
```

```
VAL Punctuation IS ['.', ',', ':', ';', '?', '!'] :
VAL SummerMonths IS ["Jun", "Jul", "Aug"] :
VAL []INT ValidRange IS [Spectrum FROM Start FOR Length] :
```

are further examples of abbreviations using arrays – the last demonstrating the abbreviation of a segment. So it is possible to have statements of the form

```
NextPieceToMove := WhiteQueen
```

instead of

```
NextPieceToMove := ChessBoard[3][0]
```

and

```
Acceptable := ValidRange
```

instead of

```
Acceptable := [Spectrum FROM Start FOR Length]
```

(where `Acceptable` is an array of the same type as `ValidRange`.)

Example 7.6

```
VAL Vowels IS ['a', 'e', 'i', 'o', 'u']:
BYTE Char :
INT VowelCount :
SEQ
  VowelCount := 0
  WHILE TRUE
    SEQ
      InChan ? Char
        IF
          IF Index = 0 FOR 5
            Char = Vowels[Index]
              VowelCount := VowelCount + 1
          TRUE
            SKIP
```

represents an occam fragment to count the number of vowels appearing in a piece of text, where the channel, InChan, is declared to be type **BYTE**.

7.1.2 Element abbreviations

This form of abbreviation is used to give a new name to an element. (Occam gives the generic title `element` to variables of the primitive data types, channel and timer types, and also to arrays – components, segments or whole arrays.) The format is

```
type name IS element :
```

where `type` is the type of the abbreviation, and which may be omitted since it may be determined from the type of the `element`. If `type` is present, the type of the element must match `type`. This type of abbreviation is not limited to constant values. Any change in the value of the abbreviation is reflected by a change in the value of the element being abbreviated. For example,

```
INT Rook IS Castle :
REAL32 Average IS Results[99] :
StatusLine IS Screen[20] :
INT Element IS Array[Subscript] :
```

So, for instance, `Results[99]` would now be referenced by `Average`.

The element abbreviated (i.e. the part after the `IS`) may not be referred to within the scope of the abbreviation.

When the abbreviation is an alias for any array component, then certain rules must be observed within the scope of the abbreviation.

• any variable selecting (i.e. indexing) the array component must remain constant. For example,

```
INT Middle :
[50]REAL32 List :
SEQ

  .
  . -- initialize array
  .

  Middle := 25
  Pivot IS List[Middle] : -- specify Pivot as an
                          -- abbreviation

  .
  . -- scope of Pivot
  .
```

The value of `Middle` may not be changed by input or assignment within the scope of definition of `Pivot`.

• no reference must be made to *any* component of the array, except via abbreviations. For example,

113

```
INT Middle :
[50] REAL32 List :
SEQ
    .
    . -- initialize array
    .
    Middle := 25
    Pivot IS List[Middle] :
    Initial IS List[0] :
    .
    . -- process array with abbreviations Pivot and Initial
    .
```

The array component List [Middle] must not be referenced as such within the scope of Pivot; any reference to List [Middle] is valid only via a reference to Pivot. Moreover, references to other components of List (e.g. List [0]) are illegal within the scope of Pivot. Other components of List may only be referenced via other abbreviations for these components; for example, declaring the abbreviation Initial for List [0] and referencing List [0] via this abbreviation.

As with the previous category of abbreviation, an array version exists for this category. The format is

```
[size] type name IS element :
```

or

```
[] type name IS element :
```

Example 7.7

```
[30] INT WholeRange :
MiddleRange IS [WholeRange FROM 10 FOR 10] :
```

declares that MiddleRange is an alias for a segment of the array, WholeRange, and may be referenced as an array. So, for example, MiddleRange [4] refers to WholeRange [14].

7.2 Retyping

Retyping is a useful feature of occam that allows a given constant or variable of one data type to be expressed as a different data type, essentially mapping the given bit pattern to a named constant or variable of the different type. Retyping differs from the previously discussed data conversion in that, as the name suggests, it only changes the *type* of the given constant or variable, and does not alter the pattern of bits used to represent the program object. On the other hand, data conversion may alter the bit pattern to produce an equivalent value of a different type. For example, the data conversion from an integer value to a real value involves the change from twos complement form to the IEEE floating point form. Retyping, moreover, is a specification and not an operation, as data conversion is. The format of retyping declarations is

VAL type name **RETYPES** expression :

or

type name **RETYPES** element :

where name is the occam identifier of the constant (expression) or variable (element) being retyped.

The retyped constant or variable is governed by the usual scoping rules. Within the scope of the retyping, the name of the constant or variable being retyped may not be used.

Example 7.8

```
INT32 PackedNumber :
[4]BYTE SmallNumber RETYPES PackedNumber :
```

retypes the integer PackedNumber as a byte array SmallNumber. Individual bytes of the integer may then be referenced via the array. The size of the array must be such so as to correspond to the word size of the integer being retyped.

The result of **RETYPES** is generally specific to the implementation of occam, and so the use of **RETYPES** should be avoided if possible.

7.3 Procedures

The *procedure* is a means of giving a name to an occam process and, as such, leads to more compact, transparent and structured programs. Instead of the statements of the same process being repeated many times within a program, the process may be defined once and then referenced many times by referring to its name.

One limitation of an occam procedure is that recursion is not supported. Memory allocation in occam is static, fixed at compile-time, and static allocation does not allow recursion.

An occam procedure is another example of a specification statement. Constant and variable declarations were earlier examples of specification statements. The procedure has the format

```
PROC name (parameters)
  procedure_body
:
```

i.e. an occam procedure definition consists of
- a procedure heading comprising the keyword **PROC**; name, the procedure identifier; and a pair of matching brackets, containing zero or more formal parameter declarations
- followed by the procedure_body (The procedure body must be indented by two spaces and may consist of a primitive or a more complex process. Like any other process, this process may contain local declarations of constants, variables, and so on, required by the procedure.)
- a colon.

The procedure, like other specifications, is terminated by a colon. However, the terminating colon of a procedure must appear on a line by itself, directly aligned with the **P** of **PROC**. The procedure is bound to the following process in the same way as a constant or variable declaration. It is governed by similar scoping rules, that is, it is defined only within the scope of the following process. Procedures must therefore be defined before any process that references them. Procedures may be nested within other procedures.

Constants and variables, specified before the specification of a procedure, but which are still in scope when the procedure is in scope, are accessible from within the procedure.

Example 7.9

```
PROC WriteErrorMessage ()
  SKIP
:
```

specifies a trivial procedure named WriteErrorMessage. The body of this procedure solely comprises the primitive **SKIP** process. Thus, essentially, this procedure behaves as a procedure *stub*, representing an as yet unwritten procedure. This is quite a general idea for the development of a working program; as yet unwritten procedures are represented by procedure stubs, to be filled in later as the development progresses.

Example 7.10

```
PROC Delay ()
  VAL Limit IS 5000 :
  INT Count :
```

```
SEQ
   Count := 0
   WHILE Count < Limit
      Count := Count + 1
:
```

depicts a procedure that produces a delay by (rather wastefully) looping until an incremented variable reaches a certain value. (A more efficient method of producing a delay is to use an occam timer; see Ch. 9.)

Procedures are executed only when invoked from another process. A procedure is invoked from another process by referring to the procedure's name – this is called an *instance* of the procedure. The format is

```
name ()
```

where name is the procedure identifier of the procedure being invoked. (The procedure brackets must be present.)

Example 7.11

```
PROC Delay()              -- |
   VAL Limit IS 5000 :    -- |
   INT Count :            -- |
   SEQ                    -- | procedure specification
      Count := 0          -- |
      WHILE Count < Limit -- |
         Count := Count + 1 -- |
:                         -- |
SEQ
   Delay()                     -- instance of procedure
```

shows an instance of the procedure Delay in a following process.

Procedure invocations are implemented with a branch and return mechanism – an instance of an occam procedure causes a branch of execution to the procedure body, which is placed elsewhere in memory. After execution of the procedure body, a return is made to the next statement after the procedure instance. However, logically, a procedure instance is equivalent to an in-line expansion of the procedure body. For example, using the Delay procedure once more, an instance of Delay() may be *effectively* viewed as an in-line expansion of the procedure body:

```
   .
   .
   .
SEQ
   VAL Limit IS 5000 :        --|
   INT Count :                --|
   SEQ                        --|  instance of
      Count := 0              --|  procedure - Delay()
                              --|  - effectively
         WHILE Count < Limit  --|  expanded in-line
            Count := Count + 1 --|
   .
   .
   .
```

7.3.1 Parameters

Procedures may have parameters that allow the effect of the procedure to be applied to different values or variables, if required, each time an instance of a procedure occurs. The *formal* parameters are specified in the procedure heading within the brackets.

```
PROC name(parameter_1, . . . parameter_n)
   procedure body
   :
```

where `parameter_1, . . . parameter_n` are the formal parameters of the procedure, each separated by a comma if there is more than one parameter. The parameters may be of any occam type. This type must be completely specified within the procedure heading. Parameters of the same type may be grouped together with a single specifier of that type.

A procedure parameter may be
- a constant
- a variable
- a channel
- a timer.

If the value of a parameter remains constant (i.e. unchanged within the procedure), then the type specification of the parameter in the procedure heading should be preceded by the reserved word **VAL**. If the value of a parameter may be changed (i.e. it is a variable within the procedure), then **VAL** should be omitted from the parameter specification. For example,

```
PROC SkipSpaces(VAL INT Number)
```

118

indicates the value of the parameter, Number, remains constant within the procedure (an instance of this procedure would use an evaluated expression as a parameter), whereas

```
PROC Exchange(INT Item1, Item2)
```

indicates the values of the parameters, Item1 and Item2, may be changed within the procedure (an instance of this procedure would use named variables as parameters), and

```
PROC MaxMin(VAL INT Item1, Item2, INT Max, Min)
```

indicates the values of the first two parameters, Item1 and Item2, remain constant, whereas the values of the second two, Max and Min, are variable and may be modified within the procedure.

Example 7.12

```
PROC SkipSpaces(VAL INT Number)
  VAL Space IS ' ' :
  BYTE Char :
  INT Skip :
  SEQ
    Skip := Number
    WHILE Skip > 0
    SEQ
      Chan ? Char
      IF
        Char = Space
          Skip := Skip - 1
        TRUE
          SKIP
  :
```

is a procedure to skip a given number of spaces, specified as the parameter value, Number. The channel, Chan, is assumed to be declared with type **BYTE**. It would be preferable to pass this channel name to the procedure as a channel parameter (see Example 7.18).

Example 7.13

```
PROC Exchange(INT Item1, Item2)
  SEQ
    Item1, Item2 := Item2, Item1
  :
```

represents a procedure to swap the values of its two parameters.

Example 7.14

```
PROC Circle(VAL REAL32 Radius, REAL32 Area, Circumference)
  VAL Pi IS 3.14159(REAL32) :
  SEQ
    Area:= Pi * (Radius * Radius)
    Circumference:= 2.0(REAL32) * (Pi * Radius)
  :
```

is a procedure to calculate the area and circumference of a circle, given the radius.

Example 7.15

```
PROC RunningAverage(VAL REAL32 Data, REAL32 Average,
                    INT Count)
  SEQ
    Average := ((Average * (REAL32 ROUND Count)) + Data)
              / (REAL32 ROUND (Count + 1))
    Count := Count + 1
  :
```

is a procedure to calculate the running average of a list of numbers, given one number at a time.

In an instance of a procedure within a process, *actual* parameters replace the formal parameters. Actual parameters must agree in type and number with the formal parameters. The format of a procedure instance with parameters is just an extension of the simple format

```
name(actual_1, . . . actual_n)
```

For example,

```
Exchange(Int1, Int2)
```

In execution, the formal parameter behaves as an abbreviation for the value of the actual parameter; a **VAL** type parameter behaving as an expression abbreviation and a non-**VAL** type behaving as an element abbreviation. For example,

```
SkipSpaces(N)
```

is formally equivalent to

```
  .
  .
  .
SEQ
  VAL INT Number IS N : -- |
  VAL Space IS ' ' :    -- |
  BYTE Char :           -- |
  INT Skip :            -- | expansion of
    SEQ                 -- | SkipSpaces(N)
    .                   -- |
    .                   -- |
    .                   -- |
```

Any change in the value of a non-**VAL** formal parameter in the procedure body produces a corresponding change in the value of the actual parameter when used in
an instance of the procedure. For example,

```
PROC Circle(VAL REAL32 Radius, REAL32 Area, Circumference)
  VAL Pi IS 3.14159(REAL32) :
  SEQ
    Area := Pi * (Radius * Radius)
    Circumference := 2.0(REAL32) * (Pi * Radius)
  :
SEQ
  Circle(R, A, C)-- instance of procedure
```

is formally equivalent to

```
  .
  .
  .
SEQ
  VAL REAL32 Radius IS R :        -- |
  REAL32 Area IS A :              -- |
  REAL32 Circumference IS C :  -- |
  VAL Pi IS 3.14159(REAL32) :  -- | expansion
  SEQ                             -- | of procedure
    .                             -- | for given instance
    .                             -- |
    .                             -- |
```

The actual parameters R, A and C are abbreviated to formal parameters Radius,
Area and Circumference, respectively, for the duration of the procedure
invocation. Any changes to the values of Area and Circumference within the
procedure will cause corresponding changes to the values of A and C.

As remarked at the beginning of the section, parameters may be of any occam type. In particular, this includes channels and arrays. In the specification of the procedure heading, occam does not require the size of any formal array parameter to be declared. Instead, an empty array dimension may be supplied. Used in conjunction with the **SIZE** operator, this allows quite general array handling procedures to be written, without having to be specific about the size of arrays catered for.

Example 7.16

```
PROC Initialize([]INT Buffer)
  SEQ Index = 0 FOR SIZE Buffer
    Buffer[Index] := 0
:
```

is a procedure that may be called with any size of array as parameter; the use of the **SIZE** operator within the procedure body catering for any size of array.

Example 7.17

```
PROC Transpose(VAL [][]REAL32 Matrix,
                   [][]REAL32 TranMatrix)
  SEQ Row = 0 FOR SIZE Matrix[0]
    SEQ Column = 0 FOR SIZE Matrix
      TranMatrix[Row][Column] := Matrix[Column][Row]
:
```

represents a procedure to calculate the transpose of a two-dimensional matrix.

Example 7.18

```
PROC Buffer(CHAN OF BYTE InChan, OutChan)
  WHILE TRUE
    BYTE Char :
    SEQ
      InChan ? Char
      OutChan ! Char
:
```

is a simple buffer process written as a procedure. The channels used by the buffer are passed as parameters. The ability to pass channel names as parameters is an important feature of occam and is frequently used in programs.

122

7.4 Functions

In addition to procedures, the occam language definition also includes *functions* that are another form of process. In common with functions in other programming languages, the occam function returns a value or values because of some computation within the function. The first format is

```
type FUNCTION name(parameters)
  declarations
  VALOF
    function_body
    RESULT expression
:
```

where
- type is one of the primitive types. The function returns a value of this type.
- name is the function identifier.
- parameters are optional parameters, separated by commas. The kind of any parameter used in a function must be **VAL**.
- function_body is an occam process that effects the computation of the function, and may be a primitive process or a more complex one. The result of the computation is returned via the value of expression (which is composed of any combination of parameters, constants, variables, etc. specified in declarations and literals). The expression must result in a value that has the same data type as type. The function_body may contain *further* local declarations of constants, variables, and so on, required by the function.
- a colon.

The occam reserved word, **VALOF**, must be indented by two spaces with respect to the first letter of the type specification; and the function body and the reserved word, **RESULT**, indented a further two spaces. Like the procedure, a function is terminated by a colon. The colon must appear on a line by itself directly underneath the first letter of the type specification.

Example 7.19

```
INT FUNCTION Maximum(VAL INT X, Y)
  INT Max :
  VALOF
    SEQ
      IF
        X > Y
          Max := X
        TRUE
          Max := Y
```

123

```
        RESULT Max
    :
```

is an integer function that delivers the maximum of two integers.

Example 7.20

```
    INT FUNCTION Factorial(VAL INT Number)
        INT Fact :
        VALOF
          SEQ
            Fact := 1
            SEQ Index = 1 FOR Number
              Fact := Index * Fact
          RESULT Fact
    :
```

depicts an integer function for calculating the factorial (n! = 1 * 2 * 3 * ... n) of a given integer.

Example 7.21

```
    REAL32 FUNCTION Average(VAL []REAL32 List)
        REAL32 Sum :
        VALOF
          SEQ
            Sum = 0.0(REAL32)
            SEQ Index = 0 FOR SIZE List
              Sum := Sum + List[Index]
          RESULT Sum / (REAL32 ROUND (SIZE List))
    :
```

represents a real function that calculates the average for a list of reals.

Instances of a function effectively behave as an in-line expansion of the function body and any formal parameters behave as expression abbreviations of the actual parameters. Also, like a procedure, a function is referenced by referring to its name. However, unlike a procedure, because the function behaves like an expression, it may be used anywhere as part of an expression, except for defining compile-time constants. The most common reference of a function is as an assignment statement

```
    variable := name(actual_parameters)
```

For example,

```
[100] REAL32 Data :
SEQ

  .
  . -- input data into array

  .
  Mean := Average(Data)    -- reference function
                           -- Average
```

A special and interesting feature of the occam function is that it is guaranteed not to produce any side-effects. To enable this feature, certain conditions must be observed in the use of the function:
  • the function body must not contain any parallel or alternation constructions
  • the function body must not contain any inputs or outputs
  • only variables declared within the function may be assigned to
  • any called procedure must observe the above rules.
More sophisticated functions may be specified that return more than one value. The simple format of the function is expanded to cater for this situation

```
type_1, . . . type_n FUNCTION name(parameters)
  declarations
  VALOF
    function_body
    RESULT expression_1, . . . expression_n
:
```

where the list of types, separated by commas, must match in type and number the list of expressions, likewise separated by commas. For example,

```
REAL32, REAL32 FUNCTION Statistics(VAL []REAL32 List)
```

would be the function heading for a function that returned the mean and standard deviation of a list of numbers.

Such a function will usually be referenced via a multiple assignment statement. For example,

```
Mean, StdDev := Statistics(Data)
```

represents an instance of this multivalued function.

Example 7.22

```
REAL32, REAL32 FUNCTION MaxMin(VAL []REAL32 Data)
  REAL32 Max, Min :
  VALOF
    SEQ
      Max := Data[0]
      Min := Data[0]
      SEQ I = 1 FOR (SIZE(Data) - 1)
        SEQ
          VAL DataI IS Data[I}
          IF
            DataI > Max
              Max := DataI
            DataI < Min
              Min := DataI
            TRUE
              SKIP
    RESULT Max, Min
  :
```

7.5 Function definitions

A function definition provides a convenient notation for the specification of simple functions that are expressible as a single expression. Essentially, function definitions have a null function body.

```
type FUNCTION name(parameters) IS expression :
```

Example 7.22

```
REAL32 FUNCTION InchesToCms(VAL REAL32 Inches) IS
  2.54(REAL32) * Inches :
REAL32 FUNCTION Area(VAL REAL32 Length, Breadth) IS
  Length * Breadth :
BOOL FUNCTION BufferFull(VAL INT Count) IS Count > 1024 :
REAL32 FUNCTION Disc(VAL REAL32 A, B, C) IS (B * B) -
  (4.0(REAL32) * (A * C)) :
BOOL FUNCTION IsaDigit(VAL BYTE Char) IS (Char >= '0')
  AND (Char <= '9') :
```

are examples of function definitions.

Like a simple function, a function definition may be generalized to deliver multiple values.

7.6 Exercises

1. Write abbreviations for
   (a) the number of degrees per radian (180 degrees = pi radians)
   (b) the number of minutes in a day
   (c) the conversion of miles per hour to kilometres per hour (50 mph = 80 kmph).

2. Comment on the validity of the following abbreviations

   (a)   **VAL [5]BYTE** Greetings **IS** "Hello" :

   (b)   **VAL []BYTE** Greetings **IS** "Hello" :

   (c)   **VAL** Greetings **IS** "Hello" :

3. Write a procedure to reverse the digits of a three-digit number.

4. Write a set of procedures necessary for manipulating a stack, for example, Push, Pop. The stack is to be implemented using an array.

5. Write a procedure to assemble characters read into an array and record the size.

6. Write a function to find the minimum of three integers.

7. Write a function to test if a word, stored as a list of characters in an array, is a palindrome or not. (A palindrome is a word that reads the same forwards as backwards.)

8. Write a function definition to convert from miles per hour to kilometres per hour (50 mph = 80 kph).

9. Write a function definition to convert a Fahrenheit temperature to a Celsius temperature (Celsius = (Fahrenheit−32) * 5/9).

10. Write a function to test whether a given character is a vowel or not.

11. Write a multivalue function that returns the mean and standard deviation of a list of values.

Chapter 8

Channel protocols

8.1 Introduction

An occam channel protocol specifies the type and format of data that may be transferred on that channel. Such a specification allows the occam system to ensure the correct usage of the channel by a process, in terms of data type and format transferred. Any misuse of the channel is treated as an error. Correct usage also implies that the protocol specifications within the corresponding output and input processes must match. This provides security for the transfer of data between concurrent processes.

To sum up, a protocol in occam terms is just the specification of the data types and number of items of data that a channel is allowed to transfer. A channel protocol may be one of the following types:
- simple
- counted array
- sequential
- variant
- anarchic.

The order specified above denotes the level of protocol complexity, successive protocols being essentially extensions of the preceding one (with the exception of the anarchic protocol).

8.2 Simple protocol

The simple protocol is used for transferring either successive single primitive data types or successive arrays of the same primitive data type. The array version is useful, for example, for communicating character strings between processes. The format of the simple protocol for communicating single values is as follows

```
CHAN OF type channel:
```

where
- `type` is the data type of the channel

128

• channel is the channel identifier.
For example,

CHAN OF BOOL Lock:

specifies a channel named Lock, which supports the successive transfers of a single Boolean value.

More than one channel of the same type may be specified within the same declaration. Each channel identifier must be separated by a comma. For example,

CHAN OF BYTE CurrentSensor, VoltageSensor:

declares two channels, CurrentSensor and VoltageSensor, which both may communicate single bytes of data.

The format of the simple protocol for communicating arrays of values is

CHAN OF [size]type channel:

where size specifies the size of the array. For example,

CHAN OF [16]**INT** Switch:

specifies a channel Switch, which may communicate 16 integer values at a time.

Example 8.1

```
CHAN OF [50]INT Stream :
  PAR
    [50]INT Results :
    SEQ
      .
      . -- initialize array
      .
      Stream ! Results
    [50]INT Data :
    SEQ
      Stream ? Data
```

shows a process that outputs the 50 elements of the array Results along the channel named Stream. The corresponding input process must declare an array of the appropriate size and type to receive the data.

Multidimensional arrays may also be used in channel specifications.

8.3 Counted array protocol

An extension to the array version allows any number of array components, up to some maximum number, to be communicated. At run-time, the actual number of array components being transferred is communicated first across the channel before any array components. The associated input process must read this count value, then the array components themselves. Thus, a channel specified in this manner can support successive variable length transfers.

```
CHAN OF count :: []type channel :
```

where count represents the occam reserved word for a byte or integer data type, that is, **BYTE, INT, INT16, INT32** or **INT64**. It specifies the maximum value of array components that can be transferred (as allowed by that data type: **BYTE** allows up to 255, **INT** allows 2 147 483 647 on 32-bit processors, and so on). Note the empty array dimensions and the double colon. For example,

```
CHAN OF BYTE :: []REAL32 RawData:
```

depicts a channel that can communicate variable length arrays of real numbers, up to a maximum of 255 (as allowed by the **BYTE** specifier). Thus, any number of successive components of the array, between 0 and 255, but always starting with the first component, may be transferred at any time.

The corresponding input and output processes that use such a protocol have a modified format, the input process having the form

```
input ? length :: array
```

and the output process having the form

```
output ! length :: array
```

where
- length is the number of actual array components being transferred. The data type of length must be the same as that declared in the protocol specification.
- array is the occam identifier of the array, of which the first length elements with be sent or received.
- input and output are the identifiers for channels with the declared counted array protocol.

The data type of the arrays in the input and output processes must be the same, and must be the same as the component type declared in the protocol specification.

Example 8.2

```
CHAN OF BYTE :: []REAL32 DataStream :
PAR
  [255]REAL32 Buffer :
  SEQ
    DataStream ! 100(BYTE) :: Buffer
  [255]REAL32 Data :
  BYTE Length :
  SEQ
    DataStream ? Length :: Data
```

shows a counted array protocol, DataStream, being used to communicate the first 100 elements of an array between two concurrent processes.

Example 8.3

```
CHAN OF INT :: []BYTE Stream :
PAR
  [1024]BYTE Buffer :
  SEQ
    Stream ! SIZE Buffer :: Buffer
  [4096]BYTE Data :
  INT Length :
  SEQ
    Stream ? Length :: Data
```

shows the use of a counted array protocol capable of supporting variable length byte transfers. The 1024 components of Buffer are transferred into the first 1024 elements of Data. The maximum theoretical length transfer supported by this protocol will be the maximum size integer allowed by **INT** – on 32-bit processors, this will be 2 147 483 647 bytes. However, any attempt to transfer an amount greater than the size defined in the array declarations will produce an error. The example also illustrates how the **SIZE** operator may be used to good effect.

Such a protocol may also be used for transferring parts of an array or string between processes. For example,

```
CHAN OF BYTE :: []BYTE Comm :
PAR
  [10]BYTE Message :
  SEQ
    Message := "Greetings!"
    Comm ! 5(BYTE) :: Message
  [5]BYTE Data :
```

```
BYTE Length :
SEQ
   Comm ? Length :: Data
```

transfers the first five characters of Message, i.e. "Greet", and so the output *corresponds* to

```
Comm ! 5(BYTE) :: [Message FROM 0 FOR 5]
```

Note: In principle, the occam 2 definition allows the use of array segments in counted array protocol input/output processes. Thus, for example, the following statements are valid:

```
Chan ! Length :: [Buffer FROM 0 FOR Length]
Chan ? Length :: [Buffer FROM 0 FOR Length]
```

However, since the publication of the definition, INMOS have revised their position. Recent releases of the occam 2 compiler (and the new occam 2.1 definition; see Ch. 11) advise that the length part should *not* appear on the array side of the counted array protocol input process, and *vice-versa*. Thus, for example,

```
Chan ? Length :: [Buffer FROM 0 FOR Length]
```

should be rewritten as

```
Chan ? Length :: Buffer
```

The rationale behind this revision of the definition is that the assignments to Length and Buffer occur in parallel; the same rules apply as for parallel assignment and so Length may not appear as a free variable in the array side of the communication. As a concession to backwards compatibility, compilers are still, at present, permitting the original form of input process.

8.4 Protocol names

Occam has a facility that allows a protocol to be given an explicit name. Such a facility is useful if, for example, the same protocol is being used by several channels. The protocol is named and specified once only. Thereafter, any channel declaration using that protocol need only specify the protocol name and not the protocol. One format is

```
PROTOCOL name IS protocol :
```

where
- name is the occam identifier of the protocol name
- protocol is the protocol specification.

By common convention, protocol names are written in capitals.

Example 8.4

```
PROTOCOL DOUBLE IS REAL64 :
CHAN OF DOUBLE Precision :
```

defines a protocol DOUBLE capable of supporting the transfer of single **REAL64** types, and a channel Precision that uses this protocol definition.

Example 8.5

```
PROTOCOL RECORD IS INT :: []BYTE :
CHAN OF RECORD Stream :
```

represents a protocol, RECORD, capable of dealing with variable length arrays of bytes (or strings).

The naming facility is also used for defining the more sophisticated protocols described in the following sections.

8.5 Sequential protocol

This protocol allows a sequence of one or more basic data types or arrays to be communicated over the channel. In essence, the sequence is a concatenation of simple protocols. The sequential protocol has the format

```
PROTOCOL name IS simple_1; simple_2; . . . simple_n :
```

where simple_1, simple_2, . . . simple_n are the names of occam basic data types or arrays, separated by semi-colons. Note that there must be at least one data type (basic or array) in the sequence and that semi-colon separators are required only when there is more than one. Channels using this protocol may then be declared by specifying the protocol name.

Example 8.6

```
PROTOCOL DIMENSIONS IS REAL32; REAL32; REAL32 :
CHAN OF DIMENSIONS Measurements :
```

defines a protocol, DIMENSIONS, for communicating three successive real values. (The protocol here means a **REAL32** followed by another **REAL32**, followed by yet another **REAL32**.) In use, the values or variables named in the associated input and output processes must match the specified protocol in type and number. As in the protocol specification, any values or variables must be separated by semicolons, if there is more than one.

Example 8.7
Given the protocol

```
PROTOCOL COORDINATES IS BYTE; BYTE :
CHAN OF COORDINATES Plotter :
```

then the sequence

```
BYTE XCoord, YCoord :
SEQ
  Plotter ! 110(BYTE) ; 50(BYTE)
  XCoord := 15(BYTE)
  YCoord := 25(BYTE)
  Plotter ! XCoord ; YCoord
```

represents an occam fragment that uses this protocol to transfer two pairs of single byte values. (The protocol here means a **BYTE**, followed by another **BYTE**.)

Protocols comprising mixed data types may also be communicated with the sequential protocol.

Example 8.8
Given the protocol

```
PROTOCOL GRIDVALUE IS BYTE; BYTE; REAL32 :
CHAN OF GRIDVALUE Chan :
```

then the sequence

```
BYTE XCoord, YCoord :
REAL32 Value :
SEQ
  XCoord := 200(BYTE)
  YCoord := 125(BYTE)
  Value := 12.5(REAL32)
  Chan ! XCoord ; YCoord ; Value
```

uses this extended protocol to transfer a real value, in addition to two single byte values. (The protocol in this example means a **BYTE**, followed by another **BYTE**, followed by a **REAL32**.)

Example 8.9

```
PROTOCOL DATASTREAM IS [256]INT; [256]REAL32 :
CHAN OF DATASTREAM Chan :
PAR
  [256]REAL32 RData :
  [256]INT IData :
  SEQ
    .
    . -- initialize arrays Idata and RData
    .
    Chan ! IData; RData
  [256]REAL32 RBuff :
  [256]INT IBuff :
  INT Length :
  SEQ
    Chan ? IBuff; RBuff
```

shows how a sequential protocol may be used to transfer two arrays. (The protocol in this example means 256 **INT**s followed by 256 **REAL3 2**s.)

8.6 Variant protocol

The variant protocol allows a channel to transfer a selection of *variant*, or different, protocols. Only one of these protocol variants may be used at any given time and the selection of which variant occurs at run-time. Each variant of the protocol is known as a *tagged* protocol because each variant is identified by a *tag*. The tag is just an occam identifier that distinguishes that variant from the others, and is used in the selection procedure. Each tag must be unique. The format of this protocol is

```
PROTOCOL name
  CASE
    tag_1; sequential_1
    .
    .
    .
    tag_n; sequential_n
  :
```

where `tag_1; sequential_1, . . . tag_n; sequential n` represent tagged protocols. A tagged protocol may comprise the tag and sequential protocol, separated by a semi-colon, or solely the tag – the sequential protocol may be omitted – as dictated by the requirements of the particular protocol. The

135

reserved word **CASE** must be indented two spaces with respect to the reserved word **PROTOCOL**. Each tagged protocol must be indented a further two spaces. The protocol is terminated by a colon on a line by itself directly under the **P** of **PROTOCOL**. Channels using this protocol may then be declared by specifying the protocol name.

In order for an associated input process to determine which tagged process is being used at any time, the output process must first communicate the tag of that protocol to the input process. Any data associated with that tag is then transmitted.

Example 8.10

```
PROTOCOL ARITHMETIC
  CASE
    add; REAL32; REAL32
    subtract; REAL32; REAL32
    multiply; REAL32; REAL32
    divide; REAL32; REAL32
:
```

represents a protocol for a process performing arithmetic operations on data received. The tags define the required arithmetic operation – *add, subtract, multiply* or *divide*. These are followed, in each case, by two real operand values.

Example 8.11

```
PROTOCOL IO
  CASE
    -- tag, length of file name, file name and open option
    Open; BYTE :: []BYTE; BYTE
    -- tag
    Close
    -- tag, length of data to be sent and data
    Put; INT :: []REAL32
    -- tag and length of data required
    Get; INT
:
CHAN OF IO File :
```

defines a protocol for communicating with a process to read or write the contents of a file (on disk, say). The required file must first be opened for reading or writing. (The example assumes that only one file is open at a time.) After the get or put operations, the file is then closed. The open, put and get operations comprise tagged sequential protocols, whereas the close operation comprises a tag-only protocol. The channel File has been defined using this protocol.

Another protocol may be declared to cater for acknowledgements from the process performing the actual I/O as shown in the next example.

Example 8.12

```
PROTOCOL IOREPLY
  CASE
    -- tag and status
    OpenAck; BYTE
    -- tag
    CloseAck
    -- tag and status
    PutAck; BYTE
    -- tag and status
    GetAck; BYTE
    -- tag, length of data sent and data
    GetReply; INT :: []REAL32
  :

CHAN OF IOREPLY Results :
```

Example 8.13

```
VAL FileName IS "Sensor.Data" :
[512]REAL32 Readings :
BYTE Status :
SEQ
  -- read sensor data
  Sensor ? Readings
  -- now file it away
  File ! Open ; BYTE (SIZE FileName) :: FileName; 'W'
  Results ? OpenAck ; Status
  File ! Put ; SIZE Readings :: Readings
  Results ? PutAck ; Status
  File ! Close
  Results ? CloseAck
```

depicts the use of the previous variant protocols, with the channels, File and Results, being declared via the protocols, IO and IOREPLY, respectively. A file is opened by sending the Open tag, and then the size of the file name, followed by the file name itself and the open option ('W' for write). Next, a block of data is written to the file using the Put tag. Finally, the file is closed; no information needs to be sent apart from the Close tag.

In order to accommodate the input of several variant protocols, a special form of the input process, the *case input*, has been defined as

```
channel ? CASE
  tag_1; sequential_1
    process_1
    .
    .
    .
  tag_n; sequential_n
    process n
```

where each tagged protocol must be indented two spaces and the associated process indented a further two spaces. Input proceeds according to which tag is received
from the output process along the named channel, the relevant component process
then being executed. If a mismatch in the tagged protocols occurs, for example the
wrong sequential protocol is used for a particular tag or an unknown tag is received,
then the case input behaves as a **STOP** process.

Example 8.14

```
[32]BYTE FileName :
[1024]REAL32 Data :
BYTE FileSize, OpenOpt :
INT Length :
BYTE Status :
SEQ
  -- respond to the relevant tag
  File ? CASE
    Open; FileSize :: FileName; OpenOpt
      SEQ
        .
        .   -- open process
        .
        Results ! OpenAck; Status
    Close
      SEQ
        .
        .   -- close process
        .
        Results ! CloseAck
    Put; Length :: Data
      SEQ
        .
        .   -- put process
        .
        Results ! PutAck; Status
```

```
Get; Length
  SEQ
    .
    .    -- get process
    .
    Results ! GetAck; Status
    .
    .    -- send data if status ok
    .
    Results ! GetReply; Length :: Data
```

depicts the use of the **CASE** input process with the tagged protocol IO. Depending on the tag received, the appropriate protocol and process will be invoked.

Another facet of the case input is its use as an alternative in **ALT** constructions. This allows such constructions to accept inputs from channels that use variant protocols. As well as the standard format, the case input may be used in conjunction with a Boolean expression in the alternative. Thus, quite sophisticated forms of alternation may be built up from combinations of case input alternatives and standard alternatives. **ALT** constructions with a case input have the format

```
ALT
  channel ? CASE
    tag_1; sequential_1
      process_1
      .
      .
      .
    tag_n; sequential_n
      process_n
```

and

```
ALT
  Boolean_expression & channel ? CASE
    tag_1; sequential_1
      process 1
      .
      .
      .
    tag_n; sequential_n
      process_n
```

where process_1 . . . process_n represent the processes to be selected for execution by the appropriate protocol variant. Any number of case inputs may be used as alternatives in the **ALT** construction.

Example 8.15

```
ALT
  RealChan ? CASE
    -- real arithmetic
    add; Real1; Real2

      . -- process to perform addition
      .
    subtract; Real1; Real2

      . -- process to perform subtraction
      .
    multiply; Real1; Real2

      . -- process to perform multiplication
      .
    divide; Real1; Real2

      . -- process to perform division
      .
  IntegerChan ? CASE
    -- integer arithmetic
    add; Integer1; Integer2

      . -- process to perform addition
      .
    subtract; Integer1; Integer2

      . -- process to perform subtraction
      .
    multiply; Integer1; Integer2

      . -- process to perform multiplication
      .
    divide; Integer1; Integer2

      . -- process to perform division
      .
```

represents an **ALT** containing two case inputs: one alternative performing real arithmetic operations, the other performing integer arithmetic operations. Which set of variants is chosen for execution depends on which case input is available first, that is, which of the channels, RealChan or IntegerChan, has an output ready first.

140

8.7 Anarchic protocol

This protocol (**ANY**) is the most general and least secure of all the types of protocol. It allows the transfer of any type and format of data, *without* any checks being performed. As such, it should be used with caution. With such a protocol, data is treated as a stream of bytes, higher-level types being decomposed for output or reconstituted on input. Typically, it is only used to communicate to external devices, such as the screen, which may be considered to be *alien* processes. The format is

CHAN OF ANY channel:

where channel is the channel identifier. For example,

CHAN OF ANY Device:

declares the channel Device to be a anarchic (special) protocol channel.

This protocol is no longer favoured, because of the problems that may easily be encountered when the protocol is misused. Indeed, INMOS strongly advise against its use.

8.8 Exercises

1. Write down a channel specification suitable for transferring:
   (a) a real array of variable size
   (b) the contents of a chess board (the components are assumed to be integers)
   (c) a variable length string of characters.

2. Write down a protocol suitable for transferring:
   (a) a complex number
   (b) single components of a real array, which may be selected at random
   (c) personal details, e.g. name, age, sex.

3. Comment on the validity of the following occam program fragments:
   (a)

```
SEQ
  Message ! "Type response now"
  Message ! "Type response"
```

where the channel is specified as

CHAN OF [13]**BYTE** Message :

(b)

```
CHAN OF INT :: [] INT Comm :
PAR
  [512] INT Buffer :
  SEQ
    Comm ! SIZE Buffer :: Buffer
  INT Count :
  [256] INT Block :
  SEQ
    Comm ? Count :: Block
```

4. Write occam processes to act as a multiplexor and a demultiplexor. (The multiplexor will need to record the channel number on which data was received.) Define suitable protocols for use with these processes.

5. Devise a variant protocol for the operations peek (read a value from a memory address) and poke (write a value to a memory address).

Chapter 9

Priority, timers, placement and ports

9.1 Priority   9.2 Timers   9.3 Placement   9.4 Ports   9.5 Exercises

9.1 Priority

Frequently in real-time applications some processes require more favourable treatment than other processes. This is arranged in occam by allowing processes in **PAR** and **ALT** constructions to be assigned a priority for execution: higher priority processes are selected in preference to lower priority processes.

To specify priority, the words **PAR** and **ALT** are preceded by the reserved word **PRI**. The component processes of such priority constructions are given a priority ordering dependent on their textual ordering within the **PAR** or **ALT**, the first-named process receiving the highest priority, and so on.

Priority **PAR**s and **ALT**s may also be replicated.

9.1.1 PRI PAR

The priority **PAR** construction provides a mechanism for specifying the priority at which the component processes of a **PAR** execute. (In a simple (non-priority) **PAR**, processes execute at the same default low priority level.) This facility uses the hardware priority levels provided by the microcoded scheduler of the transputer, as described in the Introduction. Such a construction is useful for ensuring that a high-priority device driver process, for example a disk, is properly scheduled with respect to lower-priority device driver processes. The format of a priority **PAR** construction is

```
PRI PAR
  process_1
    .
    .
    .
  process_n
```

where process_1 is the high priority process and the other component processes have decreasing priority. Although the occam language definition permits any number of priority levels, the transputer supports only *two* levels of priority: low

143

(timeslicing of processes) and high (no timeslicing). Several processes may share the priority level by being grouped within an inner **PAR** construction. For example,

```
PRI PAR
  PAR
    process_1
    process_2
  PAR
    process_3
    process_4
    process_5
```

shows how processes_1 and _2 may share the high priority level, and processes_3, _4 and _5 share the low priority level.

An interrupt handling process may be written with a **PRI PAR**, as follows:

```
PRI PAR

  .
  . -- interrupt handler process - high priority
  .

  PAR

    .
    . -- low priority processes
    .
```

9.1.2 PRI ALT

With the priority **ALT**, if input is available for more than one channel at once, the highest priority input is taken. This device may be used to solve the semantic difficulty encountered with the non-priority **ALT** (Ch. 5). When more than one input is ready at the same time, the process associated with the highest priority input guard is the one selected for execution. The priority **ALT** has the format

```
PRI ALT
  input_guard_1
    process_1

    .
    .
    .

  input_guard_n
    process_n
```

where the first alternative process

```
input_guard_1
  process_1
```

is the high priority process and the other alternatives are lower priority processes. The other forms of the alternation guard may be used besides the input guard.

Note that, with the **PRI ALT**, the alternative processes (process_1 . . . process_n) associated with the prioritized input guards are executed at the default scheduling priority level (in the transputer sense).

Although the priority **ALT** does determine which input guard will be chosen in the event of more than one being ready simultaneously, it does not solve the "fairness" problem. A solution to this problem, using the **PRI ALT**, is given in §9.2.2.1.

At the time of writing, the INMOS occam 2 implementation executes exactly the same code for the **ALT** construct as for the **PRI ALT**. The selection of a ready input is made in the order of the alternatives (which is decreasing priority order for the **PRI ALT**). The first alternative that has a ready guard is the one chosen for execution (Ch. 15). This explains why the **ALT** construct can exhibit the indefinite postponement of alternatives.

One use of **PRI ALT** is to provide a priority interrupt channel.

Example 9.1

```
WHILE Going
  PRI ALT
    Stop ? Any
      Going := FALSE
    InChan ? Char
      OutChan ! Char
```

If input is available on the Stop channel, then that alternative will be taken in preference to the InChan alternative, even if both inputs are ready at the same time.

Example 9.2

```
WHILE TRUE
  PRI ALT Index = 0 FOR 10
    InChan[Index] ? Char
      OutChan ! Char
```

represents a prioritized multiplexor, input being taken from the lowest indexed channel if more than one input is available simultaneously.

Example 9.3

```
WHILE TRUE
  SEQ
    PRI ALT
      Poll ? Message
```

145

```
.
. -- process message
.

TRUE & SKIP

.
. -- background task
.
```

depicts a polling process – on every cycle of the **WHILE** loop, a channel is polled for the availability of a message. If the message is available, it will be processed. Otherwise, a lower priority (background) process is executed.

*9.1.2.1 Unfair **ALTs*** The normal (unprioritized) **ALT** has the potential for making "unfair" selections from among the available alternatives. For example, consider the **ALT** construction:

```
WHILE busy
  ALT
    Chan1 ? Data1
      Process1
    Chan2 ? Data2
      Process2
    Chan3 ? Data3
      Process3
    .
    .
    .
```

If input arrives on Chan1 so quickly that the next input is available before Process1 has completed execution, then the semantics of occam permit the input on Chan1 always to be selected in preference to inputs on any other channels that may also be available. (In fact, as Jones (1989) points out, this is guaranteed by the transputer implementation.) This is an *unfair* selection: a particular channel can hog the selection, while the other channels starve indefinitely.

Jones describes several algorithms that achieve a fairer selection strategy. Essentially, they are variants on a theme: the **PRI ALT** construct, coupled to a resequencing of the **ALT** branches, is used to force fairness – the **PRI ALT** construct, in the event of two or more channels having input at the same time, will select the branch that occurs earliest in the textual ordering. Three of these algorithms are repeated here. Each algorithm assumes there are N branches to the **ALT** (i.e. there are N input channels forming a list of N branches or selections), with the channels and associated data values represented by the arrays Chan[N] and Data[N], respectively.

Fair **ALT** algorithm 1:

```
INT Favourite :
SEQ
  Favourite := 0
  WHILE Busy
    SEQ
      PRI ALT Index = Favourite FOR N
        VAL Shift IS Index REM N :
        Chan[Shift] ? Data[Shift]
          -- perform some task associated with this
          -- alternative - Shift
      Favourite := (Favourite + 1) REM N
```

This algorithm cyclically rotates the **ALT** branches so that, at each pass through the **WHILE** loop, a different branch is first in the list. Coupled with the **PRI ALT**, this ensures that any of the channels will be serviced after at most *N* passes through the loop.

Fair **ALT** algorithm 2:

```
INT Favourite :
SEQ
  Favourite := 0
  WHILE Busy
    PRI ALT Index = Favourite FOR N
      VAL Shift IS Index REM N :
      Chan[Shift] ? Data[Shift]
        SEQ
          -- perform some task associated with this
          -- alternative - Shift
          Favourite:= (Shift + 1) REM N
```

This variation gives the lowest priority next time around to the branch that was selected this time; that is, the **ALT** branches are resequenced, so the branch selected this time is placed at the bottom of the list.

Fair **ALT** algorithm 3:

```
INT Favourite :
SEQ
  Favourite := 0
  WHILE Busy
    SEQ
```

```
PRI ALT
  Chan[Favourite] ? Data[Favourite]
    -- perform some task associated with this
    -- alternative - Favourite
  ALT Index = 0 FOR N
    Chan[Index] ? Data[Index]
      -- perform some task associated with this
      -- alternative - Index
  Favourite := (Favourite + 1) REM N
```

This algorithm, again, cyclically rotates the first **ALT** branch so that, at each pass through the **WHILE** loop, a different one is first in the list. This guarantees that any of the channels will be serviced after at most N passes through the loop.

9.2 Timers

The timer feature in occam makes use of the real-time clock (hardware timer) facility of the transputer and is particularly useful in real-time programming applications (INMOS 1989b). The timers may be used for measuring time intervals and for real-time scheduling. As described in the Introduction, the transputer has two timers, one for each of its priority levels. The high priority timer is incremented every microsecond, and the low priority timer is incremented every 64 microseconds. The scaling factors for converting clock ticks to seconds are 1 000 000 and 15 625 for the high and low priority levels respectively. By default, occam processes execute at low priority and so access the low priority timer. The priority at which an occam process executes, and hence which priority timer it accesses, may be changed by using the **PRI** reserved word (for the **PAR** construction only).

The timer behaves as an input-only channel: its value can only be read. However, unlike channels, more than one component of a **PAR** construction may input from the same timer. Timers, in common with variables and channels, must be declared via a timer specification statement. This has the format

```
TIMER timer :
```

where `timer` is the identifier of the timer within the program. For example,

```
TIMER Clock :
```

declares a timer named `Clock`.

More than one timer may be declared in the same specification statement, and arrays of timers may be declared. For example,

```
TIMER Clock1, Clock2 :
```

148

and

[5] **TIMER** Clock :

The value of the real-time clock is regularly updated by the transputer system, and the value at any instant (the current number of clock ticks) may be read using an timer input statement. The format of the timer input statement is

```
timer ? time
```

The variable time, which receives the clock value, must be of type **INT**.

Example 9.4

```
TIMER Clock :
INT Time :
SEQ
   Clock ? Time
```

reads the current value of Clock into the variable Time.

The hardware timers for each of the transputer's two priority levels may be accessed by respective high and low priority processes in a **PRI PAR** construction. For example,

```
PRI PAR
  TIMER HiClock :
  SEQ
     .
     . -- high priority process
     .
  TIMER LoClock :
  SEQ
     .
     . -- low priority process
     .
```

The clock updating mechanism is cyclic, such that the clock value wraps round to negative values after passing through its most positive value: the clock values behave in modulo arithmetic value fashion. Consequently, modulo arithmetic must be used in conjunction with timers for calculating time delays and differences. These time delays and differences are valid only if the times compared are within a half a timer cycle of each other. The cycle time depends on the type of the transputer and also the priority level. Approximate cycle times are as follows:

low priority   high priority

149

```
T2XX        4.2 seconds     65.5 milliseconds
T4XX,T8XX 76 hours          1.2 hours
```

9.2.1 Measuring time intervals

By recording the value of the timer before and after the execution of a process, the elapsed time of process execution may be determined. For example, the process could be a benchmark. As the timer is incremented modulo fashion, the modulo arithmetic subtraction, **MINUS**, operator is used.

Example 9.5

```
TIMER Clock :
INT T1, T2, TimeInterval :
SEQ
  Clock ? T1
  .
  . run process
  .
  Clock ? T2
  TimeInterval := T2 MINUS T1
```

The time measured is elapsed time, not processor time. Any other processes running in parallel will affect the measurement. The measured interval must be less than half a timer cycle.

Using a timer in conjunction with a **PRI PAR** construction, it is possible to obtain a better measure for the elapsed time for process execution. In the following example, the process under consideration is run at high priority. This eliminates any timeslicing effects introduced by other processes if low priority was used. The **SKIP** represents a null low priority process.

Example 9.6

```
TIMER Clock :
INT Before, Now, TimeDiff :
PRI PAR
  SEQ
    Clock ? Before
    .
    . process being timed
    .
    Clock ? Now
    TimeDiff := Now MINUS Before
  SKIP
```

9.2.3 Generating delays

One use of the timer is to generate a delay in an occam program. To effect a timed delay, the timer input statement is used in conjunction with the **AFTER** keyword.

```
timer ? AFTER expression
```

causes the timer input to be held up until the current clock value is later than the value of the expression (allowing for modulo arithmetic). Again, the delay must be less than half a timer cycle.

Since the current value of the clock is not known until read, a more useful ploy is to read the current clock value and use that value as the starting point of the delay.

Example 9.7

```
VAL TicksPerSecond IS 15625 :
TIMER Clock :
INT Now :
SEQ
  Clock ? Now
  Clock ? AFTER (Now PLUS (TicksPerSecond * 10))
```

The completion of the timer input is now held off until the 10 second delay specified by the expression, *Now* **PLUS** (*TicksPerSecond* * 10) − modulo arithmetic − has elapsed. The process is descheduled for the extent of the delay. Scheduling delays, introduced by the transputer's scheduler, may slightly increase the delay (INMOS 1989b). The greatest delay that can be generated by this method is half the timer's cycle time.

Another example using a timer delay is the generation of an "event" at regular intervals of time. For example, the event could be the execution of some process.

Example 9.8

```
TIMER Clock :
INT Time :
VAL Interval IS 15625 :
  SEQ
  Clock ? Time
  WHILE TRUE
    SEQ
      . . . execute process at 1 second intervals
      Time := Time PLUS Interval
      Clock ? AFTER Time
```

After execution of the process, there is a delay of `Interval` clock ticks before the process is re-executed.

9.2.4 Generating timeouts

A timer may be used in conjunction with an **ALT** construction to build a process that will timeout after a certain delay. If no regular input occurs within a specified time, a timeout will be triggered by the timer input and the timeout component process will be executed.

Example 9.9

```
VAL TicksPerSecond IS 15625 :
VAL OneMinute IS 60 * TicksPerSecond :
TIMER Clock :
SEQ
  Clock ? Now
  ALT
    InChan ? Item
      .
      .      -- default process
      .
    Clock ? AFTER (Now PLUS OneMinute)
      .
      .      -- timeout process
      .
```

represents a process with a one minute timeout. If an input occurs on the channel, InChan, before one minute has elapsed, the default process is executed; otherwise the timeout process will be executed.

9.2.5 Interleaved processing

In conjunction with the **ALT** construct, timers can also be used to produce interleaved processing; for example, the execution of a high priority process at regular intervals of time, interleaved with the execution of a low priority process.

Example 9.10

```
TIMER Clock :
INT Time :
SEQ
  Clock ? Time
  WHILE TRUE
    SEQ
      Time := Time PLUS Interval
      PRI ALT
        Clock ? AFTER Time
          . . . process associated with high priority guard
```

152

```
InChan ? Data
    . . . process associated with low priority guard
```

A detailed description of the use of timers, with many examples and explanations of pitfalls is given in INMOS (1989b).

9.3 Placement

Usually, program objects such as constants and variables are automatically allocated memory locations by the compiler. However, in occam, the programmer is allowed to place variables, channels or arrays at specified physical memory addresses, if necessary. For program objects such as simple variables or arrays, memory placement must be regarded as being uncommon and it usually occurs when the use of memory space needs to be specially optimized or external devices need to be "attached" (memory-mapped) to occam processes. Generally, an occam compiler will try to optimize data space versus code space by attempting to allocate data objects in on-chip memory. Memory allocation is achieved with the **PLACE** statement. The INMOS occam compiler (Ch. 12) has specially extended versions of the **PLACE** statement that should be used for the optimal placement of arrays in memory. Overriding the default allocation of program variables is a non-trivial task, fraught with difficulties. For further information, the necessary compiler and system documentation should be consulted.

The main use of placement is in the allocation of transputer links to memory addresses. Such allocation is necessary for mapping logical channels to physical links (see Ch. 10).

The address space of the transputer is signed and byte addressed. Words are aligned on two-byte or four-byte boundaries depending on processor type. Table 9.1 displays the vital statistics of the transputers' memory address space. However, all this is hidden from the occam programmer. Occam views the memory of the

Table 9.1 Transputer memory address space chracteristics (byte addresses).

	T2XX	T414	T8XX, T400, T425
Word alignment boundary	two-byte	four-byte	four-byte
Start of internal address space	$8000	$80000000	$80000000
Number of bytes used by system at start of address space	36	72	112
Start of user memory	$8024	$80000048	$80000070
Range of internal address space	$8800 – $87FF	$80000800 – $800007FF	$80001000 – $80000FFF
Start of external address space	$8800	$80000800	$80001000
End of external address space	$7FFF	$7FFFFFFF	$7FFFFFFF

transputer as an array of type **INT** to provide wordlength-independent code. Memory addresses in occam are mapped into the correct address space by the compiler.

The **PLACE** statement is known as an occam *allocation*, and its format is

```
PLACE name AT address:
```

where
  • `name` is the occam identifier of the variable, and so on
  • `address` is the absolute memory address, of type **INT**.
The object being allocated memory space must be specified before the placement. For example,

```
INT Event :
PLACE Event AT 8 :
```

places `Event` at memory address 8. This address (of type **INT**) corresponds to an offset of #10 on a 16-bit T2XX (two bytes per **INT**), and an offset of #20 on a 32-bit T4XX or T8XX (four bytes per **INT**). So the end result is `Event` being placed at byte address #8010 on a T2XX, or #80000020 on a T4XX or T8XX. Similarly,

```
[8]BYTE Sensors:
PLACE Sensors AT #400:
```

corresponds to array `Sensors` being placed in memory starting at byte address #8800 (T2XX) or #80001000 (T4XX, T8XX).

9.4 Ports

Occam supports direct access to external devices via memory-mapping; the hardware registers of these devices, such as the input, output and status registers, may be allocated memory addresses, or *ports*, in the transputer's memory. The device's registers may then be treated as ordinary program variables and be accessed from an occam process; for example, performing an input or output, or checking the status of the device. However, only input and output operations are allowed with a port. Essentially, a port behaves as a very special channel and must be declared. It is important to realize that there is no synchronization provided for port access by the transputer. Any timing constraints must be explicitly catered for by the programmer; for example, when reading from a port, if the external device has not yet provided a value, then the input process will read an incorrect value.
The port declaration has the format

```
PORT OF type port :
```

where
- type is the data type of the port
- port is the occam identifier of the port

After it has been declared, the port must be *placed* at a memory address. For example,

```
VAL Address IS #20000000 :
PORT OF BYTE StatusReg :
PLACE StatusReg AT Address :
```

specifies a port, StatusReg, placed at memory address #20000000.

Example 9.11

```
VAL Address IS #20000000 :
PORT OF BYTE StatusReg :
PLACE StatusReg AT Address :
SEQ
  Clock ? Time
  WHILE TRUE
    SEQ
      Time := Time PLUS Interval
      Clock ? AFTER Time
      StatusReg ? Status
        .
        .
        .
```

is an occam fragment that shows how the register of an external device may be polled on a periodic basis using the **AFTER** timer statement.

Example 9.12

```
VAL InputAvailableMask IS #40 :
VAL Reset IS #BF(BYTE) :
PORT OF BYTE InReg :-- input register
PLACE InReg AT #20000000 :
PORT OF BYTE StatusReg :-- status register
PLACE StatusReg AT #20100000 :
PORT OF BYTE ControlReg :-- control register
PLACE ControlReg AT #20200000 :
BYTE Status, Data :
BOOL DataNotAvailable :
SEQ
```

```
ControlReg ! Reset-- initialize control register
DataNotAvailable:= TRUE
WHILE DataNotAvailable
   SEQ
     StatusReg ? Status-- examine status register
     IF
        (INT Status BITAND InputAvailableMask) = 0
          SKIP-- no data available
        TRUE
          SEQ
             InReg ? Data            -- read data
             ControlReg ! Reset      -- reset register
             DataNotAvailable := FALSE
   .
   . -- process data read
   .
   .
```

represents an occam fragment that implements a busy polling loop, testing a device status register until input in an associated input register is available, as indicated by a bit being set in the status register. The input register is then read and the data processed. (A more efficient scheme would be to employ an interrupt-driven input handler; this would do away with the unrestrained looping of busy polling.)

9.5 Exercises

1. Write an occam program to produce a delay of 2 seconds
   • at low priority
   • at high priority.

2. In a network of transputers, messages from a sending process may need to be transmitted through intervening transputers to reach the destination process. Using a **PRI PAR** construction, write a router program to do this. The router should decide whether an incoming message is for this transputer or another. Messages for other transputers should be passed on. For simplicity, assume a pipeline topology. Using a replicated **ALT** construction, extend this example to cater for a general topology; messages may be input from either of five input channels, representing four transputer links and an internal message channel. Use a look-up table to determine which of five output channels the message is to be sent along.

3. Write a program to time the execution of an addition process, e.g. C:= A + B. To minimize timing errors, time the execution of many additions.

4. Write a program to time the execution of the following process

```
INT X, Y, I :
SEQ
   X := 0
   Y := 9
   I := 0
   WHILE I <> 30001
     SEQ
       X := ((X + ((Y * Y) - Y)) / Y)
       I := I + 1
```

Chapter 10

Configuration

10.1 Introduction   10.2 Hardware description   10.3 Software description
10.4 Mapping description

10.1 Introduction

So far, all discussion has assumed that an occam program runs on a *single* transputer system. However, this need not be the case, for the logic of an occam program does not depend on the processor configuration on which it executes. One of the main attractions of the transputer is that the component parts of an occam program may be distributed for execution over a multitransputer network in order to realize true parallel processing. To achieve this, the components must be self-contained (apart from communication requirements). These independent components may then be placed on individual transputers and executed in parallel, with any required communication taking place via the transputers' physical links. (Being independent means that these components are capable of being executed in parallel.) Usually, each component part will comprise a group of occam parallel processes, with each group being placed on a separate transputer for parallel execution. The grouping of the parallel processes is important, for an optimal distribution will achieve better load sharing.

Once an occam program is proven on a single transputer, it may be distributed over a network of transputers quite safely without any effect on its logical correctness. This chapter illustrates how an occam program containing identified parallel processes may be distributed over a given network of transputers, and how the structure of these networks may be specified. Some common approaches for exploiting inherent parallelism in applications are discussed in Chapter 12. The chosen approach will, given the constraint of four links per transputer, determine the possible configurations.

When processes are being distributed over a multitransputer network, it is necessary to *configure* the processes for the network of transputers. Configuration is the mapping of processes to a topology of transputers. This configuration procedure takes place on a higher plane than the logic of the program. For best results, the configuration must be tailored to suit the application. For example, a linear configuration of transputers, rather than a tree structure, may be best suited to a pipeline of processes. But, in many applications, the optimal configuration may not be so obvious. Quinn (1994) lists several general criteria for evaluating different configurations of parallel processors:

- *The diameter of the network* This is the largest distance between two processors. Low diameter networks mean there would be less forwarding of messages between arbitrary pairs of processors.
- *The bisection width of the network* This is the minimum number of communication edges (within one) that must be removed from the network to divide it into two disconnected parts. A high bisection width is to be preferred. For algorithms requiring the movement of large amounts of data, the size of the data set divided by the bisection width puts a lower bound on the complexity of the algorithm.
- *Number of communication edges per processor* A configuration will scale more easily if the number of communication edges per processor is a constant, independent of the network size. (For most transputers, the maximum number of communication edges per processor is four.)

The most popular configurations used in transputer applications appear to be pipelines, rings, trees, grids, toroids and hypercubes. This area is subject to continuing research and development.

Currently, INMOS support an *occam configuration language* that allows the programmer to specify such a configuration (INMOS 1991a). This configuration language is an *extension* of occam and it observes the same scoping rules as occam. Although occam serves as the basis, the configuration language is not part of the occam language definition, is subject to change, and varies from system to system. Only a rudimentary description will be presented here, enough to give the reader some insight into how configurations may be specified.

To configure an occam program for execution on a network of transputers, two or three separate descriptions need to be established:

- A hardware description that specifies how the transputers are arranged as a network. Principally, this description defines how processors are connected to other processors in terms of link connections, along with declaring processor types (e.g. T805) and memory sizes.
- A software description that identifies which occam processes are to be placed on which transputer. A collection of such processes are grouped together as a *single* occam process (program) by an outermost **PAR** in the software description.
- An optional mapping between the above two descriptions, which allows an occam program to be more easily configured for a different network topology. This description maps logical processors, on which occam processes and channels have been placed, to physical processors.

10.2 Hardware description

The configuration description takes the form of a *connected graph*. In the graph, the transputers are regarded as *nodes* and the links as *arcs* or *edges*. The transputers are declared by **NODE** statements, and the links are declared as either **ARC**s or

EDGEs, depending on whether the links are internal to the network or connected to external devices. A transputer declared in the hardware section is considered to be *physical*, whereas a transputer declared in the software section is considered to be *logical*. The latter type has to be mapped to a physical transputer within a mapping description.

The specification of previously declared **NODE**s is heralded by the **NETWORK** keyword. The actual specification comprises the attributes of each node (such as memory size and link connectivity) and is constructed using two directives that are available for hardware description in the configuration language:

• **SET** – assigns **NODE** attributes such as processor type and memory size
• **CONNECT** – defines the link connections between two nodes' edges.

One or more of these directives may grouped together with the **DO** statement.

The four communication links of a transputer are numbered 0 to 3 (Fig. 10.1) and are referenced in the configuration as an array of links for a particular named processor. So, for instance, if a particular transputer has been named as `Proc` in a **NODE** statement, its links are referenced as

• `Proc[link][0]`, which refers to link 0
• `Proc[link][1]`, which refers to link 1
• `Proc[link][2]`, which refers to link 2
• `Proc[link][3]`, which refers to link 3.

Each communications link will support two channels: one input channel and one

Figure 10.1 Two processes connected by two channels.

output channel. Any link may be chosen to act as a channel to a communicating processor. A link on one transputer need not be connected to a corresponding link on another transputer. Thus, for example, link 1 on one transputer may be connected to link 1 on another transputer, but may equally well be connected to link 0, link 2 or link 3. The corresponding physical links must be connected together between transputers, as per the configuration.

As an example of a hardware description, consider a simple network: link 2 of a T400 transputer with 4 Mbytes of memory is connected to link 0 of a T805 transputer with 8 Mbytes of memory (Fig. 10.2). The hardware description for this configuration is

```
-- hardware description
VAL KBytes IS 1024 :
```

```
VAL MBytes IS KBytes * KBytes :
NODE Master, Slave :   -- declare and name two
                       -- transputers
  NETWORK Example
    DO
        -- specify the attributes for each transputer :
        -- first, the type of processor and memory size
        SET Master(type, memsize := "T400", 4 * MBytes)
        SET Slave(type, memsize := "T805", 8 * MBytes)
        -- next, the link connections
        CONNECT Master[link][2] TO Slave[link][0]
  :
```

Figure 10.2 Two transputers lined together.

Within this hardware description, the attributes for each transputer are specified. These are followed by the link connections. Symbolic names, Master and Slave, are declared using a **NODE** statement. These names are specifically associated with the T400 and T805 transputers, respectively, in the **SET** directives. The **SET** directives specify the particular processor attributes such as type and memory size. Note the use of the multiple assignment. The variables type, memsize and link are predefined in the configuration language. The **CONNECT** directive defines the link connections between the two transputers. Note that the ordering of directives is important: the **SET** must come before the **CONNECT**.

A slightly more complicated example is a pipeline of four transputers, with memory sizes 4, 8, 12, and 16 Mbytes respectively. Each transputer connects via its link 2 to the next transputer in the pipeline via its link 0 (Fig. 10.3)

```
-- hardware description
VAL KBytes IS 1024 :
VAL MBytes IS KBytes * KBytes :
VAL PipeLength IS 4 :-- number of transputers
[PipeLength]NODE PipeProcessor :-- array of processors
NETWORK Pipeline
  DO
    DO I = 0 FOR PipeLength
```

```
    SET PipeProcessor[I] (type, memsize := "T805",
                                ((I + 1) * 4) * MBytes)
 DO I = 0 FOR (PipeLength - 1)
   CONNECT PipeProcessor[I][link][2] TO
           PipeProcessor[I + 1][link][0]

:
```

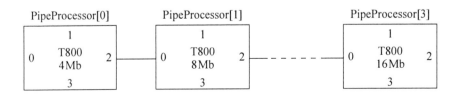

PipeProcessor[0]	PipeProcessor[1]	PipeProcessor[3]

Figure 10.3 Pipeline of transputers.

If the first transputer is connected via its link 0 to a host computer then the hardware description becomes

```
-- hardware description
VAL KBytes IS 1024 :
VAL MBytes IS KBytes * KBytes :
VAL PipeLength IS 4 :-- number of transputers
[PipeLength]NODE PipeProcessor :-- array of processors
ARC HostLink :
NETWORK Pipeline
  DO
    DO I = 0 FOR PipeLength
      SET PipeProcessor[I] (type, memsize := "T805",
                              ((I + 1) * 4) * Mbytes)
    CONNECT HOST TO PipeProcessor[0][link][0] WITH HostLink
    DO I = 0 FOR (PipeLength - 1)
      CONNECT PipeProcessor[I][link][2] TO
              PipeProcessor[I + 1][link][0]

:
```

Note that **HOST** is a predefined **EDGE**.

162

10.3 Software description

The software description comprises an overall **PAR** process that is divided into one or more sections (allocations or placements): each section representing parallel processes to be placed on an individual transputer. Each section is introduced by the keyword **PROCESSOR**. The transputer named on the **PROCESSOR** statement may be either physical or logical, and the occam process following it is placed on that processor. The whole is prefaced by the **CONFIG** keyword.

As a simple example, consider the transputer network described above (Fig. 10.2) and assume that there are two occam processes, Root and Worker, which communicate via two channels, ToWorker and ToRoot. These processes are to be placed on the transputers, Master and Slave, respectively. The software description to achieve this is as follows:

```
-- software description
#INCLUDE "prots.inc"-- INMOS preamble
#USE "Root.lku"      --
#USE "Worker.lku"    --
CONFIG
  CHAN OF PROTOCOL ToWorker, ToRoot :
  PAR -- overall PAR process
      -- place each subprocess on the required
      -- transputer
    PROCESSOR Master
      Root(ToWorker, ToRoot)
    PROCESSOR Slave
      Worker(ToRoot, Toworker)
  :
```

The two channels are automatically placed on the single, interconnecting, communications link, it being assumed that one is in each direction. For such a simple network, a mapping description is not really required. However, Section 10.4 describes how such a mapping may be constructed.

A slightly more complicated example is that of placing a pipeline of occam processes, PipeProcess, onto a pipeline of (physical) transputers, PipeProcessor (Fig. 10.3). PipeProcessor[0] executes the initialization process, whereas PipeProcessor[PipeLength - 1] executes the termination process. Processes in between these two execute the pipeline processes. The pipeline processes communicate via an array of channels, Pipe.

```
-- software description
VAL PipeLength IS 4 :
CONFIG
  CHAN OF PROTOCOL Input, Output :
```

```
[PipeLength] CHAN OF PROTOCOL Pipe :
PAR
  PROCESSOR PipeProcessor[0]
    Initialize(Input, Pipe[0])
  PAR I = 1 FOR (PipeLength - 2)
    PROCESSOR PipeProcessor[I]
      PipeProcess(Pipe[I - 1], Pipe[I])
  PROCESSOR PipeProcessor[PipeLength - 1]
    Terminate(Pipe[PipeLength - 1], Output)
:
```

10.4 Mapping description

If logical processors have been used in the software description, then a mapping description is also necessary to map these logical processors onto the physical ones contained in the hardware description.

The mapping description is introduced by the keyword **MAPPING** and the actual assignment of logical processors to physical processors is performed by the **MAP** statement.

As a simple example of a mapping, consider the simple hardware and software descriptions developed above. These are modified below to allow a mapping description to be written. In the hardware description, Master and Slave are now named MasterProc and SlaveProc: these are the *physical* processors. In the software description, two *logical* processors, RootProc and Worker-Proc, replace Master and Slave respectively in the **PROCESSOR** statements.

```
-- modified hardware description
VAL KBytes IS 1024 :
VAL MBytes IS KBytes * KBytes :
-- physical processors
NODE MasterProc, SlaveProc :
NETWORK Example
  DO
    SET MasterProc(type, memsize := "T400", 4 * MBytes)
    SET SlaveProc(type, memsize := "T805", 8 * MBytes)
    CONNECT MasterProc[link][3] TO SlaveProc[link][0]
:
-- modified software description
#INCLUDE "prots.inc"-- INMOS preamble
#USE "Root.lku"      --
#USE "Worker.lku"    --
CONFIG
  CHAN OF PROTOCOL ToWorker, ToRoot :
```

```
PAR
  -- logical processor
  PROCESSOR RootProc
    Root(ToWorker, ToRoot)
  -- logical processor
  PROCESSOR SlaveProc
    Worker(ToRoot, ToWorker)
:
```

The mapping for such a configuration is

```
-- mapping description
MAPPING
  DO
    MAP RootProc ONTO MasterProc
    MAP WorkerProc ONTO SlaveProc
:
```

In a similar manner, configuration descriptions for other network topologies, such as rings, toroids and hypercubes, may be easily written down.

Chapter 11

Extended occam 2 – occam 2.1

11.1 Introduction

Several of the extensions to the occam 2 language definition as proposed in the occam 3 reference manual (Barrett 1992) have been implemented by INMOS in an enhanced version of occam 2 known as occam 2 extensions (or occam 2.1) (SGS–THOMSON Microelectronics 1995). This extended version of the language also includes several smaller enhancements made to occam and already implemented by INMOS in the occam 2 compilers (but which do not appear in the occam 2 definition). INMOS expect these language extensions to be fully implemented in INMOS DX405 release of the occam toolset, due in 1996.

11.2 User-defined types

This extension allows the renaming of occam data types by the programmer. Such a facility means that data types may now have more specific or meaningful names, relevant to a particular application. It also increases type security in that user-defined (or *named*) types may not be accidentally mixed with any others. The syntax is

```
DATA TYPE name IS type :
```

where name is the programmer-assigned type name, and type is a standard occam 2 basic scalar or array type, or another user-defined type. In particular, for an array type, the size of the array must be a compile-time constant. Named types are used just like the basic occam 2 primitive types.

166

An example of user-defined types is illustrated in the following occam fragment:

```
DATA TYPE LONGINT IS INT64 :
DATA TYPE SHORTINT IS INT16 :
LONGINT BigOne :
SHORTINT SmallOne :
```

defines two named data types, LONGINT and SHORTINT, in terms of the occam 2 types **INT64** and **INT16** respectively. Following these statements, two variables, one of each type, BigOne and SmallOne, are declared. Similarly,

```
273(SHORTINT)
```

represents a literal value of type SHORTINT.

Note that although a named type has the same *structure* as the occam type, the two types are not directly equivalent. This means that, for example, occam 2 basic scalar types and user-defined types may *not* be mixed without an explicit type conversion. Thus, the assignment shown below is illegal if Int has been declared as an **INT16** type:

```
Int := SmallOne
```

Variables of a user-defined type (whether scalar or array) are not compatible with variables of similarly sized user-defined types. For example,

```
DATA TYPE TYPE1 IS REAL32 :
DATA TYPE TYPE2 IS REAL32 :
DATA TYPE TYPE3 IS [10]REAL32 :
DATA TYPE TYPE4 IS [10]REAL32 :
TYPE1 A :
TYPE2 B :
TYPE3 X :
TYPE4 Y :
```

In the above, the types of A and B, and of X and Y are different. For named array data types, this constraint has the consequence that array constructors for such types must have the name of the type appended if the type cannot be deduced directly by the occam compiler.

Named array tables may also be defined, with the type being appended to the end of the table declaration. For instance,

```
['A', 'E', 'I', 'O', 'U'](VOWELS)
```

represents a table accorded the type VOWELS.

11.3 RECORDs

The record is an addition to the occam 2 structured type. There are now *two* structured types in occam: the *array* and the *record*. A record allows several related data items (or *fields*) to be collected together under the umbrella of a single identifier. The syntax of the record structure is

```
DATA TYPE name
  RECORD
    field_1
    field_2
       .
       .
    field_n
  :
```

where name is the identifier of the record type being defined, and field_1, field_2, . . . field_n specify the identifiers and data types of that record's fields and must be *simple* data declarations – primitive scalar types or arrays. No channels, timers, ports, procedures, functions or protocols may be used. Each field of the record type has the format

```
type namelist :
```

where namelist is a comma-separated list of items of type type. After such a declaration, record variables of type name may then be declared in the usual fashion. The fields of a record may also be records, but only if the subrecord is expressed as a named type. Thus, records of arrays, records of records, and arrays of records may now be constructed.

Fields of a **RECORD** structure are accessed as with array elements, with the field name being used as the index.

For example, the real and imaginary parts of a complex number may be grouped together in a **RECORD** to form a new "type", COMPLEX:

```
DATA TYPE COMPLEX
  RECORD
    REAL32 Real :
    REAL32 Imag :
  :
```

A variable of type COMPLEX may be declared thus:

```
COMPLEX Z :
```

and the two fields of Z are referenced as Z[Real] and Z[Imag], respectively.

11.4 PACKED RECORDs

The packed record extension to the record type allows the programmer to control exactly how the record is mapped into memory, a necessary feature for some external hardware and communications protocols. (The occam language definition does not specify how **RECORD**s are to be implemented, and an implementation *may* introduce reordering and unwanted padding between fields, for example.)

The syntax is the same as that for **RECORD**, except that the keywords **PACKED RECORD** replace the keyword **RECORD**.

```
DATA TYPE name
  PACKED RECORD
    field_1
    field_2
      .
      .
      .
    field_n
  :
```

The compiler will lay out the fields of a packed record in memory in the order specified in the declaration, with no reordering of the fields nor introduction of padding. There may be some implementation restrictions, such as word alignment, on some fields.

11.5 BYTESIN operator

This operator is analogous to the **SIZE** operator of occam 2. However, **BYTESIN** delivers the size of a variable (scalar or structured type) expressed as a number of *bytes* (and not as a number of elements as the **SIZE** operator does). When used in conjunction with an occam variable, **BYTESIN** returns an **INT** value that contains the size of that variable. The format is

```
length := BYTESIN (variable)
```

where `variable` is an occam variable and `length` is set to the size in bytes of that variable. (The variable `length` must have been already declared as an **INT** type.) For example,

```
length := BYTESIN (Int)
```

with Int declared as an **INT32**, will set Length to the value 4.

The **BYTESIN** operator may also act on a data type, and will deliver the size of the type in bytes. The syntax is analogous to that above.

```
length := BYTESIN (type)
```

where `type` is an occam or user-defined data type and `length` is set to the size in bytes of that type. For example,

```
length := BYTESIN (LONGINT)
```

will return the value 8. (The semantics and syntax of the **SIZE** operator have also been extended to allow it to operate on named array data types as well.)

11.6 OFFSETOF operator

The **OFFSETOF** operator returns an **INT** value, which is the offset in bytes from the start of a given record to the beginning of a given field within that record. The syntax is

```
offset := OFFSETOF (record, field)
```

where `record` is a occam variable of a **RECORD** type, `field` is a field of that record, and `offset` is an **INT** variable that receives the number of bytes. For example,

```
offset := OFFSETOF (COMPLEX, Imag)
```

sets the **INT** variable `offset` to the value 4.

The next two extensions remove some cumbersome restrictions that unfortunately, at times, made occam 2 programs tedious to write and difficult to comprehend.

11.7 Typed literals

With the occam 2 extensions, INMOS have relaxed the rule that literal values must be followed by a type specification. Instead, the occam compiler will attempt to deduce types of scalar and array literals from their context within the program. A literal may now be written as

```
literal = value
```

For example, the following simplifications will be possible.

```
VAL Pi IS 3.142(REAL32) :
VAL TwoPi IS Pi * 2.0(REAL32) :
```

may be written as

```
VAL Pi IS 3.142(REAL32)  :
VAL TwoPi IS Pi * 2.0 :
```

(Note that the type of 3.142 cannot be unambiguously deduced – is it a **REAL32** or **REAL64**?) and

```
Epsilon := 1.0E-60(REAL64)
```

may be written as

```
Epsilon := 1.0E-60
```

11.8 BYTE arithmetic

The extended language definition allows integer arithmetic operations directly on **BYTE** variables. Such operations were not permitted in the original occam 2 definition. Instead, **BYTE** variables had to be converted to **INT**s for any arithmetic operations. This restriction no longer applies in the extended definition.

All the dyadic integer arithmetic operators apply, as do the conversion operators, **ROUND** and **TRUNC**. Of the three monadic operators, only negation is *not* permitted, as the result would be meaningless in **BYTE** terms (**BYTE**S are defined in the range 0–255 only).

Type conversions are allowed with **BYTE** variables. Real variables may be converted to **BYTE** types by use of the **ROUND** or **TRUNC** operator.
Overflow will occur if the value of the results is out of the range 0 to 255.

11.9 MOSTPOS and MOSTNEG BYTE

The use of the **MOSTPOS** and **MOSTNEG** operators for **BYTE**-type variables will be permitted, with

```
MOSTPOS BYTE evaluating to 255(BYTE)
```

and

```
MOSTNEG BYTE evaluating to 0(BYTE)
```

11.10 FUNCTIONs returning fixed-length objects

The type returned by a **FUNCTION** is now permitted to be *any* type, not just the basic occam types. This means **FUNCTION**s may return records and fixed-length arrays, that is, arrays whose size is known at compile time. There is no change to the syntax. As an example, consider a function, `VectorProduct`, which calculates and returns the vector product of two vectors (arrays). This may be written as

```
[3]REAL32 FUNCTION VectorProduct(VAL [3]REAL32 X, Y)
  [3]REAL32 Z :
  VALOF
    SEQ
      Z[1]  :=  (X[2]  *  Y[3])  -  (X[3]  *  Y[2])
      Z[2]  :=  (X[3]  *  Y[1])  -  (X[1]  *  Y[3])
      Z[3]  :=  (X[1]  *  Y[2])  -  (X[2]  *  Y[1])
    RESULT Z
:
```

Such a function may be invoked by a call such as

```
[3]REAL32 A, B, C :
SEQ
  C := VectorProduct(A, B)
```

11.11 Dropping FROM and FOR in segments

The occam 2 extensions will permit either the **FROM** keyword or the **FOR** keyword (*but* not both) to be omitted from its use in array segments. In either case, a suitable default value will be used. When **FROM** is dropped, the default start value will be 0. When **FOR** is omitted, this will be taken to mean "the rest of the array". Thus, besides standard syntax for array segments,

```
[array FROM first FOR count]
```

the following two variants will also be available:

```
[array FOR count]
```

when the start value for the array indexing will be taken to be 0, and

```
[array FROM first]
```

when the length of the array to be accessed will be taken to be (**SIZE** array) – first.

So, for example,

```
[512]REAL32 Source :
```

```
[256]REAL32 Destination :
SEQ
  Destination := [Source FROM 256 FOR 256]
```

can be rewritten as

```
[512]REAL32 Source :
[256]REAL32 Destination :
SEQ
  Destination := [Source FROM 256]
```

and have exactly the same effect.

11.12 RESHAPES for arrays

A new operator, **RESHAPES**, is provided, which allows a previously defined multidimensional array to be "reshaped" in another declaration, that is, to be moulded into an array of different dimensions, but of the same type. The reshaped array must have one or more dimensions variable (i.e. a dimension size not explicitly stated). The syntax is

```
[size_1] . . . [] . . . [size_n]type name RESHAPES array :
```

or

```
VAL [size_1] . . . [] . . . [size_n]type name RESHAPES
array :
```

where `[size_1] . . . [] . . . [size_n]type` specifies the dimensions and type of the reshaped array, `name` represents the occam identifier of the reshaped array and `array` is the occam identifier of the previously defined array. For example,

```
[12]INT Old1,Old2, Old3 :
[3][]INT New1 RESHAPES Old1 :
[][4]INT New2 RESHAPES Old2 :
[2][][3]INT New3 RESHAPES Old3 :
```

defines three "new" arrays, New1, New2, New3, which are reshapes of the arrays Old1, Old2 and Old3.

11.13 Scoping of PROTOCOL tags

The scope of a variant protocol tag is to be limited to the scope of the defining protocol. (They are currently treated as global names. Moreover, it is possible to re-use a tag name for an occam variable within the scope of the protocol, without any untoward effects!) This will permit more transparent occam code to be written.

11.14 Single-line FUNCTIONS as constants

The use of so-called "single-line" **FUNCTION**s as compile-time constants will be allowed, provided that all the **FUNCTION**'s parameters and free-variables are themselves compile-time constants. This feature will permit better abstraction facilities for the occam programmer.

The following extensions have already been implemented by INMOS in their occam 2 compilers.

11.15 INLINE operator

The **INLINE** operator may be used to immediately precede **PROC** and **FUNCTION** definitions to inform the compiler that the body of specified procedure or function should be expanded *inline* whenever that procedure or function is called in the code (i.e. the procedure or function body is expanded at the position of the call). Any occam procedure or function definition may be proceeded with the keyword **INLINE**. Note that it is the *definition* that is preceded with the **INLINE** keyword, but it is the *call* of the particular procedure or function that is affected. For example,

```
INT INLINE FUNCTION Area (VAL REAL32 Length, Breadth)
           IS Length * Breadth :
```

11.16 Channel RETYPEs

Retyping channels allows the channel to be retyped to another channel of a different protocol. For example,

```
PROTOCOL PROTOCOL32 IS INT32 :
CHAN OF PROTOCOL32 Chan1 :
CHAN OF REAL32 Chan2 RETYPES Chan1 :
```

This is a low-level facility, which should be used with caution.

11.17 Channel constructors

Arrays of channels may be constructed from a list of other previously declared channels. For example, if the following channels have been declared:

```
CHAN OF PROTOCOL X :
[3]CHAN OF PROTOCOL Y :
```

then an array of channels such as the following may be defined:

```
[3]CHAN OF PROTOCOL Z IS [X, Y[0], Y[1]] :
```

11.18 PROTOCOL name IS ANY

The use of the anarchic protocol **ANY** may cause channel problems if not used securely. The ability now to specify this protocol as part of a named, sequential or variant protocol goes some way in removing these problems. When used as such, a data item of any type may be transferred as part of that protocol, that is, it still behaves like **CHAN OF ANY**, but it is now a named protocol and is therefore preferred. For instance, the following is an example of the recommended usage:

```
PROTOCOL ANARCHIC IS ANY :-- ANY as a named protocol
CHANNEL OF ANARCHIC Secure :
SEQ
    Secure ! X; Y; 4 :: "PLOT"
```

11.19 Allocations

This facility allows a variable (scalar or array), a channel or port to be placed at an absolute memory address. Essentially, an allocation is a **PLACE** statement or an extension of it. The new restriction on its use is that an allocation must be written *immediately* after the declaration to which it refers. For example,

```
INT RegisterA, RegisterB :
PLACE Register AT #0800 :
PLACE RegisterB AT #0804 :
```

is valid, whereas

```
INT RegisterA :
INT RegisterB :
PLAC8E RegisterA AT #0800 :
PLACE RegisterB AT #0804 :
```

is not.

Some of the more recent releases of the INMOS occam compiler support an extension of the **PLACE** statement, which allows a variable to be placed at a specified location in a process's workspace (Ch. 13), rather than just at an absolute location.

11.20 Counted array input

The semantics of the *counted array input* have been *changed* from those described in the occam 2 language definition. The occam 2 definition permitted an input in the form of an array segment:

```
chan ? length :: [array FROM 0 FOR length]
```

that is, the length of the input buffer, `length`, was allowed to be part of the buffer expression: `array FROM 0 FOR length`. Now, INMOS advise that the length of the input buffer should not appear on the array side of the input. (The reason for this change is that the assignments to `length` and `array` occur in parallel, and, according to the rules of parallel assignment, `length` may not appear free in `array`, and vice versa.)

The preferred syntax is now

```
chan ? length :: array
```

Thus, rather than writing

```
[10] INT Array :
SEQ
  Chan ? 10 :: [Array FROM 0 FOR 10]
```

the following is recommended

```
[10] INT Array :
SEQ
  Chan ? 10 :: Array
```

For the sake of backwards compatibility, the compiler will accept a communication using the old syntax and will transform it into the preferred form.

11.21 Future directions

INMOS advocate the disuse of **CHAN OF ANY**, replacing it with a named protocol for greater program execution security (see §11.16).

11.21 Future directions

INMOS also advise that the ability to name the length of a counted array input as the length of the receiving buffer is obsolescent. The counted array input should be recoded as described in §11.18.

Chapter 12

Approaches to writing parallel programs in occam

12.1 Introduction   12.2 Algorithmic parallelism   12.3 Geometric parallelism
12.4 Process farming

12.1 Introduction

The development of a parallel program often poses a problem for programmers used to constructing programs for sequential execution; quite how to organize the program to make the best use of the parallel processing power is not always obvious. Research and development into this problem have been going on for many years, and a collection of general and quite specific paradigms have evolved. In particular, three approaches most suited to the transputer are considered in this chapter.

Fox et al. (1988) have put forward three very general features of parallel computation. (The work of Fox et al. was largely based on the *data parallel* approach to parallel computation. There are other approaches, as examined in this chapter. Nevertheless, the observations are still interesting and viable.) Such a computation is considered to comprise an algorithm applied to a large dataset forming a domain consisting of many members:

- parallelism is achieved by domain decomposition, i.e. division or partition of the domain into smaller elements
- large speed-ups can be obtained as long as each processor contains a large enough element
- each processor uses an algorithm similar to a sequential version, with two key differences: each processor operates on part or all of the dataset, and boundary conditions on the algorithm mean inter-processor communication.

Fox et al. also draw the analogy to parallel processing with the construction of a wall by several bricklayers: the wall represents the domain, and bricklayers represent the processors. There are several ways in which the bricklayers can go about this everyday task. Surprisingly, the analogy illustrates several key issues in parallel processing:

- the usefulness of domain decomposition
- the size of the problem domain
- the relation of the processor topology to that of the problem
- the difficulties encountered in irregular (non-simple geometry) domains
- the difficulties encountered in inhomogeneous (unequal grain sizes) domains

178

• the distinct speed-ups possible with local and global parallelism
• parallel input/output decomposition.

The previous chapters have concentrated on the various program constructs available in occam and have explained their use. In order to reap the most benefit from the use of occam and transputers, programs need to exhibit some degree of parallelism. Every application needs to be considered to see how the inherent parallelism may be best expressed and exploited. But this is not an easy exercise. The conventional mould of thinking and expressing the solution to a programming problem as a *sequence* of steps must be broken. Several approaches for applying parallelism to problems have yielded promising results for occam and the transputer. Basically, it is a choice between partitioning the algorithm or partitioning the data. In general, the latter is easier to do. Even so, much more experience is needed in the art and science of parallel programming.

Parallelism is expressed within an occam program by parallel constructions, **PAR**. Given the fact that each parallel process may be mapped onto a separate processor for execution, the potential benefits in terms of speed and efficiency may be enormous. Nevertheless, efficiency considerations need to be taken into account so that the benefits gained from parallelism are not lost.

The *granularity* of the application needs to be carefully assessed (see also Ch. 14). Granularity is a measure of parallelism – the number of parallel processes into which a problem is divided. A large amount of parallelism in a multiprocessor configuration is not necessarily an ideal situation. It is necessary to achieve a balance between keeping each processor busy with computation and maintaining the inter-processor communication time at a minimum. The first-generation transputers (T2XX, T4XX, T8XX) do not provide message routing in hardware; valuable computation time can be taken up by extra occam processes, which implement software message routing between processes. With a high granularity, there will be many parallel processes per processor and then the communications overhead can dominate the computation, causing the efficiency to be low. However, with a low granularity, with not so many parallel processes per processor, the computation should dominate the communications. Even so, the distribution of processes (i.e. work load) to each transputer must be carefully balanced. Otherwise, the system may operate at the speed of the transputer with the largest workload (all others being held up, waiting to communicate with it), and the efficiency will again be low. For applications with independent computation and communications, optimum efficiency may realized by matching the granularity of the process to the granularity of the processor. The transputer, with its powerful processor and communications capability, can be considered as a medium- to coarse-grain computer.

The organization of programs around the parallel paradigm has been approached in several different ways. These various approaches may be broadly classified into the following categories (all are variations of the *divide-and-conquer* approach). In the general case, these approaches are implemented using a network of transputers, collections of parallel processes being distributed among the processors:

- *Algorithmic*   In this method, quasi-independent processes execute sections of the algorithm (and, in the general case, may be non-identical), with data and partially computed results being passed among the processes as the algorithm dictates. Each process implements a part of the total algorithm, that is, it is the algorithm that is divided up (or parallelized). The data flowing between the processes can cause the communication overhead to dominate computation. Thus, good load balancing is not automatic, and care needs to be exercised when the algorithm is partitioned. The memory requirements per process are not excessive. Depending on the problem, each process may operate on all the data, but not all the data at once. Hey (1988b) quotes examples of this approach, which achieved efficiencies of 50–60 per cent.
- *Geometric*   In this method, the processes are quasi-independent but identical, with each process operating on a portion of the data, and interacting with neighbouring processes, according to the geometry of the problem (i.e. it is the data that is divided up). This approach is suited to problems that have an underlying regular geometry. Each process implements the same code. Homogeneity allows the data to be partitioned equally between the processes – each process is responsible for one element – a defined spatial area or volume. Processes communicate with nearest neighbours to simulate physical interactions. The communication load will be proportional to the size of the boundary of the element, whereas the computational load will be proportional to the volume of the element (Pritchard 1988). Typically, this approach is organized in "compute then communicate" cycles. Overlapped computation and communication is not always possible, but for many applications it is; the communication may be overlapped with useful calculation, leaving only a non-overlapped communication setup overhead.

$$T_{comm} = T_{setup} + T_{overlapped}$$

Since each process implements the whole algorithm, the memory requirements per process are greater than the previous approach. Hey (1988b) states that efficiencies greater than 80 per cent have been achieved with this approach.

- *Process farming*   In this method, fully independent but identical processes operate on parts of the data, in any order (Again, it is the data that is partitioned). The problem must be such that the solution does not depend on the order of processing the partitioned data. Each process implements the same code – so-called *worker* processes. Data is distributed to the workers by a *farmer* process. The amount of computation per part of data may vary. After processing one portion of the data, a worker process is given another portion. The approach is load balanced in that a process that has a heavy computation will not be given more data until it has finished, whereas a process with a light computation will be able to accept more data sooner. Computation and communication (the transfer of "raw" data and results) may be overlapped, so the method can be very efficient. Again, since each process implements the whole algorithm, the memory requirements per process are greater than the first approach. Hey

(1988b) quotes an example in which an efficiency in excess of 95 per cent was obtained. Pritchard (1988) has analyzed a *processor farm* in terms of three parameters:

T_{calc} = time for one processor to complete one result

T_{trans} = time for inter-processor transfer of one result

T_{setup} = time for processor to setup each transfer.

He shows that for $T_{calc} > T_{trans} > T_{setup}$, then there is a limit to the number of processors that may be gainfully employed, owing to the saturation of communications bandwidth. Hey studied three different processor configurations for a farm and found that both triple chain and ternary tree configurations had better speed-ups than a single chain of processors (pipeline), presumably because the single chain was limited by the performance of the farmer processor. Hey (1990) has also studied the optimum partitioning of the data into so-called packets. He quotes a result that for a total quantity of work of N indivisible units, then the number of packets per worker to maximize the farm efficiency is $O(N^{1/2})$.

Returning to the Fox et al. (1988) wall-building analogy, these three different approaches to parallel processing are represented as follows:

- *Algorithmic*   Each bricklayer lays a row of bricks, working simultaneously with the other bricklayers but offset in time so that the bottom row is started first, then the next row, and so on up the rows, so that an upper row always has at least one underlying row of bricks. This is achieved by the bricklayers communicating with each other.
- *Geometric*   Each bricklayer is assigned a vertical section of the wall to build, working simultaneously with the other bricklayers. In order to integrate each individual area of the wall with its neighbouring areas, the bricklayers must communicate with those responsible for these neighbouring areas.
- *Process farming*   Each bricklayer lays a brick at a time, obtaining bricks and mortar from a common pool. The wall steadily builds up, sometimes in the horizontal direction, sometimes in the vertical direction.

The analysis of a problem using *process diagrams* (akin to the *data flow diagrams* used to develop conventional sequential programs) to represent parallel processes presents a graphical method for visualizing the component processes of an occam program; the processes are represented by circles, the channels are represented by arcs connecting the circles. Such a method has been found useful in the design of occam programs. Another graphical method that may also prove useful for designing occam programs is the Petri-net notation. This technique allows the graphical expression of parallel strands of computation, so that its suitability to the design of occam programs should be apparent. CSP, the theoretical basis for occam, is an excellent notational tool for expressing the design of occam programs. A very readable example of this latter technique is provided by Mett at al. (1994).

The following sections of the chapter discuss in more detail the three approaches to writing parallel programs in occam, giving concrete examples in each case. For simplicity of presentation, the handling of process termination has been omitted in most examples. In these examples, the processes are driven "forever" by **WHILE TRUE** loops.

12.2 Algorithmic parallelism

The *algorithmic parallelism* approach, also known as *data flow decomposition*, is concerned with exploiting any parallelism that exists in the *algorithm* being used to solve the problem at hand. The algorithm may be an already existing sequential one or be totally new. Parallelism can be introduced by considering how the algorithm may be broken up into separate, quasi-independent sections. Each section can then be executed in parallel, with data flowing between the sections as necessary. Each section will perform some computation with the data, and then pass the data on to the next section. Depending on the particular algorithm, each section may perform the same computation or a different one.

The inherent parallelism is frequently found in a loop or iteration. Consider a linear search, for example. In the sequential case, each item in the list is compared one at a time as the search sequences through the list. This comparison may however be performed more efficiently in parallel; each comparison may be performed at the same time.

The algorithmic approach is modelled by occam parallel processes, each parallel process responsible for the execution of a section of the algorithm, using the synchronization and communication provided by occam channels to transfer data between the processes. The communication overhead between the parallel processes in such circumstances can become quite significant. A common example of the algorithmic approach is the pipeline; each unit of the pipeline contributes by executing a section of the algorithm. The independent units operate on separate portions of the data as the stream of data is fed down the pipeline. The overall effect of this overlapped operation is the realization of parallel execution.

12.2.1 Newton–Raphson square root estimation
As an example of the algorithmic approach, consider the Newton–Raphson estimate technique for evaluating square roots. This method starts off with the value of the number whose square root is required and an initial estimate of the square root. The Newton–Raphson formula is then applied in an iterative manner, each time producing a better estimate of the square root from the previous value. If the iteration is performed many times, the final estimate will be a close approximation to the real value.

The Newton–Raphson formula for calculating the square root of a number, x, is

$$y_{i+1} = \tfrac{1}{2}(y_i + x/y_i)$$

where y_i, y_{i+1} are successive estimations of the root y. This formula may be expressed in occam as

```
Estimate := (Estimate + (Number / Estimate)) / 2.0(REAL32)
```

where *Number* is the number whose square root is required and the initial value for *Estimate* is given. Usually, the initial value for *Estimate* is taken to be

```
Number / 2.0(REAL32)
```

If the iteration is performed *Iterations* times, then a sequential solution may be written as

```
SEQ
   Input ? Number
   Estimate := Number / 2.0(REAL32)
   SEQ Index = 0 FOR Iterations
      Estimate := (Estimate + (Number / Estimate)) /
                  2.0(REAL32)
   Output ! Estimate
```

The Newton–Raphson procedure may be written in a concurrent form by considering each iteration as an occam parallel process. (This algorithm is an example of the type in which each parallel process performs the same operation.) Each of these processes accepts the number and previous estimate as input, calculates the new estimate and produces the number and new estimate as output (Fig. 12.1).

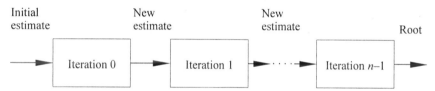

Figure 12.1   A pipeline of processes to calculate the square root of a number, using the Newton–Raphson method.

Thus, the approximation technique may be written as a pipeline of identical processes, with the necessary initialization and termination processes. The pipeline may be generated with a replicated **PAR** statement. The top level of the program will have the following form

```
global declarations
procedures comprising
   initialization process
   pipeline processes
   termination process
main process
```

The global declarations comprise the channels for the pipeline processes and the channels for the initialization and termination processes. Assuming 50 iterations, this section may be written as

```
-- global declarations
VAL Iterations IS 50 :
[Iterations + 1]CHAN OF REAL32 Pipe :
CHAN OF REAL32 InChan, OutChan :
```

The `Initialize` process inputs the number whose square root is required, and outputs the value of this number and initial square root estimate to the first pipeline process. This may be expressed in pseudo-occam as

```
WHILE data is available
  SEQ
    INPUT a number
    SEND this number and initial square root estimate
      to first pipeline process
```

In occam, this may be written as

```
PROC Initialize(CHAN OF REAL32 Input, Inject)
  WHILE TRUE
    REAL32 Number:
    SEQ
      Input ? Number
      -- feed number and initial estimate into pipeline
      Inject ! Number
      Inject ! Number / 2.0(REAL32)
  :
```

As indicated previously, the pipeline comprises *Iterations* identical processes that are generated with a **PAR** replicator. Each of these processes inputs the number and the previous estimate from the preceding pipeline process and outputs the number and new estimate to the succeeding process. Expressed in pseudo-occam, this becomes

```
WHILE data is available
  SEQ
    RECEIVE a number and previous square root estimate
      from preceding pipeline process
    SEND this number and new square root estimate to
      next pipeline process
```

Written in occam, this becomes

```
PROC Pipeline(CHAN OF REAL32 InPipe, OutPipe)
  WHILE TRUE
    REAL32 Number, Estimate :
    SEQ
      -- accept number and previous estimate
      InPipe ? Number
      InPipe ? Estimate
      -- pass on number and new estimate
      OutPipe ! Number
      OutPipe ! (Estimate + (Number / Estimate)) /
                 2.0(REAL32)
  :
```

Finally, the *Terminate* process inputs the number and final estimate of the square root from the last pipeline process and outputs this value. Writing this in pseudo-occam:

```
WHILE data is available
  SEQ
    RECEIVE a number and final square root estimate from
      last pipeline process
    OUTPUT this number and final estimate as results
```

In occam, this becomes

```
PROC Terminate(CHAN OF REAL32 Extract, Output)
  WHILE TRUE
    REAL32 Number, Root :
    SEQ
      -- extract number and root (final estimate) from
      -- pipeline
      Extract ? Number
      Extract ? Root
      -- output results
      Output ! Number
      Output ! Root
  :
```

The main process will comprise a **PAR** construction containing instances of Initialize, Pipeline and Terminate. The Pipeline process is replicated the desired number of times.

```
PAR
  Initialize(InChan, Pipe[0])
```

185

```
PAR Index = 0 FOR Iterations
  In IS Pipe[Index] :
  Out IS Pipe[Index + 1] :
  Pipeline(In, Out)
Terminate(Pipe[Iterations], OutChan)
```

The amount of computation required for the sequential and parallel solutions is the same. The benefit derived by expressing the sequential algorithm as a parallel one accrues *only* when the square roots of many numbers need to be calculated, as may happen in the compilation of a table of square root values, for example. The partial estimates for these numbers may all be within the pipeline at the same time (depending on the length of the pipeline); each pipeline process can be calculating a different partial estimate in parallel. The automatic synchronization of occam ensures the correct order of communication and, hence, the correct order of computation. Thus, the algorithmic approach only benefits when the pipeline (or whatever organization) can be continually filled with data. The example above is rather artificial, but is only used to illustrate the principle of algorithmic decomposition. An example of the algorithmic approach in which each section performs a different operation can be found in image processing (Fig. 12.2). The pipeline now may be composed of four different sections: for example, the first concerned with smoothing a raw image, the next concerned with the extraction of features from the smoothed image, the third concerned with the recognition of objects from feature descriptions, and the last responsible for displaying recognized objects.

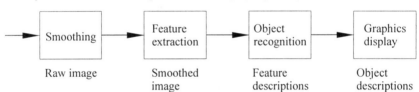

Figure 12.2   Image processing pipeline.

12.2.2 Matrix multiplication
The algorithmic approach is not limited to one-dimensional cases. For example, a *systolic array* is effectively a two-dimensional pipeline that may be used to great effect for the parallel execution of matrix operations (Jones & Goldsmith 1988).

The product AB of the $m \times p$ matrix $A = [a_{ij}]$ and the $p \times n$ matrix $B = [b_{ij}]$ is defined to be the $m \times n$ matrix $C = [c_{ij}]$ where

$$c_{ij} = a_{i1}b_{1j} + i_2b_{2j} + \ldots + a_{ip}b_{pj}$$

$$= a_{ik}b_{kj} \qquad\qquad \text{for } i = 1, 2, \ldots m; j = 1, 2, \ldots n$$

If A is thought of as consisting of m rows and B as consisting of n columns, then, in forming $C = AB$, each row of A is multiplied once and only once by each column of B. The element c_{ij} is then the product of the ith row of A and the jth column of

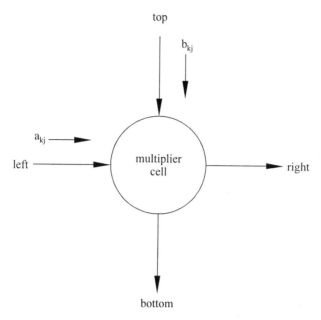

Figure 12.3 Matrix multiplication as a two-dimensional pipeline.

B. The following occam example is based on this principle.

The matrix multiplication example shown here uses two 4 × 4 matrices, the values of which have been "hardwired" into the program as **VAL** constants for convenience. The two-dimensional "pipeline" (or systolic array) is represented by the channels Horizontal and Vertical. Each row of AMatrix is fed in parallel into the left-hand side of the systolic array (using the Horizontal channels), and each column of BMatrix is fed in parallel into the top of the systolic array (using the Vertical channels). The matrix multiplication is performed by a replicated set of the MatrixMult process. This process has four channels for handling the matrix elements (Fig. 12.3). The Left and Top channels input in parallel a row and column of AMatrix and BMatrix elements, respectively. These elements are then passed on in parallel to the adjacent cells below and to the right using the channels Bottom and Right. At the same time, the cell computes its element c_{ij} of the matrix multiplication using the equation

$$c_{ij} = \sum a_{ik} b_{kj}$$

A fifth channel, Result, is assigned for the output of the resulting product element. The occam code is

```
VAL NRows IS 4 :
VAL NCols IS 4 :
```

187

```
VAL Size IS 4 :
VAL [NRows][Size]INT AMatrix IS
      [[1, 1, 1, 1], [1, 1, 1, 1],
       [1, 1, 1, 1], [1, 1, 1, 1]] :
VAL [Size][NCols]INT BMatrix IS
      [[2, 2, 2, 2], [2, 2, 2, 2],
       [2, 2, 2, 2], [2, 2, 2, 2]] :
[NRows + 1][NCols + 1]CHAN OF [Size]INT Horizontal,
                                         Vertical :
[Nrows][NCols]CHAN OF INT Result :

PROC MatrixMult(CHAN OF [Size]INT Left, Right,
                                    Top, Bottom,
               CHAN OF INT Result)
  --
  -- process computes c_ij element of multiplication
     matrix
  --
  INT Product :
  [Size]INT A, B :
  SEQ
    Product := 0
    PAR
      -- input elements from adjacent left and top cells
      Left ? A
      Top ? B
    PAR
      -- output elements to adjacent right and
      -- bottom cells
      Right ! A
      Bottom ! B
      -- calculate element for this cell
      SEQ I = 0 FOR Size
        Product := Product + (A[I] * B[I])

    Result ! Product
  :

PROC Sink(CHAN OF [Size]INT Chan)
  [Size]INT Any :
  SEQ
    Chan ? Any
```

188

```
  :

PROC DistributeRows([]INT A, CHAN OF [Size]INT Right)
  SEQ
      -- feed left-hand side of systolic array
      -- with one row of elements
      Right ! A
  :

PROC DistributeCols([]INT B, CHAN OF [Size]INT Bottom)
  SEQ
      -- feed top of systolic array
      -- with one column of elements
      Bottom ! B
  :

PROC CollectResult([][]CHAN OF INT Result)
  [NRows][NCols]INT C :
  SEQ
    PAR I = 0 FOR NRows
      PAR J = 0 FOR NCols
        Result[I][J]? C[I][J]
    --
    -- process result
    --
  :

-- main process
PAR
  PAR I = 0 FOR NRows
    -- send elements of each row in parallel through
    -- left-hand side of systolic array
    [Size]INT AVector :
    SEQ
      SEQ Col = 0 FOR Size
        AVector[Col] := AMatrix[I][Col]
      DistributeRows(AVector, Horizontal[I][0])

  PAR J = 0 FOR NCols
    -- send elements of each column in parallel through
    -- top of systolic array
    [Size]INT BVector :
```

189

```
SEQ
  SEQ Row = 0 FOR Size
    BVector[Row] := BMatrix[Row][J]
  DistributeCols(BVector, Vertical[0][J])


  -- soak up elements at bottom and right-hand side
  -- of systolic array
  PAR Row = 0 FOR NRows
    Sink(Horizontal[Row][NCols])
  PAR Col = 0 FOR NCols
    Sink(Vertical[NRows][Col])


  -- perform matrix multiplication
  PAR Row = 0 FOR NRows
    PAR Col = 0 FOR NCols
      Matrix Mult(Horizontal[Row][Col],
                  Horizontal[Row][Col + 1],
                  Vertical[Row][Col],
                  Vertical[Row + 1][Col],
                  Result[Row][Col]

CollectResult(Result)
```

Other examples of the use of the algorithmic approach are sorting (Pountain & May 1987), the generation of prime numbers (Burns 1988), compiling and solid modelling (INMOS 1989b).

12.3 Geometric parallelism

With the *geometric* parallelism approach, parallelism is introduced by making use of any regular spatial geometry or structure present in the problem. Rather like a large cube may be divided up into smaller constituent cubes, so the spatial geometry of the problem is divided up in some symmetrical fashion, assuming a uniform distribution of data over the geometry, to allow a more tractable solution to be expressed. A computation is performed for each of these small units, which act as a quasi-independent entities. The computation performed for each small unit is then summed to give an overall effect. Interactions between neighbouring units is usually incorporated to give a more realistic solution. This approach is also known as *data structure decomposition* and *data parallelism*.

The computation for each small unit is modelled by an identical occam parallel process, each process operating on the data relevant to its own domain. Interactions between nearest neighbours may be introduced with occam channels connecting the neighbouring units. The communications overhead between these communicating processes may become quite appreciable.

12.3.1 Heat conduction in a metal plate

An example of the geometric approach is its use in the simulation of thermal conduction in a two-dimensional rectangular metal plate that is being heated by a heat source at a certain point. Simulation of thermal conduction over the whole plate is difficult. So, to simplify the problem, the geometry of the situation is utilized and the plate is subdivided into rectangular areas, these areas being the quasi-independent units that will be represented by occam processes. The heat conduction (i.e. temperature of each of these areas) may be estimated and summed to give an approximate effect for the heat conduction over the whole plate. The temperature of each area will depend on that of its surroundings (i.e. the neighbouring areas). It is assumed that one of the areas contains the heat source.

For the example, consider a metal plate, n by m units (Fig. 12.4). The program is required to monitor the temperature at the centre of each of these areas. Also, for the example, consider that two boundaries (top and left-hand side) of the plate are adjacent to an infinite heat sink and that the other two boundaries (bottom and right-hand side) of the plate are adjacent to a perfect heat insulator.

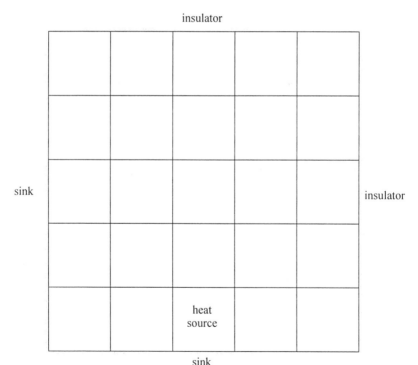

Figure 12.4 Metal plate subdivided into smaller areas.

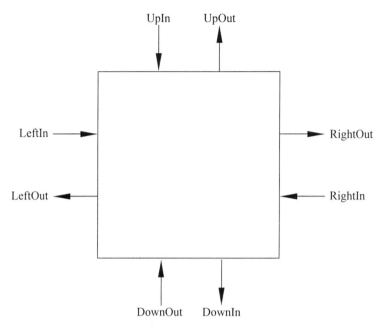

UpIn   UpOut

LeftIn ──────▶   ──────▶ RightOut

LeftOut ◀──────   ◀────── RightIn

DownOut   DownIn

Figure 12.5   Channels of a plate area.

The simulation program will comprise a set of identical parallel processes, each responsible for determining the temperature of one of the areas of the metal plate. This temperature is taken to be an average of the temperatures of the four neighbouring areas. In addition, areas on the boundaries of the plate will be affected by the type of adjacent boundary; the heat sink will maintain a constant (base) temperature and the heat insulator will reflect the temperature of the boundary areas. These boundary effects will be simulated by extra parallel processes.

Each plate area will have nine channels: an input and output channel for each of the neighbouring areas, up, down, left and right plus a result channel (Fig. 12.5). The result channel communicates with a monitor process to display the current temperature of each area on the screen.

There will be $n * m$ processes for calculating the areas' temperatures plus $n + m$ processes for each of the two different boundary effects. This number of processes may be generated by suitable replication of the following processes:

```
Sink - simulate the effect of a heat sink
Insulator - simulate the effect of a heat insulator
Source - simulate the effect of a heat source
CalcTemp - calculate the temperature of an area.
```

Account must be taken of the fact that one of the areas will contain the heat source. The top level of the program will have the following form

```
global declarations
procedures comprising
   Sink
   Insulator
   Source
   CalcTemp
main process
```

Assuming a metal plate of dimension 3 by 3 units, the global declarations are as follows

```
VAL Height IS 3 :
VAL Width IS 3 :
VAL TwiceHeight IS 2 * Height :
VAL TwiceWidth IS 2 * Width :
VAL Rectangle IS Height * Width :
VAL TwiceRectangle IS 2 * Rectangle :
VAL SourceX IS 1 :
VAL SourceY IS 2 :
VAL BaseTemp IS 50.0(REAL32) :
[TwiceRectangle + TwiceHeight] CHAN OF REAL32 Horizontal :
[TwiceRectangle + TwiceWidth] CHAN OF REAL32 Vertical :
[Rectangle] CHAN OF REAL32 Result :
```

The initial temperature, BaseTemp, is assumed to be 50 degrees. The position of the area containing the heat source at its centre is given by SourceX and SourceY. The areas communicate via the channels Horizontal, Vertical and Result. The horizontal channels are numbered in right/left pairs down the columns of the array of areas. The vertical channels are numbered in down/up pairs along the rows of the array. The result channels are numbered along the rows (see Fig. 12.6 for an example of the 3 by 3 array).

The Sink process is simulated by maintaining (outputting) a constant temperature, regardless of the adjacent temperature – the temperature input is disregarded. This constant temperature is taken to be the initial temperature of the plate. Expressing this in pseudo-occam gives:

```
WHILE simulation is required
   PAR
      RECEIVE a temperature of an adjacent area and ignore
      SEND a constant (base) temperature back to the
         adjacent area
```

Written as occam code, this gives

```
PROC Sink(CHAN OF REAL32 In, Out)
  -- left or bottom boundary
  WHILE TRUE
    REAL32 Any :
    PAR
      -- ignore adjacent temperature
      In ? Any
      -- output a steady temperature
      Out ! BaseTemp
:
```

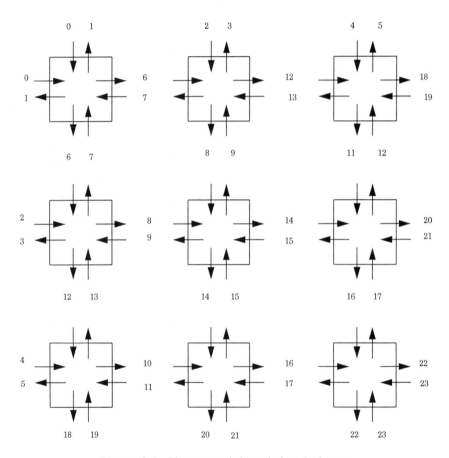

Figure 12.6   The areas and channels for a 3×3 array.

The Insulator process does not allow any heat to escape; the temperature read from the adjacent area is returned. Written in pseudo-occam, this is

```
WHILE simulation is required
  SEQ
    RECEIVE a temperature from an adjacent area
    SEND the temperature received back to the
      adjacent area
```

Rewriting in occam gives:

```
PROC Insulator(CHAN OF REAL32 In, Out)
  -- top or right boundary
  WHILE TRUE
    REAL32 Temp:
    SEQ
      -- input temperature of adjacent area
      In ? Temp
      -- return last temperature read
      Out ! Temp
  :
```

Process Source simulates a heat source by generating a temperature that increases at a steady rate: one degree higher than the previous value. This temperature is transmitted to the surrounding areas, ignoring the present temperature of these areas. The heat source will be surrounded by four neighbouring areas. Expressing these requirements in pseudo-occam gives

```
WHILE heat source is present
  SEQ
    PAR
      RECEIVE a temperature from four surrounding areas
        and ignore
      SEND new temperature back to four surrounding areas
    INCREMENT temperature by one degree
```

In occam, this may be written

```
PROC Source(CHAN OF REAL32 UpIn, DownIn,
                           LeftIn, RightIn,
                           UpOut, DownOut,
                           LeftOut, RightOut,
                           Result)
  VAL TempIncrease IS 1.0(REAL32):
  REAL32 Temp:
  SEQ
    -- initial condition
```

```
Temp := BaseTemp

WHILE TRUE
    -- output new temperature to four surrounding
    -- areas, ignoring any inputs
  SEQ
    PAR
      REAL32 Any :
      PAR
        -- area below
        DownIn ? Any
        DownOut ! Temp
      REAL32 Any:
      PAR
        -- area to left
        LeftIn ? Any
        LeftOut ! Temp
      REAL32 Any:
      PAR
        -- area above
        UpIn ? Any
        UpOut ! Temp
      REAL32 Any:
      PAR
        -- area to right
        RightIn ? Any
        RightOut ! Temp
    Result ! Temp -- output new temperature
                  -- to Monitor
    Temp := Temp + TempIncrease -- increase
                               -- temperature
                               -- of source

  :
```

(The interactions with each adjacent area have been grouped in separate **PAR** constructions for clarity.)

Process `CalcTemp` will calculate the rise in temperature of each area attributable to the temperature of the neighbouring areas. Account must be taken of the fact that one area will contain the heat source. Written in pseudo-occam, this is

```
IF area = heat source THEN
  GENERATE temperature rise
```

```
ELSE
  WHILE simulation is required
    SEQ
      PAR
        RECEIVE the temperature of four surrounding
            areas
        SEND the temperature of this area to four
            surrounding areas
        CALCULATE new temperature of this area, based
            on temperature rises of surrounding areas
```

Expressing this pseudo-occam in occam,

```
PROC CalcTemp(BOOL HotSpot,
              CHAN OF REAL32 UpIn, DownIn,
                             LeftIn, RightIn,
                             UpOut, DownOut,
                             LeftOut, RightOut,
                             Result)
  IF
    -- if area contains heat source
    HotSpot
      -- generate temperature rise
      Source(UpIn, DownIn, LeftIn, RightIn,UpOut,
             DownOut, LeftOut, RightOut, Result)
    TRUE
      -- area does not contain heat source
      REAL32 Temp :
      SEQ
        -- initial conditions
        Temp := BaseTemp
        WHILE TRUE
          REAL32 SumOfTemps, MeanTemp,
                 UpTemp, DownTemp, LeftTemp,
                 RightTemp,DeltaUp, DeltaDown,
                 DeltaLeft,DeltaRight :
          SEQ
            -- interact with neighbouring areas
            PAR
            -- area below
            PAR
              DownIn ? DownTemp
```

```
                    DownOut ! Temp
                    -- area to the left
                    PAR
                      LeftIn ? LeftTemp
                      LeftOut ! Temp
                    -- area above
                    PAR
                      UpIn ? UpTemp
                      UpOut ! Temp
                    -- area to the right
                    PAR
                      RightIn ? RightTemp
                      RightOut ! Temp
                  DeltaDown := DownTemp - Temp
                  DeltaLeft := LeftTemp - Temp
                  DeltaUp := UpTemp - Temp
                  DeltaRight := RightTemp - Temp
                  -- now average these temperatures
                  -- to find mean rise
                  SumOfTemps := ((DeltaUp + DeltaDown)
                                   + DeltaLeft) + DeltaRight
                  MeanTemp := SumOfTemps / 4.0(REAL32)
                  -- increase temperature by half average
                  -- temperature rise
                  Temp := Temp + (MeanTemp / 2.0(REAL32))
                  -- output the result to Monitor
                  Result ! Temp
     :
```

Process `Monitor` will be responsible for keeping a record of the temperature of each area, and displaying this temperature on the screen. Expressing this in pseudo-occam gives

```
WHILE heat source is available
  SEQ
    PAR
      INPUT temperature from each area
      SEQ
        IF temperature <> last temperature from each area
          THEN DISPLAY temperature
```

Writing this in occam gives

```
PROC Monitor([]CHAN OF REAL32 Result)

  [Rectangle]REAL32 LastTemp :
  SEQ
    -- initialize array holding temperatures
    SEQ Index = 0 FOR Rectangle
      LastTemp[Index] := 0.0(REAL32)
    [Rectangle]REAL32 Temp :
    WHILE TRUE
      SEQ
        -- input temperature of areas
        PAR Index = 0 FOR Rectangle
          Result[Index] ? Temp[Index]
        SEQ Index = 0 FOR Rectangle
          -- check for a temperature change
          IF
            Temp[Index] <> LastTemp[Index]
              INT Row, Col :
              SEQ
                -- display new temperature
                Row := Index / Width
                Col := Index REM Width
                Display ! Row; Col; Temp[Index]
                LastTemp[Index] := Temp[Index]
            TRUE
              SKIP
  :
```

The overall structure of the main process will be an outer **PAR** enclosing the requisite number of instances of CalcTemp, Sink and Insulator processes. In addition, there will be an instance of the Monitor process. Thus, the main process may be expressed in pseudo-occam as

```
PAR
  Monitor process
  n * m CalcTemp processes
  n + m Sink processes
  n + m Insulator processes
```

This process may be rewritten in terms of nested replicated **PAR**s (assuming n rows by m columns of rectangular areas – the index Row moving from top to bottom, the index Column moving from left to right) as follows

```
PAR
  Monitor process
  PAR Row = 0 FOR n -- left-hand side areas
    Sink process
  PAR Column = 0 FOR m
    PAR
      -- top side areas
      Insulator process
      -- middle areas
      PAR Row = 0 FOR n
        CalcTemp process
      -- bottom side areas
      Sink process
  PAR Row = 0 FOR n -- right-hand side areas
    Insulator process
```

Using the (more meaningful) constants Height (for *n*) and Width (for *m*) as specified in the global declarations, this may be rewritten as

```
PAR
  Monitor(Result)
  PAR Row = 0 FOR Height-- left-hand side areas
    VAL Out IS Row + Row :
    VAL In IS Out + 1 :
    Sink(Horizontal[In], Horizontal[Out])
  PAR Col = 0 FOR Width
    PAR
      -- top side areas
      VAL Out IS Col + Col :
      VAL In IS Out + 1 :
      Insulator(Vertical[In], Vertical[Out])
      -- middle areas
      PAR Row = 0 FOR Height
        VAL Up IS ((TwiceWidth * Row) + Col) + Col :
        VAL Down IS ((TwiceWidth * (Row + 1)) + Col) +
                    Col :
        VAL Left IS ((TwiceHeight * Col) + Row) + Row :
        VAL Right IS ((TwiceHeight * (Col + 1)) + Row) +
                     Row :
        VAL Hot IS (Row = SourceY) AND (Col = SourceX) :
        SEQ
          CalcTemp(Hot,
                   Vertical[Up],
                   Vertical[Down +1],
```

200

```
                    Horizontal[Left],
                    Horizontal[Right + 1],
                    Vertical[Up + 1],
                    Vertical[Down],
                    Horizontal[Left + 1],
                    Horizontal[Right],
                    Result[(Width * Row) + Col])
         -- bottom side areas
         VAL In IS (TwiceRectangle + Col) + Col :
         VAL Out IS In + 1 :
         Sink(Vertical[In], Vertical[Out])
   PAR Row = 0 FOR Height    -- right-hand side areas
      VAL In IS (TwiceRectangle + Row) + Row :
      VAL Out IS In + 1 :
      Insulator(Horizontal[In], Horizontal[Out])
```

12.3.2 Cellular automata

Cellular automata (CAs) are *n*-dimensional lattices of cells, with each cell being in one of a finite number of *states*. These states change at discrete time steps, according to a set of predefined *rules*. Usually these rules take into account the current state of a cell, together with the states of its immediately adjacent cells. The states of all cells are updated simultaneously (i.e. in parallel), at each time step.

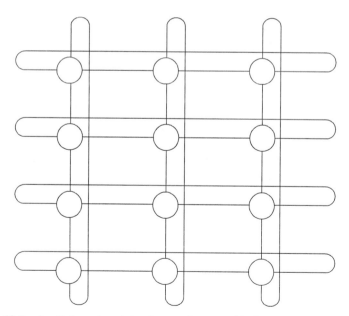

Figure 12.7 A cellular automata implemented as a toroid of occam processes; channel in the horizontal and vertical directions are wrapped around at the edges.

Cellular automata were originally developed in the 1950s by Ulam (1962) and von Neumann (1966). They received a resurgence of interest after Wolfram republicized them (1983). CAs have been used in a wide range of applications, such as fluid flow simulation, particle diffusion, crystal growth and immune system modelling. Probably the most popular implementation of CAs is Conway's *Game of life* (Gardner 1971), which is a simple expression of the basic processes of living systems. It comprises a rectangular grid of cells with vertical, horizontal and diagonal connections to neighbouring cells, giving a neighbourhood of six cells. Any cell may be in one of two states: alive or dead. The rules that govern the state of each cell at each time step simulate population change:
   • a living cell with zero or only one living neighbour dies from isolation
   • a living cell with four or more living neighbours dies from overcrowding
   • a dead cell with exactly three living neighbours becomes alive
   • all other cells remain unchanged.
A random, initial configuration of cells eventually reduces to constant and cycling patterns of groups of cells.

As an example of the implementation of a CA using occam, consider a two-dimensional, 50 by 50, lattice of cells, with cyclic wrap-around at the boundaries. This grid of cells may be generated in occam using nested replicated **PAR**s, as follows:

```
PAR X = 0 TO 49 REM 49
  PAR Y = 0 TO 49 REM 49
    CA()
```

where CA() is an occam procedure representing a single CA site. The replication code generates a grid of 50 by 50 of these processes, each executing in parallel with the others.

State updating must be performed in parallel by each process, typically using the information from the previous state of the process and those of neighbouring processes. Thus, each process needs to interact (i.e. exchange information) with neighbouring processes on the grid to allow state updating. The code for the CA process may be simply written in occam. For example, consider nearest-neighbour interactions in four directions: *up*, *down*, *right* and *left* (Fig. 12.8).

Each direction has two channels: one for receiving state information from neighbours, and one for sending state information to neighbours. For simplicity, it is assumed the state information comprises an integer value. The occam code for CA is then

```
PROC CA(CHAN OF INT FromUp, FromDown,
                    FromRight, FromLeft,
                    ToUp, ToDown,
                    ToRight, ToLeft)
  SEQ
```

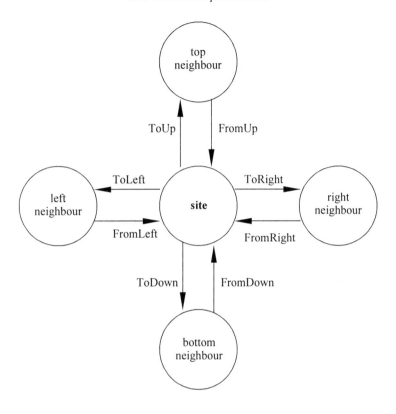

Figure 12.8   Channels for cellular automata site.

```
.     --
.     -- initialization code
.     --
WHILE TRUE
  SEQ
    --
    -- exchange state information with four
    -- nearest neighbours
    --
    PAR
      PAR
        FromUp ? UpState
        ToUp ! MyState

      PAR
        FromDown ? DownState
```

```
        ToDown ! MyState

    PAR
        FromRight ? RightState
        ToRight ! MyState

    PAR
        FromLeft ? LeftState
        ToLeft ! MyState
.           --
.           -- update MyState value according
.           -- to rules using own state and
.           -- neighbours' state information
.           --
:
```

The main cycle of CA is enclosed in the **WHILE TRUE** loop. Each pass through this loop represents a time step of the CA; nearest neighbour interactions precede the calculation of the new state value according to the given CA rules. These rules are usually expressed in terms of the state of a cell and those of its nearest neighbours.

12.3.2 Wave equation
The simulation of the wave equation in two dimensions on a square region is another good example of geometric decomposition (Wadsworth et al. 1990). The general wave equation (i.e. for N dimensions) is given by the following differential equation:

$$c^2 \Delta^2 \Phi = \frac{\partial^2 \Phi}{\partial t^2}$$

or, for two dimensions, x and y,

$$\frac{\partial^2 \Phi}{\partial x^2} + \frac{\partial^2 \Phi}{\partial xy^2} = \frac{1}{c^2} \frac{\partial^2 \Phi}{\partial xt^2}$$

where Φ is the deviation of a medium from the equilibrium position (for example, height or pressure), x and y are the spatial coordinates, t is the time, and c the speed of the wave in the medium. There are various boundary conditions that may be applied; the simplest being Φ fixed on a square boundary of length L, i.e.

$$\Phi(x, 0) = \Phi(x, L) = 0, \text{ where } 0 \le x \le L$$

$\Phi(0, y) = \Phi(L, y) = 0$, where $0 \le y \le L$

The partial derivatives may be approximated by a method known as *finite differences*. This effectively transforms the problem from a continuous value one (as per the differential equation approach) to a discrete value one, mapped to a uniform grid of points. To differentiate between the continuous and discrete domains, the notation $\Phi(x,y)$ in the continuous domain is replaced by $F(i,j)$ in the discrete one, where i and j are integers representing crossing points on the grid. The finite difference method gives a formula relating the value of F at the point (i,j) to F evaluated at the four nearest-neighbour grid points (Fig. 12.9).

After some approximation, the discrete version of the wave equation may be written as

$$F(t+1) = 2F(t) - F(t-1) + \tfrac{1}{4}(F(i+1,j) + F(i-1,j) + F(i,j+1) + F(i,j-1) - 4F(i,j))$$

relating the value of F at time $t+1$ to the values of F at times t and $t-1$, and to the values of F evaluated at the grid point (i,j) and the four nearest neighbours.

After some rearrangement, the above equation may be expressed in a form suit-

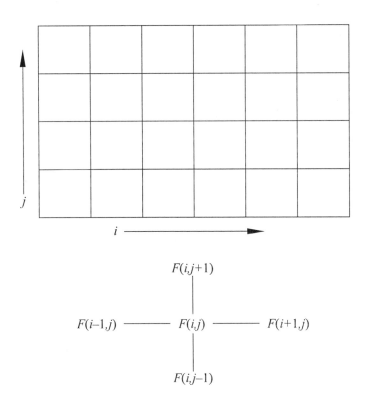

Figure 12.9 Grid used for discretization of wave equation.

205

able for computation. If A is an array that holds the values of $F(t-1)$ over the grid and B is an array that holds the value of $F(t)$, then the values of $F(t+1)$ (the new values for A) are given by

```
A[i,j] := B[i,j] - A[i,j] +
    0.25(REAL32)*(B[i+1,j] + B[i-1,j] + B[i,j+1] +
    B[i,j-1])
```

The program actually optimized the occam by making use of **RETYPES** to linearize the arrays, and aliasing array constants in loops via abbreviations.

The configuration used for the implementation was a pipeline of 16 transputers, with a graphics processor attached to one end. The choice for the configuration of the transputer pipeline links for efficient communication of the results for display by a transputer-driven graphics display proved to be an interesting problem, demonstrating the trade-off between resources and network topology. For example, some possible options are:

• The simplest choice was a doubly linked chain of transputers in the pipeline: one chain of links was used to exchange nearest neighbour information between transputers, whereas the other set of links was used for the return of result data from each transputer to the graphics processor. This meant a large communication overhead. Results from transputers at the far end of the pipeline had to pass through intermediate transputers to reach the graphics processor.

• Another choice was to link every fourth transputer in the pipeline directly to the graphics processor. This configuration quartered the communication overhead of the previous scheme. A variant of this scheme would be to link the middle transputer of each group of four directly to the graphics processor. This further cuts down the total number of intermediate links en route to the graphics processor.

• A further choice was to use *logarithmic funnelling*: result data from pairs of transputers are funnelled into a special "transfer" transputer; the data from pairs of these transfer transputers are then funnelled into yet another transfer transputer; and finally the data from this last layer of transfer transputers is funnelled into the graphics processor. This option produces the best throughput; each "compute" transputer can communicate its results immediately to the graphics subsystem. However, the option is wasteful of transputers, using some solely for the transfer function.

• A fourth choice would be to use a dynamic configuration. Each transputer in a group of four adjacent transputers may be dynamically linked to the graphics processor, with this dynamic linkage rotating with the passage of time. Such a scheme allows four transputers to deliver their results simultaneously to the graphics processor and has a low latency: all result data travel only one link.

This last example is a very good illustration that the design and implementation of the processor network is sometimes just as challenging and interesting as writing the parallel program.

Other examples of the use of the geometric approach are the modelling of statistical mechanical "spin" systems, as may be found in liquid crystal films (Askew 1986) and magnetic materials (INMOS 1989b). INMOS quote a particularly interesting and telling result. Their program, which was a lattice divided into sixteen 4×64 strips, was run on a network of 17 transputers. The efficiency was measured to be an increase of 80 per cent for the 17 transputer simulation over that of a single transputer. It was estimated that the simulation, which took 60 hours, would have taken about 3 months on a VAX 11/780!

12.4 Process farming

The *process farm* approach is applicable to problems whose data will succumb to a decomposition into many smaller parts and where the solution of each part is independent of the others. As the data parts are independent, each may be operated on concurrently, in isolation, and the effect summed to give a solution to the whole problem. The approach is analogous to a farmer supervising the toil of many farm workers, each worker performing any given task in isolation from the other workers – hence the name.

A farm is modelled by a set of occam processes. One process is nominated the farmer. The farmer process controls the organization and allocation of work. This controlling process farms or hands out work to its subordinate worker processes (Fig. 12.10). The worker processes are modelled as identical parallel occam processes. As and when each worker process completes the given task, the farmer process will issue further work for completion. Thus, a farm of worker processes toil away on parts of the problem, finishing one task and starting another, until the whole problem is complete. Typically, little interprocess communication is needed in such applications. However, depending on the number of worker processes and their configuration (e.g. whether they are organized in a linear or tree fashion), the routing of messages between the farmer and workers may well cause communications overhead problems.

When the farm is implemented on a network of processors, the term *processor farm* may be used.

12.4.1 Mandelbrot set
An example of the process farm approach is its use in producing a graphical representation of the Mandelbrot set, or more exactly, a graphical representation of those points that lie within and without the Mandelbrot set (Mandelbrot 1983, Peitgen & Richter 1987). This set comprises all complex numbers, $c = a + ib$, for which the recurrence relation

$$z_{n+1} = z_n^2 + c \quad \text{for n} = 1, 2, 3, \ldots \tag{12.1}$$

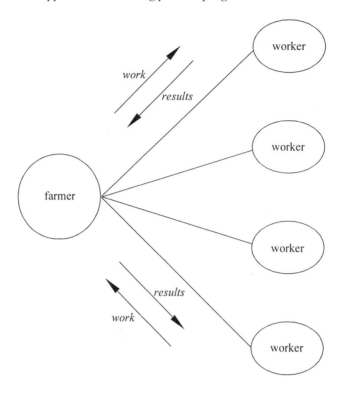

Figure 12.10   Process farm principle.

converges to a finite complex number (where z_n and z_{n+1} are complex numbers computed in successive iterations of the recurrence relation, and $z_0 = 0$ is the initial condition). It can be demonstrated that, if for some n,

$$|z_n| > 2$$

then the iteration diverges and hence c does not belong to the Mandelbrot set.

In practice, the iteration is performed a given number of times, m, and c is considered to belong to the Mandelbrot set, M, if

$$|z_n| < 2. \quad \text{for all } n \le m \tag{12.2}$$

The graphical display of the members of M produces quite vivid and intriguing self-similar shapes known as *fractals*.

For display purposes, the complex number, $c = a + ib$, is taken to be a graphics screen pixel with coordinates (a,b), the graphics screen representing the complex plane. For every screen pixel the recurrence relation is applied. If the pixel belongs to the Mandelbrot set, it is coloured black, otherwise it is allocated a colour from the graphics palette, which is graded according to the speed at which the iteration diverges, that is, the smallest natural number $n < m$ for which

$$|z_n| \geq 2.$$

Such computation is quite intensive for a suitable number of iterations and, depending on the size of the graphics screen and hence the number of pixels, needs to be performed many times. The actual computational task to be performed for each pixel is the same, but the amount of computation will vary depending on whether or not the sequence of recurrence values for that pixel converges or diverges.

The general form of a farm in terms of pseudo-occam is as follows:

```
global declarations
PAR
   Farmer process
   PAR Index = 0 FOR NumberOfWorkers
   Worker process
```

Each worker process requests and accepts data from the farmer process, works with this data and then sends the result back to the farmer process, becoming available to accept more data. In the current context this work will be the calculation of the recurrence relation for the given data, that is, pixel coordinates (a,b). The result of the calculation will give the colour for the pixel at the given position in the Mandelbrot set.

Assuming a graphics area of 512 by 512 pixels, with 5 workers, the global declarations section may be written as:

```
VAL NumberOfWorkers IS 5 :
VAL XPixels IS 512 :
VAL YPixels IS 512 :
VAL XStart IS -1.0(REAL32) :
VAL XEnd IS 1.0(REAL32) :
VAL YStart IS -1.0(REAL32) :
VAL YEnd IS 1.0(REAL32) :

PROTOCOL PACKET
  CASE
     Request
     RawData; [2]INT; [2]REAL32
     Results; [2]INT; INT; INT
     Terminate; INT
  :
[NumberOfWorkers + 1] CHAN OF PACKET ToWorker,
                            FromWorker, ForWorker :
CHAN OF PACKET FromFarmer :
```

The tagged protocol, PACKET, is defined for the data that is sent to and received from the worker processes. The tag RawData corresponds to the transfer of two integers (pixel position on the screen) and two reals, corresponding to the position in a drawing square (from −1.0 to 1.0) for the Mandelbrot set. The tag Results corresponds to the transfer of three integers (the pixel position and its colour). In addition, there is a tag to request work from the farmer and a tag that is used to pass a termination notice to the participating processes at the end of the calculation. The channels, ToWorker and FromWorker, allow the farmer process to send data to the worker processes and receive results from the worker processes.

The main process will comprise a **PAR** construction containing instances of the Farmer process and several replicated Worker processes:

```
PAR
    Farmer(ToWorker[0], FromWorker[0]
           ForWorker[0], FromFarmer)
    PAR Index = 0 FOR NumberOfWorkers
        Worker(ToWorker[Index], ToWorker[Index + 1],
               FromWorker[Index+1], FromWorker[Index],
               ForWorker[Index], ForWorker[Index + 1])
```

In practice, to improve the efficiency trade-off between computation and communications, each worker would be given a line of pixels as data. The processor overhead setting up a transmission over a transputer link is the same for many bytes as for a few bytes. (Once a data transfer has been initiated, the transfer of data over the link is autonomous of the processor.) For simplicity, this example considers the data to be a single pixel. Also, in practice, it may be advantageous to have a division of labour in the farmer process, having a farmer process proper and a separate graphics process. The function of the farmer process would be to hand out pixel coordinates to the worker processes, whereas that of the graphics process would be to accept the results (pixel coordinates and colour) and display them on the graphics screen.

Rather than allowing a worker process to idle while the farmer issues new work, the worker process may buffer an extra unit of work so that it may proceed immediately with this new work once it has completed the previous work. This scheme keeps the workers constantly busy.

Logically, each worker process may be connected via a channel to the farmer. Practically, since the transputer has only four links and if the workers are distributed over several transputers, there may be many tiers of worker processes. Because of this, each worker process will not just be concerned with the iteration of the recurrence relation. It will also act as a message switch, passing on data to processes further down the farm. The whole farm process becomes self-regulating, message-passing being synchronized by the occam input/output primitives. In addition to forwarding work to outlying workers, the worker process will gather results from these workers for onward delivery to the farmer (or graphics) process.

A simplistic farmer process, which assumes that the farm is arranged as a chain of worker processes, is presented below. The farmer awaits requests for work from the worker processes. The farmer then sends a pixel (the unit of work) to the first worker in the chain for redistribution. As each pixel is processed, the worker sends the result (the colour of the pixel in the Mandelbrot set) back to the farmer. Eventually, the colour of the pixels at all screen positions will be determined. At this point, a termination notice is issued to the farm of worker processes and the farmer waits to receive this back before finally terminating itself. In pseudo-occam this is

```
SEQ
  PAR
    loop :
      RECEIVE request for work from worker
      SEND work to worker
    UNTIL pixels exhausted
    RECEIVE completed work from worker
  SEND termination notice
  RECEIVE termination notice back
```

Writing this in occam gives

```
PROC Farmer(CHAN OF PACKET ToWorker, FromWorker,
                       ForWorker)
  BOOL Running :
  INT Result :
  [2]REAL32 Data :
  REAL32 DeltaX, DeltaY :
  REAL32 XInc, YInc :
  SEQ
    DeltaX := (XEnd - XStart) / (REAL32 ROUND XPixels)
    DeltaY := (YEnd - YStart) / (REAL32 ROUND YPixels)
    Running := TRUE
    PAR
      -- distribute work to workers
      [2]INT Coords:
      SEQ
        -- send work to workers on request
        SEQ NY = 0 FOR YPixels
          SEQ
            YInc := (REAL32 ROUND NY) * DeltaY
            Coords[1] := NY
            SEQ NX = 0 FOR XPixels
              SEQ
                XInc := (REAL32 ROUND NX) * DeltaX
```

```
                   Coords[0]  := NX
                   Data[0]  := XStart + XInc
                   Data[1]  := YStart + YInc
                   ForWorker ? CASE
                     Request
                         ToWorker ! RawData; Coords: Data
            -- send termination notice
          ForWorker ? CASE
            Request
              ToWorker ! Terminate; NoWorkers - 1
     -- collect results from workers
     [2] INT Coords:
     SEQ
        WHILE Running
           SEQ
              FromWorker ? CASE
                 Results; ResultCoords; Result
                 --
                 -- process results
                 --
                 Terminate; Any
                    Running := FALSE
     :
```

Each worker process comprises three processes: ReceiveWork, SendResult and Calculate (Fig. 12.11). The first two are "communication" processes, concerned with requesting and receiving work from the farmer, and sending results back to the farmer. The third process is a "computation" process, concerned with the actual Mandelbrot set calculation. This division of labour is an example of how communication and computation should be separated out into different processes. The communication processes are given high priority, allowing the computation process to "soak up" the remaining processor time. This arrangement may be expressed in pseudo-occam as

```
   PROC Worker
     PRI PAR
       PAR
         ReceiveWork process
         SendResult process
       Calculate process
     :
```

This arrangement of processes in the PRI PAR construction ensures a high throughput for communications. This is important for processes that may use the

212

transputer links, so that messages are transmitted without delay. If a high priority process was not used, the message would not be examined until the message switch was scheduled by the low priority round-robin scheduler of the transputer. The `Worker` process may now be rewritten with the addition of channels:

```
PROC Worker(CHAN OF PACKET FromFarmer,ToOthers,
                           FromOthers,ToFarmer,
                           ForOwn, ForOthers)
    CHAN OF PACKET ToCalculate, FromCalculate,
                   ForCalculate :
    PRI PAR
      PAR
        ReceiveWork(FromFarmer, ForOwn,
                   ToOthers, ForOthers,
                   ToCalculate, ForCalculate)
        SendResult(FromCalculate, FromOthers, ToFarmer)
      Calculate(ToCalculate, ForCalculate, FromCalculate)
```

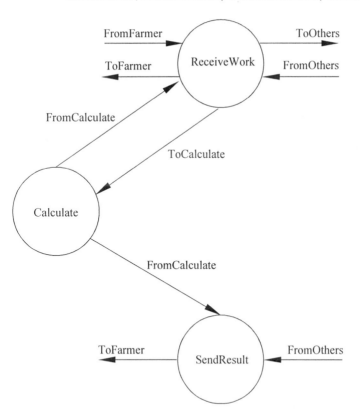

Figure 12.11　The component processes of a worker process.

213

:

The `ReceiveWork` process is responsible for forwarding requests for work from the `Calculate` process to the `Farmer` process and accepting pixels (work) from the `Farmer` process. As the farm is arranged in a chain, each `ReceiveWork` process may also forward requests from and accept work for `Worker` processes further down the chain. Expressing this in pseudo-occam gives

```
WHILE pixels are available
  SEQ
    ALT
      RECEIVE request from Calculate for work
      RECEIVE request from another Worker for work
    SEND request to Farmer
    RECEIVE work from Farmer
    SEND work to Calculate OR next Worker
```

Such a structure with more than one input to react to may be conveniently programmed using an **ALT** construction. The actual code will be slightly more complicated than the above pseudo-code because of the need to watch out for and pass on the termination notice to the `Calculate` process and the next worker. This is just a matter of reacting to the relevant tag of the channel protocol. The occam for the process is

```
PROC ReceiveWork (CHAN OF PACKET  FromFarmer, ToFarmer,
                                  ToOthers, FromOthers,
                                  ToCalculate,
                                  FromCalculate)
  BOOL Running, Terminated, OwnBusy, OthersBusy:
  INT Tag:
  [2] INT Coords:
  [2] REAL32 Data:
  SEQ
    OwnBusy := TRUE
    OthersBusy := TRUE
    Terminated := FALSE
    Running := TRUE
    WHILE Running OR OwnBusy OR OthersBusy
      SEQ
        ALT
          -- a request for more work from Calculate
          FromCalculate ? CASE
            Request
              OwnBusy := FALSE
```

```
                 -- a request for more work from other workers
                 FromOthers ? CASE
                   Request
                     OthersBusy := FALSE
            IF
               NOT Terminated
                 SEQ
                     -- send request for work to farmer
                     ToFarmer ! Request
                     -- receive response from farmer
                     FromFarmer ? CASE
                       RawData; Coords; Data
                         IF
                            -- send to Calculate
                           NOT OwnBusy
                             SEQ
                                ToCalculate ! RawData; Coords;
                                                        Data
                                OwnBusy := TRUE
                            -- send to next Worker
                           NOT OthersBusy
                             SEQ
                                ToOthers ! RawData; Coords;
                                                        Data
                                OthersBusy := TRUE
                       Terminate; Tag -- termination notice
                         SEQ
                            Running := FALSE
                            Terminated := TRUE
                            IF
                               -- last worker in chain
                               Tag = 0
                                 OthersBusy := FALSE
                               TRUE
                                 SKIP
               TRUE
                 SKIP
-- termination notice received
-- pass it on if not last worker
IF
   Tag > 0
     ToOthers ! Terminate; Tag - 1
   TRUE
     SKIP
```

```
-- terminate Calculate
ToCalculate ! Terminate; Tag
:
```

In the above process, the Boolean variable `Running` records whether or not a termination notice has been received from the farmer, whereas the Boolean variable `OwnBusy` marks whether or not the `Calculate` process has requested more work. The Boolean variable `OthersBusy` says whether or not a worker further down the chain has requested work.

The termination notice will pass down the chain of worker processes via the `ReceiveWork` processes, causing each `ReceiveWork` process to terminate on receipt. Before terminating, each process will inform its `Calculate` process to terminate, which in turn will inform the `SendResult` process of a local termination. When the termination notice reaches the end of the chain of worker processes (signified by the value 0 of the integer sent with the termination notice), it is returned to the farmer process via the `SendResult` processes, causing each `SendResult` process to terminate (provided the local termination has also been received).

The `Calculate` process performs the iteration procedure for a given pixel and assigns that pixel a colour dependent on the degree of convergence. The actual computation of the recurrence relation is performed by the procedure `Mandelbrot`, which is called by `Calculate`:

```
PROC Calculate(CHAN OF PACKET FromReceiveWork,
                ToReceiveWork, ToSendResult)
  BOOL Running :
  INT Result, Any :
  [2]INT Coords :
  REAL32 X, Y :
  [2]REAL32 Data :
  SEQ
    Running := TRUE
    WHILE Running
      SEQ
        -- request work from farmer
        ToReceiveWork ! Request
        -- await reply
        FromReceiveWork ? CASE
          -- data
          RawData; Coords; Data
            SEQ
              X = Data[0]
              Y = Data[1]
              Mandelbrot(Result, X, Y)
```

```
              -- send result back to farmer
              ToSendResult ! Results; Coords; Result
      -- terminate notice
      Terminate; Any
          Running := FALSE
  -- send terminate notice to SendResult
  ToSendResult ! Terminate; Any

:
```

Again the actual code will be complicated by the termination condition. This time the termination notice is passed on to the SendResult process.

With a little rearrangement, the recurrence relation may be simplified for computation within the Mandelbrot process. Substituting $z = x + iy$, then Equation 12.1 may be written as

$$x_{n+1} = x_n^2 - y_n^2 + a$$

and

$$y_{n+1} = 2x_n.y_n + b$$

Since

$$|z_{n+1}| = \sqrt{(x_{n+1}^2 - y_{n+1}^2)}$$

the condition for Mandelbrot set occupancy (Equation 12.2) may be written as

$$x_{n+1}^2 + y_{n+1}^2 \le 4$$

Pixels are passed from the Calculate process each time the Mandelbrot process completes the previous calculation and requires more work. Completed work, in terms of the pixel colour, is passed on to the SendResult process. In pseudo-occam, the Mandelbrot process is

```
SEQ
    loop:
        COMPUTE next iteration of recurrence relation
        IF iteration count = maximum THEN
            ASSIGN black to colour
            EXIT
        IF modulus squared > constant THEN
            ASSIGN count to colour
            EXIT
    RETURN pixel and colour to Calculate
```

Expressed in occam (assuming a graphics palette of 256 colours, with the colour black having a value of 0, and a maximum number of iterations of 255), this gives

```
PROC Mandelbrot(INT Colour, VAL REAL32 X, Y)
  VAL Threshold IS 4.0(REAL32) :
  VAL Two IS 2.0(REAL32) :
  VAL MaxIterations IS 255 :
  VAL Black IS 0 :
  INT Iteration :
  REAL32 ZReal, ZImag, ZSquared :
  SEQ
    ZReal := 0.0(REAL32)
    ZImag := 0.0(REAL32)
    Iteration := 0
    ZSquared := 0.0(REAL32)
    -- calculate next iteration of recurrence
    -- relation and test for divergence
    WHILE (Iteration < MaxIterations) AND
          (ZSquared <= Threshold)
      SEQ
        ZReal := ((ZReal * ZReal) - (ZImag * ZImag)) + X
        ZImag := (Two * (ZReal * ZImag)) + Y
        ZSquared := (ZReal * ZReal) + (ZImag * ZImag)
        Iteration := Iteration + 1
    IF
      Iteration = MaxIterations -- pixel in
                                      -- Mandelbrot set
        Colour := Black
      ZSquared > Constant -- pixel outside
                                -- Mandelbrot set
        Colour := Iteration
  :
```

The SendResult process multiplexes the results from its Calculate process and those received from other workers on the farm, and feeds them back to the Farmer process. Putting this in pseudo-occam

```
WHILE pixels are available
  ALT
    RECEIVE pixel and colour from Calculate
      SEND pixel and colour back to farmer
    RECEIVE pixel and colour from other workers
      SEND pixel and colour back to farmer
```

The code may be succinctly expressed in occam using an **ALT** construction. This time the treatment of the terminating condition needs more effort. The termination notice is only passed on when one has been received from *both* the local Calculate process and the next worker (Jones & Goldsmith 1988).

```
PROC SendResult(CHAN OF PACKET FromCalculate, FromOthers,
                                ToFarmer)
  BOOL MoreFromCalculate, MoreFromOthers :
  INT Result, Tag :
  [2]INT Coords :
  [2]REAL32 Data :
  SEQ
    MoreFromCalculate := TRUE
    MoreFromOthers := TRUE
    WHILE MoreFromCalculate OR MoreFromOthers
      ALT
        MoreFromCalculate & FromCalculate ? CASE
          -- result from Calculate
          Results; Coords; Result
            -- pass on to Farmer
            ToFarmer ! Results; Coords; Result
          -- termination notice from Calculate
          Terminate; Tag
            SEQ
              MoreFromCalculate := FALSE
              IF
                Tag = 0
                  MoreFromOthers := FALSE
                TRUE
                  SKIP
        MoreFromOthers & FromOthers ? CASE
          -- result from another worker
          Results; Coords; Result
            -- pass on to Farmer
            ToFarmer ! Results; Coords; Colour
          -- termination notice from another worker
          Terminate; Tag
            MoreFromOthers := FALSE
    ToFarmer ! Terminate; Tag
  :
```

In the above process, Boolean variables, MoreFromCalculate and More-FromOthers, record whether or not a termination notice has been received from the local worker or another worker respectively. Only when a termination notice has been received from both these processes does the SendResult process terminate.

The implementation of the process farm is sometimes called a *farm harness*.

There are many ways in which such a harness may be implemented:
- the farmer sends out a work packet on receipt of a result (after the farm has initially been primed)
- the farmer sends out a targeted work packet on receipt of a result (after the farm has initially been primed)
- each worker explicitly requests work from the farmer
- each worker explicitly requests work from its neighbour nearest to the farmer so that work gets pulled through the system.

A local buffer of work packets, maintained by each worker, is also a good idea. How large this should be, and what the buffering strategy should be, are both interesting questions!

12.4.2 Ray tracing

Another example of process farming is its application to ray tracing to generate realistic images of scenes (INMOS 1989b, Wadsworth et al. 1990). Such an application requires considerable amounts of processing power. It has been shown that the processing speed is directly proportional to the number of transputers used for this method of image generation.

Ray tracing is a means of producing very high quality, life-like computer graphics. It can deal with objects that are matt, reflective and refractive. Essentially, a ray is traced back from a point on the screen to any object in the field of view. The colour of the object is plotted at this point on the screen, If the object is reflective or refractive, the new path of the ray is calculated, and the process repeated. The whole procedure is repeated for every point on the screen. Ray tracing is extremely ˙ computation intensive. As an example of this, the time required to produce enough frames for a 60 second animated sequence was 12 hours on a network of 16 T800s, and the estimated time for producing the same sequence on a PC is 300 days!

Again, as in the Mandelbrot set example, this application involves a calculation for each pixel of the screen. The distribution of work (i.e. the unit of computation for each worker) may be organized in several ways, some more efficient in terms of communication overhead between the farmer and the worker processes than others. For example, the following are possible units of computation:
- Single pixels could be farmed out. Such a choice would generate a great deal of communication overhead.
- A group of adjacent pixels could be packeted together, and the work packet farmed out. The smallest size of grouping is such that the number of packets equals the number of workers. With this choice, however, the communication overhead is minimized but the computation load balance of the workers is not necessarily optimal. Packets, where there is more detail in the scene or where rays have to be traced to a greater depth, will require more computation than others.

The best choice for computation/communication load balancing is to choose the size of the grouping so that there are many more packets than worker processes. Experience has shown that, typically, the number of packets should be greater than

50 times the number of workers, but less than 500 times (Wadsworth et al. 1990). For a particular implementation, using 16 transputers (with one worker process per transputer) and a pixel grid of 768 by 512, the number of packets was set at 1536 (which is approximately 96 times the number of transputers). Each packet contained 256 pixels, managed as a 16 by 16 pixel square (or *patch*).

The farm is implemented as a pipeline of transputers. In common with the Mandelbrot set example, each worker process comprises a **PRI PAR** construct encompassing a communications part – reception of work packets and sending of results – and a computation part – the ray trace calculation.

```
Worker process

. . . declarations
PRI PAR
  PAR
      . . . receive work packets
      . . . send results
  . . . ray trace calculation
```

The farmer process is responsible for generating the patches and collecting the results.

This application is very scalable, with almost 100 per cent efficiency – 16 transputers performing the calculation nearly 16 times faster than one transputer.

Chapter 13

Coding for performance maximization

13.1 Efficiency factors   13.2 Coding issues for performance maximization

13.1 Efficiency factors

Even after designing a parallel algorithm, there are several competing factors to be taken into consideration for an efficient implementation.

- *Processor connectivity*   The transputer has only *four* physical links. Depending on the distribution of processes on processors, communications between processes may need to pass through several intervening transputers. This routing of messages imposes an extra overhead on each transputer, and the balance between computation and communication needs to be carefully assessed.
- *Processor loading*   The processing load of each transputer in a network must be taken into consideration. The system is likely to run at the speed of the transputer with the highest processing load, as the other transputers in the system will probably be held up, waiting to communicate with this transputer. So the processing load should be shared as evenly as possible among the available transputers, and not left to chance or haphazard placement. The farm approach (Ch. 12) semi-dynamically balances the load for each processor, since a processor receives more work only when it becomes idle. The algorithmic approach (Ch. 12) needs especial care, as an overloaded processor may create a bottleneck in the pipeline or whatever configuration is chosen.
- *Processor type and memory*   There are different types of transputer available with different word sizes and floating point capabilities. The choice of transputer for a particular function within a network needs to be carefully considered to match applications with suitable processors. For example, computation-bound tasks involving floating-point operations will obviously benefit from the use of a T800 processor. As regards memory, the program memory requirement must be balanced against the use of internal memory (fast but finite) and external memory.

Some key facts to keep in mind are:
- There is a small but finite overhead involved in the execution of **PAR** processes on a single transputer. This is attributable to the context switch as each **PAR** process is executed.
- Communicating processes are blocked until both processes are at a point

whereby the communication can proceed. The communication is *not* buffered.
- Communication between processes on different transputers requires extra "communication" processes such as multiplexors and routers. If a message has to pass through several intermediate transputers, the communications overhead is increased. (Current INMOS software now provides for message routing and multiplexing/de-multiplexing.)

13.2 Coding issues for performance maximization

In order to maximize performance of an occam program, INMOS have issued guidelines on how best to arrange occam programs (INMOS 1989c). These guidelines fall into two classes, depending on whether the performance of a single transputer or a network of transputers is being maximized. However, it should be noted that some of the code optimizations suggested by INMOS are implementation (i.e. compiler) dependent. Some of the more generally applicable optimizations are discussed here.

13.2.1 Single transputer performance
- When using transputer systems that have both internal and external memory, it is important that optimal use is made of internal memory, since frequent memory references to off-chip memory can seriously degrade the effective memory speed, off-chip memory being significantly slower than on-board memory – a ratio of 1:5 or worse. (The internal memory of a T80 transputer is 4 Kbytes.) After system workspace allocation, the occam compiler utilizes memory in the following order: process workspace, code space and vector space. For a large occam program, the code space and vector space (for arrays) may well be placed off-chip.

The memory layout of code should be organized so that frequently accessed variables are placed on-chip. Or rather, process workspaces should be kept on-chip (since occam variables are referenced via a workspace pointer; see Ch. 15).

Care should be exercised over the cavalier use of the **PLACE** statement for the allocation of memory for variables. If the variable is placed accidentally outside the workspace of the process that accesses it, then even more code is required to generate the necessary access, which then takes longer to execute. The placement of variables may also lead to untoward effects if the placement accidentally overwrites a workspace location.

The more recent releases of the INMOS occam compiler have an extension to the **PLACE** statement. The recommended procedure for variable placement is to use **PLACE** in conjunction with the **IN WORKSPACE** compiler directive. For example,

```
[2048] INT Data :
PLACE Data IN WORKSPACE :
```

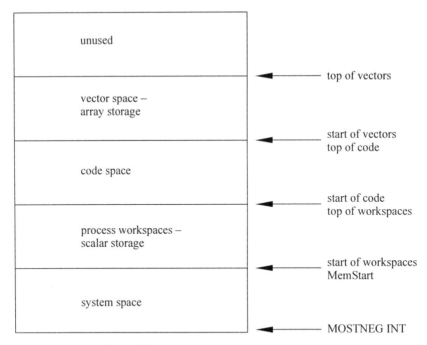

Figure 13.1 Memory layout of occam program.

Placement may be critical for some arrays. Frequently accessed global variables and arrays should be brought into local scope via abbreviations or by passing them as parameters if accessed in a procedure. Generally, the occam compiler tries to place scalar values and pointers in internal memory, rather than code and arrays. The memory layout of an occam program is shown in Figure 13.1, which illustrates three distinct areas: process workspaces, program code and array storage. Each occam process has its own workspace. For any occam process, the compiler places the most recently declared variables in the lowest workspace addresses.

• Abbreviations are a powerful feature of occam for producing efficient code, particularly in terms of memory space and execution time for handling large arrays. For example, rather than writing

```
VAL Start IS 1000 :
[5000]Vector :
SEQ
  Vector[Start + Offset1]  := Value
  Vector[Start + Offset2]  := Value
  .
  .
  .
```

(where `Offset1`, `Offset2`, etc. have been declared as type **INT** constants), it is better to write

```
VAL Length IS 3000 :
VAL Start IS 1000 :
[5000]INT Vector :
Array IS [Vector FROM Start FOR Length]:
SEQ
  Array[Offset1]  := Value
  Array[Offset2]  := Value
  .
  .
  .
```

where the large array, `Vector`, has been abbreviated by the segment, `Array`, and the segment is indexed by a constant. Thus, the occam compiler has no need to generate run-time range-checking code. All the checking may be performed at compile time. This leads to efficiency in saving memory space (shorter code is produced) and execution time (the shorter code executes more quickly).

Abbreviations are also useful for speeding up large array accesses by "opening out loops". For example, in a replicated **SEQ**, which performs an addition of two large arrays:

```
SEQ I = 0 FOR 20000
  Sum[I]  := A[I] + B[I]
```

execution speed is increased if the addition is performed on slices of the array, instead of the whole array as shown above.

• The use of array segments rather than the use of replicated constructs to access large arrays can increase the efficiency of the compiled occam code. For example, instead of using a replicated **SEQ** to copy an array (whole or part) as shown below

```
[10000]INT Original :
[5000]INT Copy :
SEQ Index = 0 FOR 3000
  Copy[Index]  := Original[Index]
```

it is better to write

```
[10000]INT Original :
[5000]INT Copy :
SEQ
  [Copy FROM 0 FOR 3000]  := [Original FROM 0 FOR 3000]
```

225

The segment version is compiled using a *block move* instruction, and speed improvements of nearly 50 per cent have been recorded. The efficiency of an array transfer across a channel is also improved using this technique.

13.2.2 Multitransputer performance

All of the issues discussed in the previous section are pertinent to the maximization of multitransputer performance. In addition, there are several separate factors that need to be considered for a network of transputers.

- The transputer's communication links operate autonomously from the processor and each other. To attain maximum link throughput, the processor and the links need to be kept as busy as possible. Decoupling the communication part of the program from the computation part in some way helps to achieve this. In practice, this means writing these two parts as parallel processes:

```
PAR
    communication
    computation
```

- Processes responsible for communicating with other processes across a transputer link should be executed at high priority. This minimizes any communication delay that might otherwise hold up a transputer awaiting the communication. So the code above now becomes

```
PRI PAR
    communication
    computation
```

- Inter-transputer messages should be kept as long as possible, so that link setup time overheads are minimal compared to the actual data transfer time. So, for example, lots of small messages are better batched up and sent as a longer message.

226

Chapter 14

Software design issues

14.1 Deadlock   14.2 Load balancing   14.3 Routing   14.4 Performance analysis

14.1 Deadlock

Deadlock is a problem that has been plaguing system designers ever since the dawn of computing. Books dealing with operating system principles usually include a chapter on deadlock. With the advent of parallel processing, deadlock problems reached new insidious heights. Needless to say, the study and resolution of deadlock problems is an active research area.

In occam, deadlock occurs when a process is prevented indefinitely from proceeding: from proceeding with an input/output operation because, for some reason, the other communicating process never executes its corresponding output/input operation. Often the reason is that the communicating process itself is deadlocked on some different channel. This form of deadlock has been termed *communication deadlock*. Very careful use of the occam input/output primitives has to be exercised in order to avoid deadlock situations. A simple illustration of deadlock in an occam program is the following, in which two processes are linked by a channel in each direction. However, the ordering of the input/output operations for the different channels in each **SEQ** process do not match, and deadlock ensues:

```
PAR
  SEQ
    Chan1 ! Data1 -- this process blocked here
    Chan2 ? Data2
  SEQ
    Chan2 ! Data2 -- this process blocked here
    Chan1 ? Data1
```

A related problem is to ensure the absence of *livelock* in occam programs. Livelock occurs when a program becomes too busy to terminate properly. In a livelock situation, a process continues to execute in an endless loop, unable to exit the loop. For example, the following occam fragment illustrates livelock:

```
WHILE TRUE
  SKIP
```

227

The external effect is similar to that of deadlock. However, deadlock imposes no load on the system, whereas livelock imposes a continuous demand. Willcock & Welch (1992) have classified various forms of deadlock and livelock:

- *primitive deadlock* occurs when a process executes a **STOP** process
- *structured deadlock* is the situation outlined in the deadlock example above
- *primitive livelock* is the situation outlined in the livelock example above
- *structured livelock* occurs when two communicating processes both enter an endless loop, within which they only communicate with each other. The example below illustrates this effect:

```
WHILE TRUE
    SEQ
        .
        .
        .
        Chan1 ? Data1
        .
        .
        .
        Chan2 ! Data2
        .
        .
        .
WHILE TRUE
    SEQ
        .
        .
        .
        Chan1 ! Data1
        .
        .
        .
        Chan2 ? Data2
        .
        .
        .
```

To an outside observer, all classes appear the same: they fail to communicate any further with the environment.

14.1.1 The I/O graph for deadlock detection

Communication deadlock may be detected with *communications state graph*, a *directed* graph that models the *ungranted* I/O requests of communicating processes. The processes are represented by the nodes of the graph and the ungranted

Figure 14.1   Communication state graph.

I/O requests by the edges. Assuming that all the processes are non-terminating and individually deadlock-free, it may be shown that a necessary condition for deadlock is a cycle in this graph. Such a graph is known as a *busy network* (Fig. 14.1).

De Carlini & Villano (1991a) advocate the use of the *I/O graph* for detecting *possible* deadlock situations in occam programs. The I/O graph is a graphical representation that models I/O requests of communicating processes. In this representation, a communicating process is modelled by a vertex and a channel by an undirected edge. The edges of an I/O graph are *undirected* to account for the fact that an ungranted request may be an input or output. In a deadlock situation, the *ungranted* requests of communicating processes will form a cycle in the I/O graph.

The following condition is given for a *possible* deadlock situation:

- a necessary condition for a busy occam program to be deadlock prone is that its I/O graph contains at least one cycle. (Note, however, that, since at any point in time only a subset of edges in an I/O graph may be ungranted requests, a cyclic graph *may* not represent a deadlock: the condition is *not* sufficient. Indeed, if the above occam fragment is rewritten to remove the deadlock, the resulting I/O graph is still the same as in Fig. 14.2!)

De Carlini & Villano go on to refine the I/O graph concept for problems that perform their inputs via an **ALT** construct. An **ALT** is non-blocking with regard to input (*if* it contains a catch-all guard). In such cases, the edges of the I/O graph may now be directed, corresponding to outputs only. The condition above may also be restated in terms of this directed I/O graph. The authors illustrate the use of the I/O graph to design a deadlock-free routing algorithm, based on **ALT**s, for a square mesh network of transputers.

Figure 14.2   I/O graph.

The I/O graph, then, is a simple but useful graphical means for indicating *possible* problem areas in communicating process code.

14.1.2 I/O-SEQ, I/O-PAR *and client–server models*

In a series of articles, Welch et al. (1993) have introduced paradigms for developing deadlock-free programs. (These paradigms are based on the concept of *directed* graphs for modelling communicating processes, in which the directed edges represent I/O relationships between communicating processes and the nodes represent processes.):

- the **I/O-SEQ, I/O-PAR** model
- the client–server model

14.1.2.1 The **I/O-SEQ, I/O-PAR** *model*   As discussed above, a loop of communicating processes *may* create a deadlock situation. To study such situations, Welch (1987) categorizes certain processes with fixed cyclic communication patterns into two classes:

- **I/O-SEQ** processes: any processes that, every cycle, have sequenced input and output, performing one after the other; that is, all inputs are performed in parallel, and *then* (in sequence) all outputs are performed in parallel.

For example, the following code is **I/O-SEQ**:

```
WHILE TRUE
   SEQ
      PAR
            In1  ?  Data1
            In2  ?  Data2
            .
            .
            .

      PAR
            Out1  !  Data1
            Out2  !  Data2
            .
            .
            .
```

- **I/O-PAR** processes: any processes that, every cycle, perform all input and output in parallel.

The following code is **I/O-PAR**, for example:

```
WHILE TRUE
   SEQ
      . . . compute values for Data1, etc. from
            NewData1, etc.
```

```
PAR
    In1 ? NewData1
    In2 ? NewData2
    .

    .

    .

    Out1 ! Data1
    Out2 ! Data2
    .

    .

    .
```

Using these concepts, Welch proves several theorems. (The theorems are stated in terms of a *connection diagram*: a directed graph, which has a node for every process, and an edge for every channel.)

- a network of **I/O-SEQ** processes with an acyclic connection diagram *will not* deadlock, and may itself be treated as **I/O-SEQ**; but a cyclic network of such processes *will* deadlock
- any network of **I/O-PAR** processes *will not* deadlock
- any network of mixed **I/O-SEQ** and **I/O-PAR** processes *will not* deadlock *provided* that there is no cycle of just **I/O-SEQ** processes in the connection diagram
- any network of mixed **I/O-SEQ** and **I/O-PAR** processes like the one above, which also has an **I/O-PAR** process on every path from each input to each output, may be treated as **I/O-PAR** itself.

14.1.2.2 The client–server model   The *client–server* principle refers to a certain pattern of bi-directional communication between two occam processes: one process (the *client*) send requests on a channel to the other process (the *server*), which sends back replies on a different channel. The transaction is always initiated by the client process. Such a pattern of I/O requests between processes may, again, be modelled by a *directed* graph, in which a single directed edge (from client to server) represents the bi-directional communication.

A server has typically the following pattern of input/output operations:

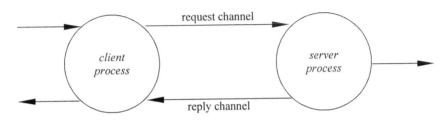

Figure 14.3   Example of client–server communication.

```
WHILE Servicing
  SEQ
    Request ? Parameters -- receive request from client
    --
    -- perform computation
    --
    Reply ! Answer -- send reply to client
```

The server process may service several client processes via different pairs of channels. A server process may itself be a client of another server process. Note that each client–server connection defines an ordering between two processes. A process must not indefinitely refuse to communicate with one of its clients, unless it is itself waiting indefinitely to communicate with one of its servers. Welch et al. (1993) prove the following theorem:

- any network of client–server connections that is acyclic with respect to the client–server digraph is deadlock/livelock free
- any collection of processes that communicate only using the client–server paradigm and has an acyclic topology (with respect to client–server relationships) itself communicates with its environment by the client–server paradigm.

Observing these rules in occam program development will lead to deadlock-free programs.

14.2 Load balancing

In order for performance to scale as more transputers are added to a network, the computational loads of the transputers must be balanced. Partitioning an application into several independent processes and dealing with the communications between them are key factors in the design of parallel programs (Qingping & Paker 1990). More independent processes should mean more parallelism in the system. However, increasing the degree of parallelism means more communication and other overheads, as there are more messages for the transputers in the system to forward. Thus, there is a balance to be achieved between increasing the level of parallelism and minimizing the communication overhead in order to reap the most benefit of parallelism. The amount of computation performed by a process before communication should be sufficiently high, so that communication costs are relatively low.

A computational load imbalance will also produce a poor increase in performance on a multitransputer system. Indeed, if the load imbalance is so bad, then the system may perform at the rate of one transputer, the one with the largest load; the other transputers may be blocked waiting to communicate with this busy one. On the other hand, a near-perfect load balance should produce linear improvements in performance.

Important questions are how much a task should be partitioned into parallel processes and how should the processes then be distributed among the available processors? If the task is decomposed into many processes and these distributed among many processors, the amount of communication between processes may be increased unnecessarily. If the task is divided up into a few processes and these distributed among few processors, there may be large differences in processing load per transputer so that at the end there may be some transputers still computing, whereas others have nothing left to do.

A key concept in load balancing is *granularity* (Qingping & Paker 1990): the average number of independent processes distributed to each processor. The granularity is said to be "high" if the average number of processes per processor is large, and otherwise "low". Another concept, inversely related to granularity, is *grain size*: a measure of the processing size (or load) of a task. (Note that some authors use the terms *grain size* and *granularity* interchangeably.) For a process, grain size is defined as the ratio of the number of computations to communications performed in unit time. A system with few processes per processor is said to be "coarse grained", whereas one with many processes per processor is said to be "fine grained".

The notion of grain size made be applied to the processors themselves. The grain size of a processor is determined by the ratio of its computing power to its communication ability. Processors, in general, may be regarded as being relatively very powerful or less powerful. Those belonging to the former class are called *coarse grained*, and belonging to the latter are known as *fine grained*. Typically, a parallel system will comprise few coarse-grained processors or many fine-grained processors. Fox et al. (1988) regard fine-grained processors to have memories with upwards of about 1 Kbyte, and coarse-grained processors typically to have at least 100 Kbyte of memory. The transputer, with its powerful processor and significant communications capability, qualifies as being medium grain-sized.

For optimum performance, the grain size of the processing task executed on a processor must match that of the processor. If the grain size of the task is greater than that of the processor, then the communication capacity of the processor may be under-utilized. If the grain size of the task is less than that of the processor, then the processing capacity of the processor may be under-utilized. The under-utilization of communication capacity may be tolerated, but not the under-utilization of processing capacity. The grain size of a task should be as small as possible, consistent with low communications and processor utilization, to reap the most parallelism from the problem.

In order to make efficient use of processing capacity, processors should not be idle while waiting for communication. Increasing the communication speed helps, but cannot always eliminate the problem. For the transputer, the use of *hidden parallelism* (May 1990) is advocated when possible to hide any delays in communication; that is, communication and computation should be overlapped so that they proceed in parallel, whenever possible. This may be organized in occam by use of a **PRI PAR** construct:

```
PRI PAR
    PAR
        . . . receive next data item
        . . . send previous data item
    compute with current data item
```

Communication is handled as the high priority process. This ensures that communications are dealt with immediately. The processor is kept busy while data is being communicated. Any communication delays are masked by the computation, which proceeds at low priority.

14.3 Message routing

Regardless of the configuration of transputers in a network, the *routing* (or *forwarding*) of messages from one transputer to another is an important and necessary requirement. The transputer is a *distributed-memory, message-passing* architecture: all information exchange between processes and transputers must be done by explicit message passing. Obviously, the delivery of messages from one process to another should be reliable and efficient. However, it is not a trivial task to ensure that the routing software is deadlock-free. A network of transputers is quite prone to message deadlock unless some design steps in the routing algorithm are taken to prevent it. The problem derives from the fact that the transputer link supports only two channels, one in either direction. The application may require that there be several channels between processes on each linked transputer. In the past, the onus for developing efficient, deadlock-free routing software has fallen to the programmer, the older transputer development environments not providing any. This state of affairs may have curtailed, or at least constrained, several multitransputer developments. However, these problems have now disappeared. Deadlock-free routing support is now provided by INMOS. Current INMOS software provides automatic routing and multiplexor/de-multiplexor processes. The introduction of the second-generation T9000 series transputer and its communications-support devices has aided this progress.

The availability of general algorithms for the deadlock-free routing messages between (possibly) non-adjacent transputers in a network is an important area in the development of transputer systems. A message may have to pass through several intermediate transputers in order to arrive at its destination. Some authors (e.g. Wexler & Prior 1989) rely on *generous buffering* to alleviate the effects of deadlock; the buffers are used to store messages that temporarily cannot be delivered. But even these authors admit that this does not prevent deadlock, only maybe postpone it long enough for the program to complete its task!

Several tried-and-tested methods have been designed for routing networks in general. All methods assume that the message is labelled somehow with the destination address (and sometimes also the source address). This addressing information is used to route the message through the network. Usually the address information is prepended to the start of the message (the *header*). De Carlini & Villano (1991a) list the following representative examples of routing techniques:

- *Store-and-forward routing*   This is a classical method for routing messages, developed for wide-area networking. The whole of each message is assembled (stored) in each intermediate processor before being transmitted (forwarded) to the next one. This method requires each processor to have large buffers, large enough to hold the largest message likely to be received. The storing of the message in each intermediate processor increases the *message latency*: the time it takes for a message to be delivered.
- *Wormhole routing*   In this scheme, a message is split up into several smaller units called flow-control digits (*flits*), and transmitted as such. This means that the size of the buffers in the intermediate processor can be correspondingly smaller. The addressing information in the header flit is interpreted as soon as it is read in by the intermediate processor, that is, a routing decision is made before the rest of the message is read. Each following flit of the message can thereby be forwarded as soon as it is received by the intermediate processor. Hence, the overall message latency is reduced: the whole message is no longer buffered in the intermediate processors. This method has been adopted by INMOS for the functioning of the C104 routing switch, part of the T9000 chip set (see Ch. 16).
- *Virtual cut-through routing*   This technique is a hybrid mixture of the store-and-forward and wormhole methods. It behaves as in wormhole routing, but, if the forwarding of a flit is blocked by a busy output channel, the intermediate processor may elect to buffer the whole message for later retransmission. Thus, virtual cut-through routing dynamically adjusts its behaviour according to the network loading.
- *Mad postman routing*   A variant of wormhole routing that tries to reduce the message latency further. The first flit entering an intermediate node is immediately routed in the same continuing direction, even before the whole flit has been received. Once the whole flit has been received with the full routing address, the intermediate node reconsiders its "arbitrary" routing decision. If this decision is good, then the following flits of the message are routed in the same direction. Otherwise, the transmission is aborted and the flits are rerouted in the correct direction. The reduction of message latency thus gives rise to a possible additional communications cost for any possible misrouting.

For transputer networks, INMOS have chosen the wormhole routing technique; it is used by the C104 routing switch. The actual routing algorithm used by the C104 is based on *interval labelling* (see Ch. 16). It is possible to show that an optimal, deadlock-free routing algorithm can be constructed for regular networks, such as trees, hypercubes and grids (INMOS 1993).

A particular application may not require a full-blown router, but others will. For the first-generation transputers, general routing software will comprise a multiplexing process and a de-multiplexing process. Each transputer link will be driven by such a combination, with the two channels supported by the link transferring the multiplexed messages in either direction.

A simple, general multiplexor may be built using an **ALT** construct, with a tag being communicated before each packet of data, for example:

```
ALT
  InChan1 ? Data1
    MuxChan ! 1; Data1
  InChan2 ? Data2
    MuxChan ! 2; Data2
  InChan3 ? Data3
    MuxChan ! 3; Data3
  .
  .
  .
```

The general de-multiplexor may be built using a **CASE** construct, with selection of the branch based on the packet tag, for example:

```
MuxChan ? PacketTag; Data
CASE PacketTag
  1
    OutChan1 ! Data
  2
    OutChan2 ! Data
  3
    OutChan3 ! Data
  .
  .
  .
```

The routing protocol may be made more sophisticated by, for example, having the destination specified in the packet header and using a look-up table to route the packet to its destination.

Note: the newer versions of the INMOS occam toolset now incorporate a virtual routing and multiplexing feature; the occam configurer will automatically add the necessary occam processes if they are required by a multitransputer configuration. This enables the programmer to a write a configuration connecting channels in the program without regard to the number of transputer links available. The configurer inserts extra processes for the multiplexing and routing of messages to support the requested channel connections.

14.4 Performance analysis

One of the potential benefits of parallel processing is the ability to increase performance by adding more processing power. There are two important ways to distinguish applying parallelism to a problem:
- parallel processing can be used to solve a larger problem in the same time – so-called *scale-up*
- parallel processing can be used to solve the same problem in less time – so-called *speed-up*.

The concept of scaling may be used in two distinct ways. An algorithm is said to be *scalable* if the level of parallelism increases at least linearly with the problem size. An architecture is scalable if it continues to yield the same performance per processor, albeit used on a larger problem size, as the number of processors increases. This means that it is possible to solve larger problems in the same time by adding more processors.

Speed-up is defined as the ratio between the time needed for the algorithm to be computed sequentially on a single processor and the time needed to perform the same computation on a network of parallel processors. A measure closely related to speed-up is *efficiency* of a network of parallel processors, defined as the speed-up per processor (i.e. the ratio of speed-up to the number of processors constituting the network). These two measures allow the performance of a network of parallel processors to be gauged.

It is possible to calculate the performance of a network of transputers using a simple but yet useful model. The following analysis is that of De Carlini & Villano (1991b), based on work by Fox et al. (1988) and Pritchard et al. (1987). Let T_{seq} be the time required for an algorithm to be computed sequentially (on a single processor), and $T_{par}(N)$ be the time need to perform the same computation on a network of N parallel processors (indicating explicitly the dependency on the number of transputers, N). Using the definitions above, then speed-up, $S(N)$, may be written as

$$S(N) = \frac{T_{seq}}{T_{par}(N)}$$

and efficiency, ε, as

$$\varepsilon = \frac{S(N)}{N}$$

Substituting for speed up, $S(N)$, in the equation for efficiency, gives

$$\varepsilon = \frac{T_{seq}}{N \times T_{par}(N)}$$

In practice, the efficiency may be reduced by several different factors:
- algorithmic overhead: an algorithm that performs optimally executing sequentially on a single transputer may not be so optimal for parallel execution on a network of transputers

237

- software overhead: the distribution and control of an algorithm executing in parallel on a network of transputers introduces a performance overhead
- load imbalance overhead: if the computational load is not equally distributed among all transputers in the network, then some transputers may be idle
- communication overhead: communication between transputers does introduce a small penalty in performance overhead; communication is not totally overlapped with computation.

Assuming that the communication overhead is the major contribution to efficiency reduction (i.e. the other factors may be neglected), then the overall computation time, $T_{par}(N)$, can be considered to be composed of two parts:
- the actual calculation time, $T_{calc}(N)$
- the communication time, $T_{comm}(N)$.

Thus, $T_{par}(N)$ may be written as

$$T_{par}(N) = T_{calc}(N) + T_{comm}(N)$$

Now, if the computation and communication workload is well balanced over the network of N transputers, then

$$t_{calc} = T_{calc}(N)$$

and

$$t_{comm} = T_{comm}(N)$$

where t_{calc} and t_{comm} are the calculation and communication times respectively for each individual transputer. Hence, $T_{par}(N)$ may be written as

$$T_{par}(N) = t_{calc} + t_{comm}$$

Invoking once more the assumption that the algorithmic and software overheads may be neglected and that the network is well load balanced (i.e. the algorithm is scalable), then T_{seq} may be written as

$$T_{seq} = N \times t_{calc}$$

that is, the time for the sequential computation, T_{seq}, on a single transputer is N times the calculation time for any one of the transputers, t_{calc}, when the algorithm is distributed over a network of N transputers.

So, substituting for T_{seq} and $T_{par}(N)$, the equation for the efficiency now becomes

$$\varepsilon = \frac{t_{calc}}{t_{calc} + t_{comm}}$$

Defining the fractional communication overhead, f_c, as the ratio of the time spent on communication per transputer to the time spent on calculation per transputer

$$f_c = \frac{t_{comm}}{t_{calc}}$$

then the efficiency may be written as

$$\varepsilon = \frac{1}{1+f_c} \approx 1 - f_c$$

If the fractional communication overhead is kept constant as the number of transputers, N, in the network increases, then the efficiency will remain constant (i.e. the efficiency is independent of N). This condition requires that the computation and communication loads per transputer remain the same, which means the problem size must increase with any increase in the number of transputers.

Fox et al. give a graphical illustration of the dependency of speed-up on (a) a fixed grain size (Fig. 14.4) and (b) a fixed problem (domain) size (Fig. 14.5).

For a fixed grain size (which is large enough to keep the processor busy) –that is, the problem size is proportional to the number of processors –then the speed-up is linear with respect to the number of processors.

For a fixed problem size, in which the grain size is inversely proportional to the number of processors, then the speed-up saturates as communication and control become the limiting factors.

For the transputer, interprocessor communication may sometimes be overlapped with processor calculations. (This is not always the case – it depends upon the approach adopted for organizing the parallelism. This subject is explored in Ch. 12.). However, communication is not entirely independent of processor activity. There is a small but finite amount of communication setup that is performed by the processor and is not overlapped. Thus, t_{comm} may be written as the sum of two parts:

$$t_{comm} = t_{setup} + t_{overlap}$$

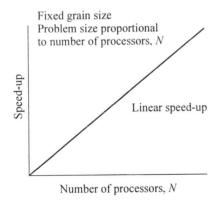

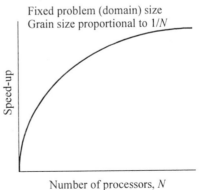

Figure 14.4 Sketch of the dependence of the speed-up on the number of processors, assuming fixed grain size.

Figure 14.5 Sketch of the dependence of the speed-up on the number of processors, assuming fixed problem size.

where t_{setup} is the non-overlappable time to set up the communication, and $t_{overlap}$ is the time the communication actually overlaps with processoractivity. Substituting for t_{comm} in the equation for efficiency gives, finally,

$$\varepsilon = \frac{t_{calc}}{t_{setup} + MAX(t_{calc}, t_{overlap})}$$

Pritchard et al. measured values for t_{setup}, t_{calc} and $t_{overlap}$ for some particular application:

t_{setup}: 50 ns (T4, T8-20 MHz)

$t_{overlap}$: 1.95 μs per byte (T4 with 10 MHz link)
1.18 μs per byte (T4 with 20 MHz link)
1.13 μs per byte (T8 with 10 MHz link)
0.57 μs per byte (T8 with 20 MHz link)

t_{calc}: 10-20 μs per flop (T4-20 MHz, internal RAM)
0.66 μs per flop (T8-20 MHz, internal RAM)

Chapter 15

The transputer

15.1 Transputer architecture

The Introduction gave an overview of the architecture of the transputer. This chapter contains a more detailed description of the transputer register set, its instruction set and how microcoded functions are implemented (INMOS 1992).

The basic "register" set of the transputer processor comprises six registers, as follows (Fig. 15.1):
- instruction pointer, I, which points to the next instruction to be executed for the currently executing process.
- workspace pointer, W, which points to that area of memory where the local variables of the process are stored
- operand register, O, used to form instruction operands
- three registers, A, B, C, which are used for integer and address arithmetic and form a conventional evaluation stack for holding operands and intermediate results for expression evaluation. (The floating-point unit of the T8XX family has a complementary set of registers, AF, BF and CF.)
In addition, there are two one-bit flags:
- error flag, E, which is set when an arithmetic overflow occurs
- halt-on-error flag, H, which enables the transputer to be halted if the error flag, E, is set.
Besides the execution of occam code, these registers are also used for implementing the microcoded functions of the transputer.

15.2 The transputer instruction set

The transputer is a minimal instruction set processor, with each instruction having the same basic format, independent of the transputer type: 1 byte in length, with a 4-bit function code and a 4-bit data field (Fig. 15.2). At first sight, this may seem unusual. However, measurements by INMOS showed that about 80 per cent of

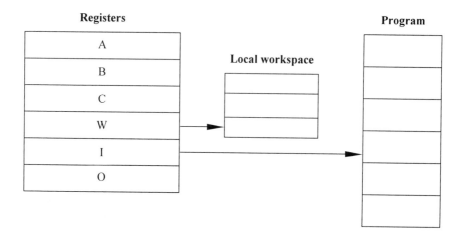

Figure 15.1 Transputer register set.

instructions used in programs may be encoded in a single byte. Thus, by choosing this instruction format, the transputer machine code is very compact compared to that of more conventional processors, and most operations may be executed very quickly. Most instructions, in fact, execute in one cycle (50 ns on a 20 Mhz transputer), with many of the rest executing in two cycles. Some complex functions, such as a block move, take an arbitrary number of cycles.

The 4-bits allocated to the function code means that there are 16 basic functions available. These are allotted as follows:

- 13 *normal* functions such as load constant, store local variable, etc., plus
- *operate*, which causes the 4-bit data field to be interpreted as an operation on the evaluation stack, giving rise to 16 arithmetic and comparison operations, and
- *prefix* and *negative prefix*, which allow the data field to be extended.

All instructions execute by the loading of the data field into the operand register, which is then used as the instruction's operand when the instruction is executed (Fig. 15.3). With the exception of the two prefix instructions, all instructions end by clearing the operand register. The prefix instructions shift the four data bits left four places. Consequently, operands may be extended to more than four bits in length by a sequence of prefix instructions. The negative prefix complements the operand register before shifting.

Figure 15.2 Instruction format.

242

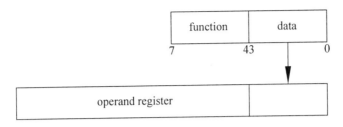

Figure 15.3   Instruction operand register.

The T805 has extra instructions for manipulating the floating-point stack. The T400, T425, T450 and T805 contain further instructions for supporting colour graphics, pattern recognition and implementing error-correcting codes. All these instructions except for 2-D block moves are on the T225.

15.3 The process scheduler

The microcoded process scheduler permits the concurrent execution of any number of processes through time sharing. At any moment, a process is *active* (either executing or ready to execute) or *inactive* (i.e. suspended: waiting for an input or output, or waiting for an event such as a timer). Processes ready to execute are held on a linked *FIFO* queue (a *round-robin* queue), awaiting execution. The queue is a linked list of process workspaces. There are *two* such queues, one for high-priority processes and the other for low-priority processes. The scheduler chooses a process for execution from these queues on a priority basis. The head and tail of each queue are pointed to by two special registers, *front* and *back*. When an executing process is descheduled, the next instruction register, I, of that process is stored in the process's workspace and the process at the head of the queue (the one pointed by *front*) is scheduled (i.e. chosen for execution; its saved I register is restored). The descheduled process (if it has been time-sliced) is put at the back of the queue. Low priority processes are scheduled only if the high-priority queue is empty.

In Figure 15.4, process S is the currently executing process; the transputer's register set is allocated to this process. The queue of waiting processes (active but waiting turn to execute) holds three processes, P, Q and R, with process P at the head of the queue. This example corresponds to the following occam code:

```
PAR
    P
    Q
    R
    S
```

Registers   Local workspaces   Programs

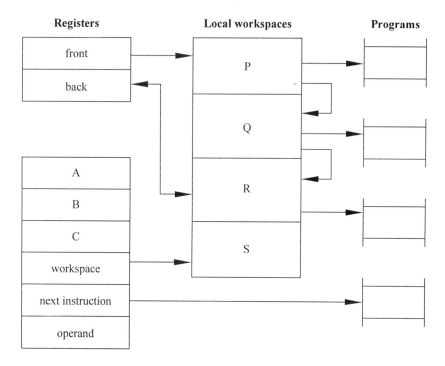

Figure 15.4   Linked process list.

15.4 Priority scheduling

Low-priority processes are scheduled only if the high-priority queue is empty. High-priority processes run to completion or until the execution of an input/output process or a timer interrupt, at which point they are descheduled. Low-priority processes execute for a time-slice period (5120 internal clock cycles = 1.224 ms). After holding the processor for a time-slice or executing an input/output process, low-priority processes are descheduled and the process at the front of the process queue is selected for execution. (Actually, descheduling occurs only after certain instructions, so the time-slice is slightly variable – between one and two time-slice periods after the process started executing.) The execution of low-priority processes may be pre-empted by a high-priority process becoming ready.

15.5 Implementation of the SEQ process

The implementation and execution of a SEQ process is supported by the six transputer registers. Registers A, B and C form an evaluation stack, the register W points to that part of memory (the Workspace) where the local variables of the process are stored, and register I points to the next code instruction in memory.

15.6 Implementation of the PAR process

Execution of a **PAR** process requires more overhead than a **SEQ** process – a single transputer time-slices concurrent processes and this consumes a finite amount of time each time it happens. Only one process can be executing at any time and this involves a *context switch* every time a different concurrent process is chosen to be the one that executes. During the context switch, the register set of the previously active process has to be saved, the register set of the newly active process has to be loaded and the queue of waiting concurrent processes adjusted. Even though the context switch is microcoded, it takes a small but finite time – about 10 to 20 processor cycles, depending on memory speed.

The constituent processes of a **PAR** process are held ready, awaiting execution in the FIFO queue. When the currently executing constituent process is descheduled, its I register is saved in the process's workspace and the process pointed to by the FIFO queue front register becomes active (once its saved I register has been restored).

15.7 Implementation of the ALT process

The **ALT** construct allows an occam process to wait until an input occurs on any one of several specified channels. As the normal occam instructions would cause such a process to be descheduled until input on a *specific* channel is available, a special set of instructions are used to implement the **ALT**.

Within an **ALT**, each alternative channel input guard is "enabled", then an "alternative wait" is executed if no channel is ready – the **ALT** process is descheduled. When an input is available, the process is rescheduled and each channel input is "disabled". The "disable" instruction tests each alternative channel input in turn (textual ordering of the alternatives). The first one found to be ready is selected for execution.

The execution of an **ALT** – especially large, replicated **ALT**s – can be slow. Each time the **ALT** is executed, all of the operations described above have to be performed. Although individual operations may be fast, the cumulative effect can be quite pronounced. In fact, the execution time of the **ALT** construct has a linear dependence on the number of channels.

15.8 Implementation of TIMERs

The transputer has two timers (hardware clocks), one for each priority level:
- the high-priority timer ticks, that is, the value of the timer is incremented every 1 microsecond (1 second is equivalent to 1 000 000 clock ticks of the high-priority timer)
- the low-priority timer ticks every 64 microseconds (1 second is equivalent to 15 625 clock ticks of the low-priority timer)

Each timer is incremented in modulo fashion; for example, with the value continually cycling from the most negative integer through zero to the most positive integer, then wrapping round to the most negative integer to start the cycle once more.

For the occam programmer, these timers may be regarded as *special, read-only* channels, which are accessible from *any* process. Alternatively, the timer may be viewed as a special location, holding an integer value that continually changes.

Processes that are awaiting the elapse of a TIMER delay are placed in a queue of such processes. The queue is ordered according to the delay each process has requested, so that the process at the front of the queue is the one with smallest delay. When this delay has expired, the process is rescheduled.

15.9 Transputer link communications protocol

To achieve reliable communication between two transputers, a handshaking *communications* protocol is implemented in the firmware of each transputer link. This protocol (which should not be confused with a *channel* protocol) is quite simple, offering no error detection or correction. Data is transmitted as a *data packet* of one byte at a time across the link, each byte being sandwiched between two start bits (1) and a stop bit (0). Each byte received must be acknowledged by an *acknowledge packet* before the next byte is sent (Fig. 15.5). The acknowledgement means that the receiving process did actually receive the data byte and is ready to receive another.

On the T212 and T414 transputers, the acknowledgement is sent *only* after the *whole* data packet is received; this limits the maximum link transfer rate to 1.6 Mbytes at 20 Mbps. On later transputers, an overlapped acknowledgement is employed; the acknowledge packet is sent as the data packet is being received. This achieves a much higher transmission rate of 2.4 Mbytes at 20 Mbps, which amounts to an almost continuous transmission of data packets across the link.

Each transputer link behaves independently of the others; data is transferred autonomously across each link. Usually, one of three different link transmission speeds is selectable. The communications protocol is compatible across the family range of T2XX, T4XX and T8XX transputers, so that, for example, a T414 transputer may be linked with a T800 transputer.

In addition to communications links, the transputer also has an event channel, a special link used as an interrupt channel for external devices.

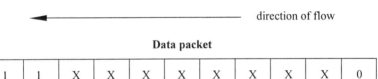

direction of flow

Data packet

1	1	X	X	X	X	X	X	X	X	0

Acknowledgement packet

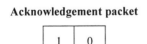

1	0

Figure 15.5   Link protocol.

15.10 Implementation of channels

Communication between occam processes, whether on the same or different transputers, occurs via a *channel*. If the processes are on the same transputer, then the channel is termed a *soft channel*; otherwise it is called a *hard channel*. The communication is point-to-point between two processes, synchronized and unbuffered. There is no message queue, no process queue or message buffer maintained by the system.

15.10.1 Soft channels
Each *soft* channel defined between two processes, P and Q, in an occam program is allocated a word of memory, which acts essentially as a synchronization flag. This channel word is initialized to the value "empty", signifying that there is no waiting message (Fig. 15.6).

When process P wishes to send a message to process Q via the channel, a process identifier (actually the pointer to its workspace) for P is deposited in the channel word and P is descheduled (i.e. suspended from execution; Fig. 15.7).

When process Q eventually becomes ready to communicate, it inspects the channel word and recognizes that it contains a process identifier (i.e. that process P is waiting to communicate). The contents of the message are then copied directly from the workspace of process P to the workspace of process Q, and the channel word reset to "empty" (Fig. 15.8).

During the communication, process Q remains active, and afterwards process P becomes active again, that is, it is placed on the queue of processes awaiting scheduling for execution. (If process Q is ready to communicate before process P, a similar procedure occurs.)

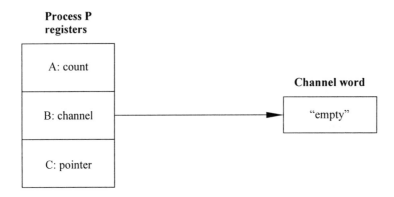

Figure 15.6 Process P ready to communicate.

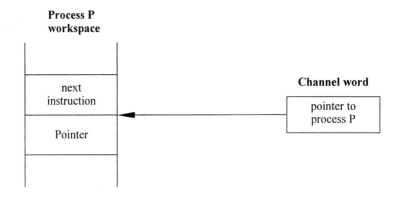

Figure 15.7 Pointer to Process P's workspace stored in channel word.

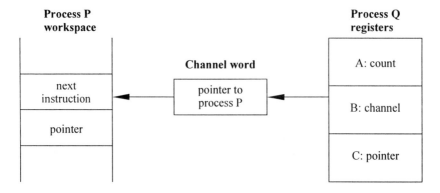

Figure 15.8 Process Q ready to communicate.

15.10.2 Hard channels

In the case of a *hard* channel, the responsibility for communication is delegated to the autonomous link interface of each communicating transputer. Each interface participates in the transfer of the message and reschedules its communicating process, which has been suspended for the duration of the transfer. When process P wishes to send a message to process Q on another transputer, the pointer to its workspace is stored in the channel word in memory, the pointer to the message and the byte count for the message length are deposited in the link registers and the process is descheduled (Fig. 15.9).

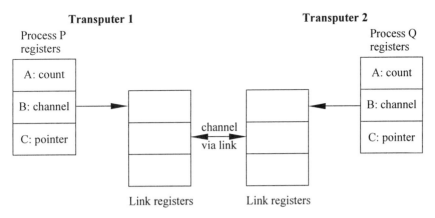

Figure 15.9   Channel communication via transputer link-initialization.

A similar procedure occurs when process Q is ready to receive a message. When both processes are in this state, the message is copied directly between process workspaces using a mixture of DMA from and to the memory of the transputers and serial transmission across the link (Fig. 15.10).

In addition to the four communication channels, the transputer also has a separate event "channel" available, which is used for external device interrupts.

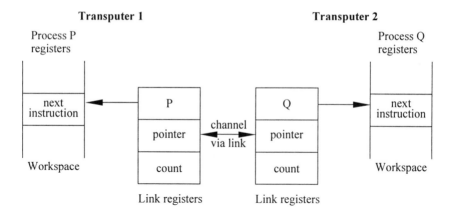

Figure 15.10   Channel communication via transputer link – data transfer.

Chapter 16

The T9000 transputer

16.1 Overview of the T9000 transputer   16.2 The T9000 processor pipeline
16.3 T9000 memory organization   16.4 The virtual channel processor
16.5 The packet routing switch   16.6 T9000 message routing algorithms

16.1 Overview of the T9000 transputer

The T9000 is the latest member of the transputer family (INMOS 1991b). In fact, it is the second generation, the T2XX, T4XX and T8XX families representing the first generation. It was announced by INMOS in 1991. The T9000 architecture contains many of the features of the previous generation transputers, but also has several innovative additions (Fig. 16.1). It is the highest-performance member of the transputer family: a 50 MHz T9000's rated peak computation performance is equivalent to ten 20 MHz T805s.

The major components of the T9000 architecture are as follows:
- A 32-bit superscalar integer processor (ALU), rated at a maximum performance of 200 Mips.
- A 64-bit floating-point processor (FPU), rated at a maximum performance of 25 Mflops. It operates as specified by the IEEE 754 standard.
- 16 Kbyte internal memory, which acts as a high bandwidth instruction and data cache, capable of accessing 800 Mbytes per second. This RAM can be configured as 16 or 8 Kbytes of cache. The latter allows code and data to be locked into fast on-chip memory for time-critical processes. A programmable memory interface allows the addition of external memory up to 4 Gbytes, capable of accessing 200 Mbytes per second.
- A communications processor – the *virtual channel processor* (VCP) –to manage the external communications; its main function is the implementation of a packet protocol for messages being passed over the communication links.
- Four communications links with a maximum transmission speed of 100 Mbits per second, full-duplex. The maximum bi-directional throughput over the four links amounts to 80 Mbytes per second.
- Two additional links for system control and monitoring. These allow all the transputers in a network to be "daisy-chained" together, allowing code to be loaded, monitored and debugged completely separately from what is going on with the four communications links.
- Four event channels.
- Submicrosecond interrupt response and context switching times.

251

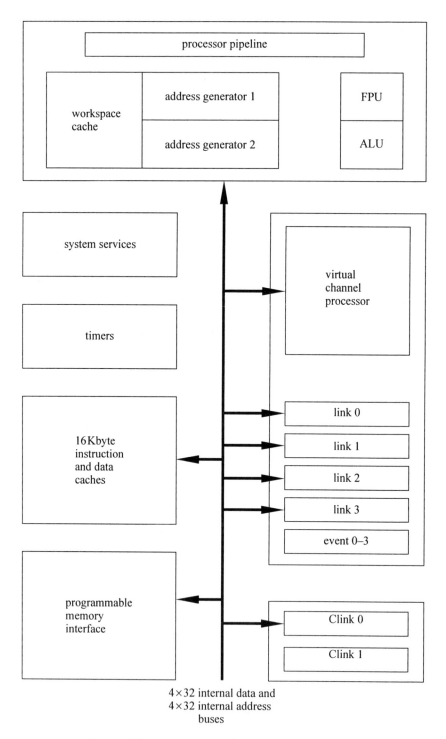

Figure 16.1 Schematic of T9000 transputer architecture.

16.2 The T9000 processor pipeline

The T9000 has a so-called *pipelined, superscalar* CPU, comprising the integer and floating-point processors, a 128 byte workspace cache and two address generators, which functions transparently to the programmer. It is able to operate on multiple instructions per cycle. Instructions are executed in a pipeline, comprising five stages, allowing several instructions to be executed per processor cycle. These stages are as follows:

- fetch two local variables
- perform two address calculations for accessing non-local or subscripted variables
- load two non-local variables
- perform an ALU of FPU operation
- perform a write or conditional jump operation.

After instructions are fetched from memory, but before they are passed into the pipeline, they are passed through an *instruction grouper*. The instruction grouper is essentially an execution optimizer in hardware. Its function is to examine the stream of instructions being fetched and to form them into groups that allow optimum use of the pipeline (Fig. 16.2).

The T9000 instruction set is broadly a superset of that of the T8XX, but is not binary compatible with it. Therefore, binary code generated for first-generation transputers will not execute on the T9000. A recompilation is required.

Each priority level has its own evaluation stack, so there is now no need to save the stack on a high-priority process interrupt, resulting in a reduced interrupt latency – interrupts can be handled faster.

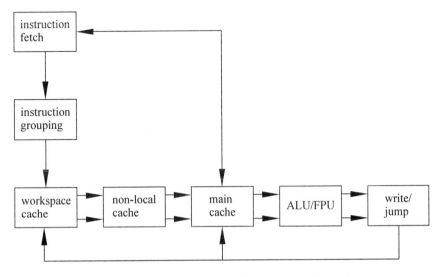

Figure 16.2 Block diagram of T9000 grouper and pipeline.

16.3 T9000 memory organization

In order to reduce the bandwidth requirements on the memory system, the T9000 uses two levels of caching. The first level is within the processor itself, which provides a 32 word (128 byte) data cache for the workspace of the currently executing process. As most accesses are for data in the workspace, this has a major effect. The second level of caching is in the on-chip RAM (the main cache: 16 Kbyte), to speed up access to data normally located in external RAM.

By default, the on-chip RAM acts as ordinary memory, but it may be configured as part memory/part cache or all cache (with external memory acting as ordinary memory in this case). This facility means that, since most memory accesses will be to cache, then slow external memory will not significantly degrade performance.

The on-chip RAM is organized as four banks, each bank caching one quarter of the address space. Whenever an address is presented to the memory system, the request is directed via an internal cross-bar switch to the appropriate memory bank.

16.4 The virtual channel processor

It has been recognized that the first generation of transputers *do* have a communications link support problem. The onus for the development of routing software for inter-transputer messages and multiplexor/de-multiplexor software for increasing the channel capacity of the links –each link supporting just two channels – fell on the software developer (although, with the later versions of the occam toolset, multiplexing and routing software is automatically added by the INMOS configurer/collector, if needed). This problem has been addressed in the design of the T9000 with the provision of the *virtual channel processor* (VCP). The VCP supports the *multiplexing* of any number of *virtual channels* over each physical communications link (Fig. 16.3).

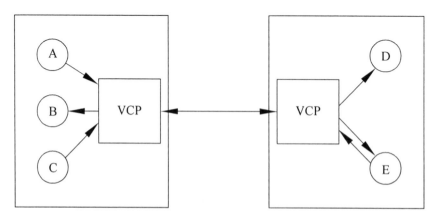

Figure 16.3   Shared links supported by VCP.

In conjunction with the C104 routing device, the T9000 allows the communication of messages between many pairs of processes, no matter on which transputer in a network they are located. The programmer no longer has to be concerned with such details.

16.4.1 Communications link protocol

With the VCP, a completely new (and different) link communications protocol has been introduced. Each inter-transputer message is transmitted over the link by the VCP as one or more packets. A packet can contain up to 32 bytes of data, so longer messages are split up and sent as several packets, with the last packet possibly containing less than 32 bytes. Packets from different virtual channels are interleaved, that is, multiplexed on the link.

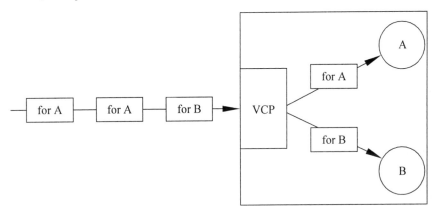

Figure 16.4   Multiplexing of packets for different channels.

Part of the VCP functionality is a multiplexing/de-multiplexing capability for packets being sent to and received from a link. *Every* data packet contains
- a header, containing a destination address used to route the packet through a network of C104 switches and deliver it to the intended process
- up to 32 bytes of data
- a trailer, signifying either the end of a packet or the end of the message.

In order to maintain synchronized communication, each packet sent on a virtual channel is acknowledged before another one is sent. This acknowledgement comprises a special packet, the *acknowledge* packet, consisting of a header and end-of-packet token. The acknowledge packet is sent along on a virtual channel paired to the one that was used to send the data packet. This pair of virtual channels is termed a *virtual link* and can be used to transmit interleaved data and acknowledge packets in both directions at the same time.

In order to prevent hold-ups by any channel using the link, a one-packet buffer for each virtual channel is maintained by the VCP. A packet for any channel that is not in a state to be transmitted will not hold up the transmission of packets from other channels. Besides the obvious differences in the communications protocol between the two generations, the hardware method of transmission is also completely different. Mixed networking between the two generations is thus problematical. In order to interconnect transputers from the two generations, a C101 parallel link adaptor can be used. This device converts the T9000 link protocol to a high-speed parallel interface, which can be memory-mapped to a first-generation transputer.

16.5 The packet routing switch

To allow the operation of T9000 transputer networks, an extra external device is required. This device is the C104 packet routing switch, which is a dynamically switching, 32-link, cross-bar switch, with submicrosecond switching latency. It allows inter-transputer messages to be passing on all links at the same time. Each link operates at 100 Mbits per second. Coupled with the T9000, this switch allows desktop supercomputer performance to be attained easily. For example, 16 fully connected T9000s would be capable of delivering performances of 3200 Mips and 400 Mflops. Multiple C104 switches may be connected to allow the construction of networks of any number of T9000s. (Detailed information on the C104 switch, together with performance issues, is to be found in INMOS 1993.)

16.6 T9000 message-routing algorithms

The routing of messages between interconnected T9000s is delegated to the C104 packet-routing switch. The routing algorithm employed provides efficient, deadlock-free communications. The *wormhole* routing method is used to route packets (see Ch. 14), in which a routing decision (i.e. the determination of the link to be used to output the packet) is made as soon as the packet header has been read. This means that the header may be entering the next switch or destination T9000, even before the final portion of the packet has passed through the first switch. If the output link is not free, then the packet is buffered until it is so. The passage of the packet header creates a temporary path through the network, which disappears with the passage of the packet trailer (Fig. 16.5). Wormhole routing reduces message latency – packets are not stored until the whole message has been received – and obviates the need for message buffers in the switch.

The addressing/routing scheme used by the C104 for making routing decisions is called *interval labelling* (Fig. 16.6). In this scheme, each destination process is labelled with a number (the virtual input channel) and this number is used as the destination process address in the packet header. *Each* link of a C104 switch is assigned a contiguous interval (or range) of possible destination addresses, and only those packets that have a destination address in their headers falling within an interval are output via the link associated with that interval. It is possible to label

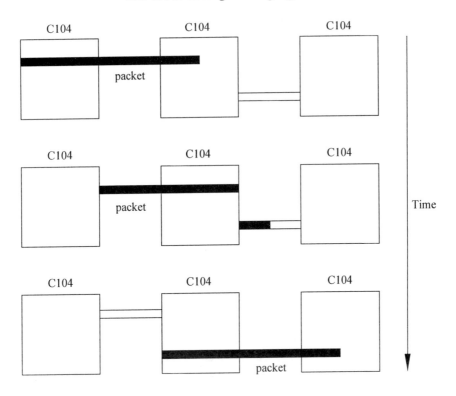

Figure 16.5   Wormhole routing: passage of packet through several router switches.

all major network topologies such that packets follow an optimal route through a
network of transputers, and such that the network is deadlock free.

The destination address of a packet may comprise any number of headers. This
feature allows a network to be labelled in hierarchical ways. If a network is labelled
using one 2 byte header, then the virtual channels of all transputers in the network
would have to be numbered uniquely in the range 0 to 65535. However, if two
1 byte headers are used, all transputers can label their virtual channels in the range
0 to 255, with the first header labelling each transputer (again, in the range 0 to
255). Additional headers can be added to give more structure. A feature of the
C104 switch that supports this hierarchical addressing is *header deletion*, which
means that the output link of the C104 can delete the first header of the packet
before transmitting the rest of the packet; the data immediately following the
deleted header becomes the new header. Using packets with multiple headers
implements a multi-level (or indirect) mode of addressing, with the first header
byte being deleted before the packet is output, revealing the second header to complete the next level of addressing.

Any number of headers can be prepended to a packet to allow addressing schemes
to cover hierarchies of networks, each header identifying a particular subnetwork.

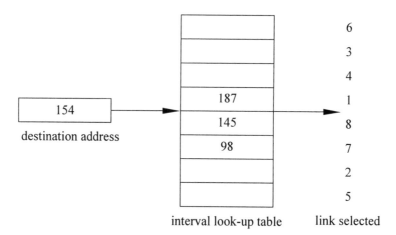

Figure 16.6   Interval labelling.

Heavy communications traffic through any link will cause message congestion and delivery hold-ups. Such a situation is termed a *hot-spot*, and is alleviated in the C104 switch by a two-phase routing algorithm known as *universal routing*. This algorithm works by first sending every packet to a randomly chosen interme-diate switch; from here the packet is then sent to its true destination. This scheme is implemented by generating a header containing a random destination address. This header is prepended to the packet, and is stripped off by the intermediate switch. The logic behind the algorithm is that, by sending the packets first to ran-dom switches, the packets will eventually be forwarded to the destination trans-puter via different links, so easing the congestion on any link.

Answers to exercises

Chapter 1

1.

```
PAR
  Chan ! Limit - Index
  Chan ? Left
```

2.
- (a) Invalid: variable Item is being assigned in two components of a parallel process without being communicated via a channel.
- (b) Invalid: same channel is being used for both input and output in the same sequence.
- (c) Problem: as deadlock will occur - first **SEQ** process will wait for second **SEQ** process to input, and second **SEQ** process will wait for first **SEQ** process to input.
- (d) No problem: no deadlock occurs as component processes are executing in parallel not in sequence.
- (e) Problem: as deadlock will occur - first process will wait for second process to output on channel Chan1, and second process will wait for first process to input on channel Chan2.

3.
  (a)

```
PAR
  SEQ
    Chan1 ? A
    Chan2 ? B
  SEQ
    Chan1 ! D
    Chan2 ! C
```

  (b)

```
PAR
  PAR
    Chan1 ? A
    Chan2 ? B
```

```
SEQ
    Chan2 ! C
    Chan1 ! D
```

(Either or both **SEQ**s may be replaced by a **PAR** if the inputs and outputs are independent.)

Chapter 2

1.

   (a) Valid.

   (b) Invalid: occam reserved word.

   (c) Valid.

   (d) Invalid: space not permitted in identifier.

   (e) Invalid: underscore not permitted in identifier.

2.

   (a) Valid: variable Limit re-declared as type **BYTE**.

   (b) Invalid: assignment should be Small := 55(**BYTE**)

   (c) Invalid: **BYTE** values are valid only in the range 0–255.

   (d) Valid.

   (e) Invalid: variables INDEX and Index are not the same.

   (f) Invalid: variable Char of second process not declared. Char is only in scope of first sequential process.

   (g) Invalid: channel protocol is specified as single byte, but input process variable is specified as an integer.

   (h) Valid: identifiers Item as type **INT** and Item as type **BYTE** have separate scope and use different channels for input/output. (But code will deadlock as Chan1 has no output within its scope, nor has Chan2 an input.)

   (i) Valid: second declaration of identifier Item as **BYTE** supersedes the first declaration in scope. (But better to declare variables before a **SEQ**.)

   (j) Invalid: value of variable Count not defined.

   (k) Valid: variable Count is in scope of variable Index.

   (l) Valid: variables Index and Count are in scope.

Chapter 3

1.

   (a) Invalid: needs precedence brackets, for example 100 − (5 * 5)

   (b) Invalid: precedence brackets wrongly placed, for example 100 − ((5 * 5) + 20)

   (c) Invalid: needs precedence brackets, for example (100 − (5 * 5)) > Limit

(d) Invalid. Mixed arithmetic and Boolean types.

(e) First assignment is invalid: arithmetic overflow, result too large.
Second assignment is invalid: mixed arithmetic types. A valid statement is

```
Result := 33(INT16) * 10(INT16)
```

Third assignment is invalid: arithmetic overflow, result too large.

2.

   (a) **FALSE**

   (b) **TRUE**

   (c) BooleanValue

If **TRUE** is replaced by **FALSE**, then

   (a) **TRUE**

   (b) BooleanValue

   (c) **FALSE**

3.

   (a) 1

   (b) 0

   (c) FALSE

   (d) 3

   (e) 3

   (f) 3.0

   (g) 3.0

4.

```
VAL BitNumber IS 4 :
INT Number :
SEQ
  Number := 3-- for example
  Number := Number BITOR (1 << BitNumber)
```

5. An AND gate is

```
CHAN OF BOOL InPin1, InPin2, OutPin :
BOOL Level1, Level2 :
SEQ
  PAR
    InPin1 ? Level1
    InPin2 ? Level2
  OutPin ! Level1 AND Level2
```

Similarly for the OR and NOR gates. (The example may also be expressed using integer types, together with the appropriate channel specifications and bitwise operators.)

6.

```
VAL Number IS 123 :
INT Hundreds, Tens, Units :
SEQ
  Hundreds := Number / 100
  Tens := (Number REM 100) / 10
  Units := Number REM 10
```

7.

```
CHAN OF INT InPin1, InPin2, OutPin :
INT A, B, Part1, Part2 :
SEQ
  PAR
    InPin1 ? A
    InPin2 ? B
  Part1 := (BITNOT A) BITAND B
  Part2 := A BITAND (BITNOT B)
  OutPin ! Part1 BITOR Part2
```

(The example may also be expressed using Boolean types, together with the appropriate channel specifications and Boolean operators.)

Chapter 4

1.
  (a) [3]BYTE TrafficLights :
  (b) [8][8]INT ChessBoard :
  (c) [66][132]BYTE PrinterPaper :
  (d) [15][15]BYTE ScrabbleBoard :
  (e) [12][3]BYTE Months :

2. The first specification is an array of eight channels, each capable of transmitting a single REAL64 value; the second is a single channel capable of transmitting an array of eight REAL64 values.

3.

```
CHAN OF [25]REAL32 Chan :
PAR
  [25]REAL32 X :
  SEQ
```

```
    Chan ! X
    [25]REAL32 Y :
    SEQ
      Chan ? Y
```

4.

  (a)

```
  ScrabbleBoard[7][7]
```

(Rows and columns take values between 0 and 14.)

  (b)

```
  ScrabbleBoard[7][6]  :=  'A'
  ScrabbleBoard[7][7]  :=  'C'
  ScrabbleBoard[7][8]  :=  'E'
```

5. Num1 is assigned a value 5, Num2 is assigned a value 10, and Num3 is assigned a value 15.

6.

  (a) Invalid: mixed data types.
  (b) Invalid: first component of table is primitive data type, and second component is another table.
  (c) Invalid: strings are unequal lengths.

Chapter 5

1.

```
  IF
    Data < 0

      .
      . -- some process
      .

    Data = 0

      .
      . -- some process
      .

    Data > 0
      SKIP
```

2.

```
BOOL Running
  IF
    Running
        .
        .
        .
    NOT Running
      SKIP
```

3.

```
INT Int1, Int2, Min, Max :
SEQ
    .
    . -- assign values to Int1 and Int2
    .
  IF
    Int1 >= Int2
      Max, Min := Int1, Int2
    Int1 < Int2
      Min, Max := Int1, Int2
```

4.

```
[10]BYTE Digits : -- assume maximum of ten digits
INT Index, Number :
SEQ
  Number := 12345-- for example
  Index := (SIZE Digits) - 1
  -- store digits in array in reverse order, ready for
  -- output
  WHILE Number <> 0
    SEQ
      Digits[Index] := BYTE((Number REM 10)+INT '0')
      Number := Number / 10
      Index := Index - 1
  -- fill in any leading spaces
  WHILE Index >= 0
      SEQ
      Digits[Index] := ' '
      Index := Index - 1
  -- output digits
```

```
-- (use replicated SEQ construction - see Ch. 6)
SEQ Count = 0 FOR Index
  Output ! Digits[Count]
```

5.

(a)

```
CHAN OF BYTE Chan, In, Out :
PAR
  WHILE TRUE
    BYTE Char :
    SEQ
      In ? Char
      Chan ! Char
  WHILE TRUE
    BYTE Char :
    SEQ
      Chan ? Char
      Out ! Char
```

(b)

```
CHAN OF BYTE In, Out :
BYTE Char1, Char2 :
SEQ
  In ? Char1
  WHILE TRUE
    SEQ
      PAR
        In ? Char2
        Out ! Char1
      PAR
        In ? Char1
        Out ! Char2
```

6.

```
CASE Month
  February
    IF
      (Year REM 4) = 0
        Days := 29
      TRUE
        Days := 28
```

```
    April, June, September, November
      Days := 30
    ELSE
      Days := 31
```

7.

```
    VAL Message1 IS "a or A typed" :
    VAL Message2 IS "e or E typed" :
    VAL Message3 IS "i or I typed" :
    VAL Message4 IS "o or O typed" :
    VAL Message5 IS "u or U typed" :
    BYTE Vowel :
    SEQ
      Input ? Vowel
      CASE Vowel
        'a', 'A'
          Output ! Message1
        'e', 'E'
          Output ! Message2
        'i', 'I'
          Output ! Message3
        'o', 'O'
          Output ! Message4
        'u', 'U'
          Output ! Message5
```

8.

```
    WHILE TRUE
      BOOL Flag :
      BYTE Char :
      SEQ
        Flag := TRUE
        ALT
          Flag & InChan1 ? Char
            SEQ
              .
              . -- perform process
              .
              -- switch flag value
              Flag := FALSE
          NOT Flag & InChan2 ? Char
            SEQ
```

```
  .
  . -- perform process
  .
  -- switch flag value
  Flag := TRUE
```

Chapter 6

1.

```
SEQ Index = 0 FOR 20
  Screen ! '**'
```

2.

```
VAL Alphabet IS "ABCDEFGHIJKLMNOPQRSTUVWXYZ":
SEQ Index = 0 FOR SIZE Alphabet
  Display ! Alphabet[Index]
```

3.

```
VAL Char IS 'm':-- for example
VAL String IS "example":-- for example
INT Position :
IF
  IF Index = 0 FOR SIZE String
    String[Index] = Char
      Position := Index
  TRUE
    Position := -1
```

4.

```
VAL N IS 8 : -- for example
[N][N]INT A, B, C :
SEQ Row = 0 FOR N
  SEQ Col = 0 FOR N
    SEQ
      C[Row][Col] := 0
      SEQ Index = 0 FOR N
        C[Row][Col] := C[Row][Col] + A[Row][Index] *
                  B[Index][Col]
```

(A more efficient solution would be to have an abbreviation for *C [Row][Col]* as follows

```
VAL N IS 8 : -- for example
[N] [N] INT A, B, C :
SEQ Row = 0 FOR N
  VAL ARow IS A[Row] :
  VAL Crow IS C[Row] :
  SEQ Col = 0 FOR N
    Sum IS CRow[Col] :
    SEQ
      Sum := 0
      SEQ Index = 0 FOR N
        Sum := Sum + ARow[Index] * B[Index][Col]
)
```

5.

```
Pipe

  PAR Index = 0 FOR 1024
    BOOL Terminate :
    SEQ
      Terminate := FALSE
      WHILE NOT Terminate
        INT Item :
        SEQ
          Buffer[Index]? Item
          IF
            Item = Eof
              Terminate := TRUE
            TRUE
              SKIP
          Buffer[Index + 1] ! Item

Termination

  BOOL Terminate :
  SEQ
    Terminate := FALSE
    WHILE NOT Terminate
      INT Data
      SEQ
        Buffer[1024] ? Data
```

```
IF
  Data = Eof
    Terminate := TRUE
  TRUE
    SKIP

  .
  . -- consume or output an item of data
  .
```

6.

```
VAL N IS 10 :-- for example
[N + 1]CHAN OF INT Pipe :
PAR Index = 0 FOR N
  INT Number, LastPower, NextPower
  SEQ
    Pipe[Index] ? Number
    Pipe[Index] ? LastPower
    NextPower := LastPower * Number
    Pipe[Index + 1] ! Number
    Pipe[Index + 1] ! NextPower
```

7.

```
VAL Chan1 IS 1 :
VAL Chan2 IS 2 :
VAL Chan2 IS 3 :
VAL Chan2 IS 4 :
INT Data :
WHILE TRUE
  ALT
    Inchan1 ? Data
      SEQ
        OutChan ! Chan1
        OutChan ! Data
    InChan2 ? Data
      SEQ
        OutChan ! Chan2
        OutChan ! Data
    InChan3 ? Data
      SEQ
        OutChan ! Chan3
        OutChan ! Data
    InChan4 ? Data4
```

```
SEQ
  OutChan ! Chan4
  OutChan ! Data
```

where the channels InChan1, InChan2, InChan3, InChan4 and OutChan are specified as type **INT**.

8.

```
VAL QSize IS 20 : -- for example
ALT
  (Count < QSize) & Enqueue ? Item
    --enqueue item
    SEQ
      Queue[Head] := Item
      Head := (Head + 1) REM QSize
      Count := Count + 1
  (Count > 0) & Dequeue ? Any
    --dequeue item
    SEQ
      Item := Queue[Tail]
      Tail := (Tail + 1) REM QSize
      Count := Count - 1
      Result ! Item
```

where *Queue* is declared as
```
[QSize]INT Queue :
```

and the global variables, Head, Tail and Count, are all initialized to 0. Channel Enqueue is used to enqueue an item provided the queue is not full. Channel Dequeue is used to request an item be dequeued provided the queue is not empty; the item being returned via channel Result.

Chapter 7

1.

  (a)

```
VAL DegPerRad IS 180.0(REAL32) / 3.142(REAL32) :
```

  (b)

```
VAL MinutesInDay IS 60 * 24 :
```

(c)

```
VAL MphToKmph IS 80.0(REAL32) / 50.0(REAL32) :
```

2.
   (a), b), (c) Valid. All three alternatives are equally acceptable.
3.

```
PROC Swap(VAL INT Number, INT Reverse)
  SEQ
    Hundreds := Number / 100
    Tens := (Number REM 100) / 10
    Units := Number REM 10
    Reverse :=(100 * Units) + ((10 * Tens)+ Hundreds)
  :
```

4.

```
PROC CreateStack()
  SEQ
    Top := -1
  :
PROC Push(VAL INT Item)
  SEQ
    Top := Top + 1
    Stack[Top] := Item
  :
PROC Pop(INT Item)
  SEQ
    Item := Stack[Top]
    Top := Top - 1
  :

BOOL FUNCTION StackEmpty() IS Top = -1 :

BOOL FUNCTION StackFull() IS Top = (SIZE Stack) - 1 :
```

where Stack is declared as

```
[StackSize]INT Stack :
```

and variable Top is global.

5.

```
PROC Assemble([]BYTE String, INT Length)
  VAL EndOfString IS '.' :
  VAL MaxLength IS SIZE String :
  BOOL EoS :
  SEQ
    EoS := FALSE
    Length := 0
    WHILE (NOT EoS) AND (Length < MaxLength)
      BYTE Char :
      SEQ
        InChan ? Char
        IF
          Char = EndOfString
            EoS := TRUE
          TRUE
            SEQ
              String[Length] := Char
              Length := Length + 1
  :
```

6.

```
INT FUNCTION MinOfThree(VAL INT Int1, Int2, Int3)
  INT Minimum :
  VALOF
    SEQ
      IF
        Int1 <= Int2
          Minimum := Int1
        TRUE
          Minimum := Int2
      IF
        Int3 < Minimum
          Minimum := Int3
        TRUE
          SKIP
  RESULT Minimum
  :  ·
```

7.

```
BOOL FUNCTION IsaPalindrome(VAL []BYTE Word)
```

272

```
INT I, J :
BOOL Palindrome :
VALOF
  SEQ
    I := SIZE Word
    J := 0
    WHILE (J < I) AND (Word[J] = Word[I])
      SEQ
        I := I - 1
        J := J + 1
    IF
      J >= I
        Palindrome := TRUE
      TRUE
        Palindrome := FALSE
  RESULT Palindrome
:
```

8.

```
REAL32 FUNCTION ToKmph(VAL REAL32 Mph) IS
  Mph * (80.0(REAL32) / 50.0(REAL32)) :
```

9.

```
REAL32 FUNCTION ToCelsius(VAL REAL32 Fahrenheit) IS
  (Fahrenheit - 32.0(REAL32)) * (5.0(REAL32) /
  9.0(REAL32)) :
```

10.

```
BOOL FUNCTION IsaVowel(VAL BYTE Char)
  BOOL Vowel :
  VALOF
    IF
      (Char = 'a') OR (Char = 'A') OR
      (Char = 'e') OR (Char = 'E') OR
      (Char = 'i') OR (Char = 'I') OR
      (Char = 'o') OR (Char = 'O') OR
      (Char = 'u') OR (Char = 'U') OR
        Vowel := TRUE
      TRUE
        Vowel := FALSE
    RESULT Vowel
```

:

(A better solution is to use a **CASE** selector:

```
CASE Char
  'a', 'A', 'e', 'E', 'i', 'I', . . .
    Vowel := TRUE
  ELSE
    Vowel := FALSE)
```

11.

```
REAL32, REAL32 FUNCTION Stats(VAL []REAL32 List)
  REAL32 Mean, StdDev, Sum, SumSq, Size :
  VALOF
    SEQ
      Sum := 0.0(REAL32)
      SumSq := 0.0(REAL32)
      SEQ Index = 0 FOR SIZE List
        VAL ListI IS List[Index]:
        SEQ
          Sum := Sum + ListI
          SumSq := SumSq + (ListI * ListI)
          Size := REAL32 ROUND (SIZE List)
          Mean := Sum / Size
          StdDev:= SQRT((SumSq / Size)- (Mean * Mean))
    RESULT Mean, StdDev
  :
```

Chapter 8

1.

(a)

```
CHAN OF INT :: []REAL32 Chan :
```

(b)

```
CHAN OF [8][8]INT Chan :
```

(c)

```
CHAN OF INT :: []BYTE Chan :
```

2.
   (a)

   PROTOCOL COMPLEX **IS REAL32**; **REAL32** :

   (b)

   PROTOCOL ARRAYCOMPONENT **IS INT**; **REAL32** :

(component index followed by component value)

   (c)

   PROTOCOL PERSONAL **IS BYTE** :: [] **BYTE**; **INT**; **BYTE**

(number of characters in name followed by name, age and sex)

3.
   (a) First message is invalid: too long; second message is valid.
   (b) Invalid: size of receiving array, Block, is too small.

4.

   PROTOCOL MUXDEMUX **IS INT**; **REAL32** :

Multiplexor

   ALT Channel = 0 **FOR** Number
      In[Channel] ? Data
         Out ! Channel; Data

De-multiplexor

   SEQ
      In ? Destination; Data
      Out[Destination] ! Data

5.

   PROTOCOL PeekAndPoke
      CASE
         -- peek a memory address (supplied as an integer)
      peek; **INT**
         -- data resulting from peek request (assumed to be

275

```
    an integer)
  result; INT
  -- poke a memory address with data (both assumed
     to be integers)
  poke; INT; INT
```

Chapter 9

1.

  (a)

```
  VAL TicksPerSecond IS 15625 :
    VAL TwoSeconds IS 2 * TicksPerSecond :
    TIMER Clock :
    INT Now :
    SEQ
      Clock ? Now
      Clock ? AFTER (Now PLUS TwoSeconds)
```

  (b)

```
    VAL TicksPerSecond IS 1000000 :
    VAL TwoSeconds IS 2 * TicksPerSecond :
    TIMER Clock :
    INT Now :
    PRI PAR
      SEQ
        Clock ? Now
        Clock ? AFTER (Now PLUS TwoSeconds)
      SKIP
```

2.

```
    PRI PAR
      -- router process
      SEQ
        InChan ? Destination; Data
        IF
          Destination = Me
            Internal ! Data
          TRUE
            OutChan ! Destination; Data
      SEQ
```

```
.
. -- internal process
.
```

3.

```
VAL INT NumberOfAdds IS 1000 :
TIMER Clock :
REAL32 A, B, C :
INT Before, Now, TimeDifference, TimeOfAdds :
SEQ
  A := 100.0 (REAL32)
  B := 10.0 (REAL32)
  Clock ? Before
  SEQ Index = 0 FOR NumberOfAdds
    C := A + B
  Clock ? Now
  TimeDifference := Now MINUS Before
  TimeOfAdds := TimeDifference / NumberOfAdds
```

(Assuming no other processes are running on the transputer and ignoring the overhead of the replication.)

4.

```
TIMER Clock :
INT Start, End, Time :
SEQ
  Clock ? Start
  .
  . -- program
  .
  Clock ? End
  Time := End MINUS Start
```

References

Askew C., D. Carpenter, J. Chalker, A. Hey, D. Nicole 1986. Simulation of statistical mechanical systems on transputer Arrays. *Computer Physics Communications* **42**, 21–6.

Barrett G. 1992. *Draft occam 3 reference manual* [INMOS Internal Report]. Marlow, Bucks: SGS-THOMSON Microelectronics Ltd.

Burns A. 1988. *Programming in occam 2*. Wokingham: Addison-Wesley.

Debbage M., M. Hill, S. Wykes, D. Nicole 1994. Southampton's portable occam compiler (SPOC). In *Proceedings of 17th World occam and Transputer User Group Technical Meeting [WoTUG–17]*, R. Miles and A. Chalmers (eds), 40–55. Amsterdam: IOS Press.

De Carlini U. & U. Villano 1991a. The routing problem in transputer-based parallel systems. *Microprocessors and Microsystems* **15**(1), 21–33.

— 1991b. *Transputers and parallel architectures*. Chichester: Ellis Horwood.

Flynn M. 1972. Some computer organizations and their effectiveness. *IEEE Transactions on Computers* **C–21**, 948–60.

Fox G., M. Johnson, G. Lyzenga, S. Otto, J. Salmon, D. Walker 1988. *Solving problems on concurrent processors*, vol 1. Englewood Cliffs, New Jersey: Prentice-Hall.

Gardner M. 1971. Mathematical games. *Scientific American* **224**(February) 112; (March) 106; (April) 114.

Gurd J. 1988. A taxonomy of parallel computer architectures. In *Proceedings of the IEE conference on design and applications of parallel digital processors*, no. 298, 57–61.

Hey A. 1988a. Parallel decomposition of large scale simulations in science and engineering. In *Proceedings of UNICOM Conference: major developments in parallel processing*.

— 1988b. Practical parallel processing with transputers. In *Proceedings of 3rd Conference on hypercube concurrent computers and applications*, 115–21. Reading, Massachusetts: ACM Press.

— 1990. Scientific applications on transputer arrays – some experiments in MIMD parallelism. In *Proceedings of the 3rd Japanese occam User Group Technical Meeting [OUGJ–3]*, T. Kunii & D. May (eds), 103–121. Amsterdam: IOS Press.

Hoare A. 1985. *Communicating sequential processes*. Englewood Cliffs, New Jersey: Prentice-Hall.

Hockney R. & C. Jesshope 1988. *Parallel computers 2*. Bristol: Adam Hilger.

INMOS 1988a. *occam 2 reference manual*. Englewood Cliffs, New Jersey: Prentice-Hall.

— 1988b. *Transputer instruction set: a compiler writer's guide*. Englewood Cliffs, New Jersey: Prentice-Hall.

— 1989a. *The transputer development and iq systems databook* [INMOS handbook]. Marlow, Bucks: SGS-THOMSON Microelectronics Ltd.

— 1989b. *The transputer applications notebook – architecture and software* [INMOS handbook]. Marlow, Bucks: SGS-THOMSON Microelectronics Ltd.

— 1989c. *The transputer applications notebook – systems and performance* [INMOS handbook]. Marlow, Bucks: SGS-THOMSON Microelectronics Ltd.

— 1991a. *Occam 2 toolset (IMS D7205) – user manual* [INMOS handbook]. Marlow,

References

Bucks: SGS-THOMSON Microelectronics Ltd.

— 1991b. *The T9000 transputer products overview manual* [INMOS handbook]. Marlow, Bucks: SGS-THOMSON Microelectronics Ltd.

— 1992. *The transputer databook*, 3rd edn. [INMOS handbook]. Marlow, Bucks: SGS-THOMSON Microelectronics Ltd.

— 1993. *Networks, routers and transputers*, D. May, P. Thomson, P. Welch (eds). Amsterdam: IOS Press.

Jones G. 1987. On guards. In *Proceedings of the 7th occam User Group [OUG–7] Technical Meeting*, T. Muntean (ed.), 15–24. Amsterdam: IOS Press.

— 1989. Carefully scheduled selection with ALT. *Occam User Group [OUG] Newsletter* (10).

Jones G. & M. Goldsmith 1988. *Programming in occam 2*. Englewood Cliffs, New Jersey: Prentice-Hall

Kumar V., A. Grama, A. Gupta, G. Karypis 1994. *Introduction to parallel computing – design and analysis of algorithms*. Reading, Massachusetts: Benjamin/Cummings.

Kutti K. 1985 Taxonomy of parallel processing and definitions. *Parallel Computing* **2**, 353–9.

Mandelbrot B. 1983. *The fractal geometry of nature*. San Francisco: W. H. Freeman.

May D. 1990. Towards general-purpose parallel computers. In *Natural and artificial parallel computation*, M. Arbib & J. Robinson (eds), 31–46. Cambridge, Massachusetts: MIT Press.

Mett P., D. Crowe, P. Strain-Clark 1994. *Specification and design of concurrent systems*. New York: McGraw-Hill.

Milner R. 1980. *A calculus of communicating systems*. Berlin: Springer.

Pountain D. & D. May 1987. *A tutorial introduction to occam programming*. Oxford: Blackwell Scientific.

Peitgen, H-O. & P. Richter 1987. *The beauty of fractals*. Berlin: Springer.

Poole M. 1993. An implementation of occam 2 targeted to 80386, etc. *WoTUG News* [*World occam and Transputer User Group Newsletter*] (18), xiv–xv.

Pritchard D. 1988. Mathematical models of distributed computation. In *Proceedings of the 7th occam user group [OUG–7] Technical Meeting*, T. Muntean (ed.), 25–36. Amsterdam: IOS Press.

Pritchard D., C. Askew, D. Carpenter, I. Glendinning, A. Hey, D. Nicole 1987. Practical-parallelism using transputer arrays. In *Proceedings of the PARLE Conference*, 278–94. Berlin: Springer.

Quingping G. & Y. Paker 1990. Concurrent communication and granularity assessment for a transputer-based multiprocessor system. *Computer Systems – Science and Engineering* **5**(1), 21–8.

Quinn M. 1994. *Parallel computing – theory and practice*, 2nd edn. New York: McGraw-Hill.

Roscoe W. & A. Hoare 1986. *The laws of occam programming*. Technical Monograph PRG–53, Programming Research Group, University of Oxford.

SGS-THOMSON 1995. *occam 2.1 reference manual* [SGS-THOMSON Internal Report]. Marlow, Bucks: SGS-THOMSON Microelectronics Ltd.

Skillicorn D. 1988. A taxonomy for computer architectures. *Computer* (November), 46–57.

Ullam S. 1962. In *Essays on cellular automata*, A. Burks (ed.). Urbana–Champaign: University of Illinois Press.

Valiant L. 1990. A bridging model for parallel computation. *Communications of the ACM*

33(8), 103–111.

von Neumann J. 1966. *Theory of self-reproducing automata*, A. Burks (ed.). Urbana–Champaign: University of Illinois Press.

Wadsworth C., D. Johnston, B. Henderson 1990. *Parallel processing techniques course notes*. Parallel Processing Group, Rutherford Appleton Laboratory, Didcot.

Welch P. 1987. Emulating digital logic using transputer networks. In *Proceedings of the PARLE Conference*, 357–73. Berlin: Springer.

Welch P. 1989. Graceful termination – graceful resetting. In *Proceedings of the 10th occam User Group Technical Meeting* (OUG–10), A. Bakkers (ed.), 310–17. Amsterdam: IOS Press.

— 1992. The role and future of occam. In *Transputer applications – progress and prospects*, M. Jane, R. Fawcett, T. Mawby (eds), 152–72. Amsterdam: IOS Press.

Welch P. & D. Wood 1996. KROC – the Kent retargetable occam compiler. In *Proceedings of the World occam and Transputer User Group 19th Technical Meeting* (WoTUG–19), B. O'Neil (ed.). Amsterdam: IOS Press.

Welch P., G. Justo, C. Willcock 1993. High-level paradigms for deadlock-free high-performance systems. In *Proceedings of the 1993 World Transputer Congress*, R. Grebe, J. Hektor, S. Hilton, M. Jane, P. Welch (eds), 981–1004. Amsterdam: IOS Press.

Wexler J. & D. Prior 1989. Solving problems with transputers: background and experience. *Microprocessors and Microsystems* **13**(2), 67–78.

Willcock C. & P. Welch 1992. *Deadlock avoidance in parallel design*. Computing Laboratory Report, University of Kent.

Wolfram S. 1983. Statistical mechanics of cellular automata. *Reviews of Modern Physics* **55**, 601–644.

Index